SCARBOROUGH

THROUGH TIME

Mike Hitches

AMBERLEY PUBLISHING

First published 2011

Amberley Publishing
The Hill, Stroud,
Gloucestershire, GL5 4EP

www.amberleybooks.com

ISBN 978 1 84868 254 2

British Library Cataloguing in Publication Data.
A catalogue record for this book is available from
the British Library.

Typeset in 9.5pt on 12pt Celeste.
Typesetting by Amberley Publishing.
Printed in the UK.

Appointed GPSR EU Representative: Easy Access
System Europe Oü, 16879218
Address: Mustamäe tee 50, 10621, Tallinn, Estonia
Contact Details: gpsr.requests@easproject.com,
+358 40 500 3575

Introduction

Famous as a seaside holiday resort, Scarborough was believed to have been established by Norsemen around 966 AD, although the area had been attacked several times before the Norman Conquest. Indeed, a century later the King of Norway, Harold Hardrada, and his army waded ashore, burning and pillaging as they went, and totally destroyed Scarborough. The town did not even appear in the Domesday Book of 1086. The name attached to the town is believed to come from twin Norse brothers, Kormak and Thorsgills, who were marauding along the coast. Thorgills saw that the location was a good place to settle and he was seen as a man with 'good taste'. He was born with a hare-lip and was given the nickname 'Scarthi'. As the Norse name for a hill (on which the castle now stands) was 'Burg', the settlement would have been known as 'Scarthi's Burg', which would eventually mutated to Scarborough.

In 1225, Henry III granted use of forty royal oaks to be used for construction of a harbour here and also granted Scarborough its Charter in 1251. Edward I asked for two warships to be built in the harbour in 1301, to take on the Scots off Berwick-upon-Tweed. The castle had been built in around 1136, but fell into disrepair some seventy years later, as construction costs proved expensive. It was not until the reign of Henry II that the castle was restored to its former glory.

During the late nineteenth century, cheap travel and some leisure time brought the prospect of seaside holidays, or day visits, to the working classes, and Scarborough became attractive as an escape from the industrial towns of the West Riding. It was during this period that guest houses sprang up, along with entertainment and attractions, to keep such visitors amused. These were usually centred on the south side, being close to the railway station where many excursions terminated. As most of the town was built on a plateau overlooking the two bays, three cliff railways were built on the South Bay, which still operate.

The major feature of South Bay is the Grand Hotel, opened in 1867. This multi-storey hotel once had 365 rooms and stands on a site previously occupied by No. 2 The Cliff. This was where Anne Brontë died. The promontory on which the castle stands divides the North and South Bays, which are linked by the Marine Drive, opened in 1908, following construction of Foreshore Road and Royal Albert Drive a few years earlier. A small toll-house, close to the east pier at the harbour, is a reminder that road tolls were collected from those who used the new Marine Drive.

South beach is the most commercialised, due to the proximity of the railway station, and the harbour also lies on this side. In its heyday, the harbour was an important port for fishing boats that would discharge their cargos on the west pier, the oldest part of the harbour. On the east pier, yachts and cruisers are moored and it also has the amusement park with its funfair. On the lighthouse pier, two pleasure boats offer trips to places like Ravenscar and Filey. Near the harbour, on Quay Street, are buildings which date back to 1300, including Richard III's house at Sandside.

Along with the tourist industry, Scarborough also has other industries, which are important to the town's economy. Over at Eastfield, there is the Plaxton coach building company, established in 1936 by Frederick Plaxton, a joiner, on Seamer Road. His son, Eric, bought a 45-acre site at Eastfield in 1961 to expand the works, which, by 1972, was employing some 1,300 local workers. In the late 1960s, McCain Foods, who are famous as the manufacturers of oven chips, established their new factory at Eastfield, and also provide employment for the local population. Several other smaller firms and department stores are also present in Scarborough.

The town also has a proud sporting history. Cricket is played at North Marine Road and Yorkshire County Cricket has its Scarborough Festival here. Olivers Mount is famous for its motor-cycle racing with events being held in July. Lastly, Scarborough Football Club was formed in 1879 by members of the local cricket club. The team went on to become quite successful, winning the FA Trophy three times in the 1970's and becoming members of the Football League in 1987. However, the club went into steep decline when they were relegated from the Football League in 1999, and ceased to exist in 2007, when the High Court wound them up with debts of £2.5 million. A new club, Scarborough Athletic, has since been formed, playing their games at Bridlington Football Club's ground. It is hoped that they will one day return to the town and bring back some glory once again.

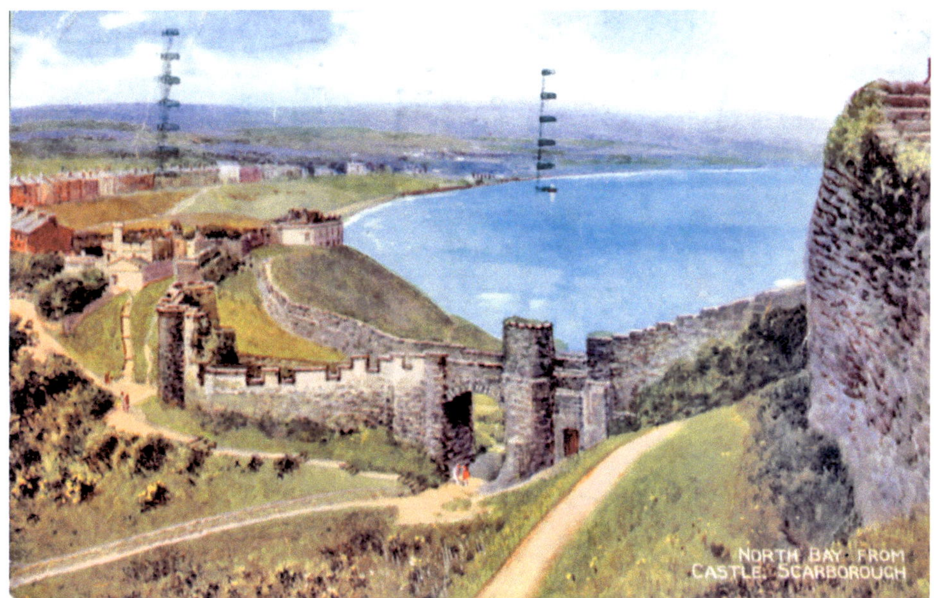

North Bay

North Bay viewed from the castle before the Second World War, and looking from North Bay to the castle with the Marine Drive in the foreground. The castle dates back to the twelfth century when, in 1136, William le Gros obtained permission from King Stephen for its construction. Since that time, the castle has been besieged twice during the English Civil War and was shelled by German ships during the First World War; the whole town also suffered from this attack at that time. It was this shelling which destroyed what remained of the curtain wall.

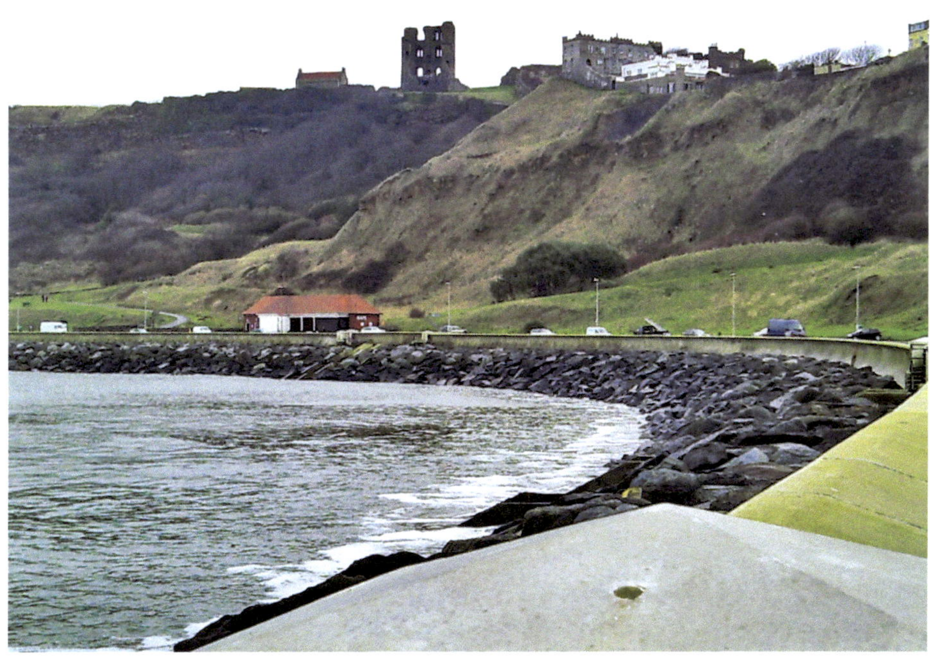

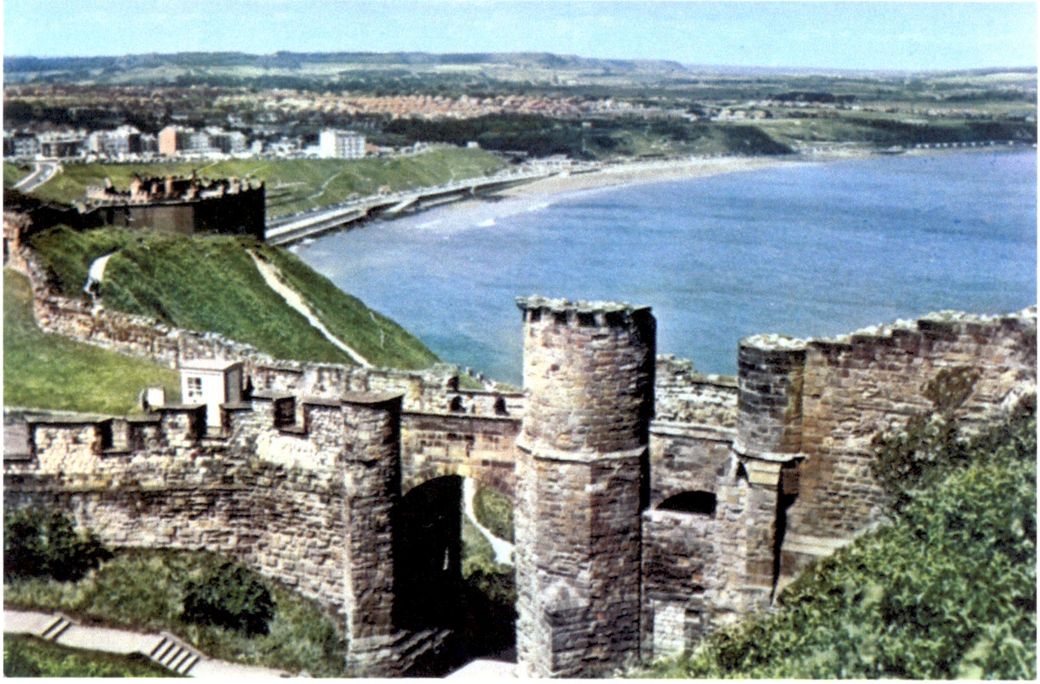

North Bay

The castle walls and North Bay in the 1950s. Below, the ornate toll booth at the entrance to North Bay is now situated next to the fairground, seen here in 2011.

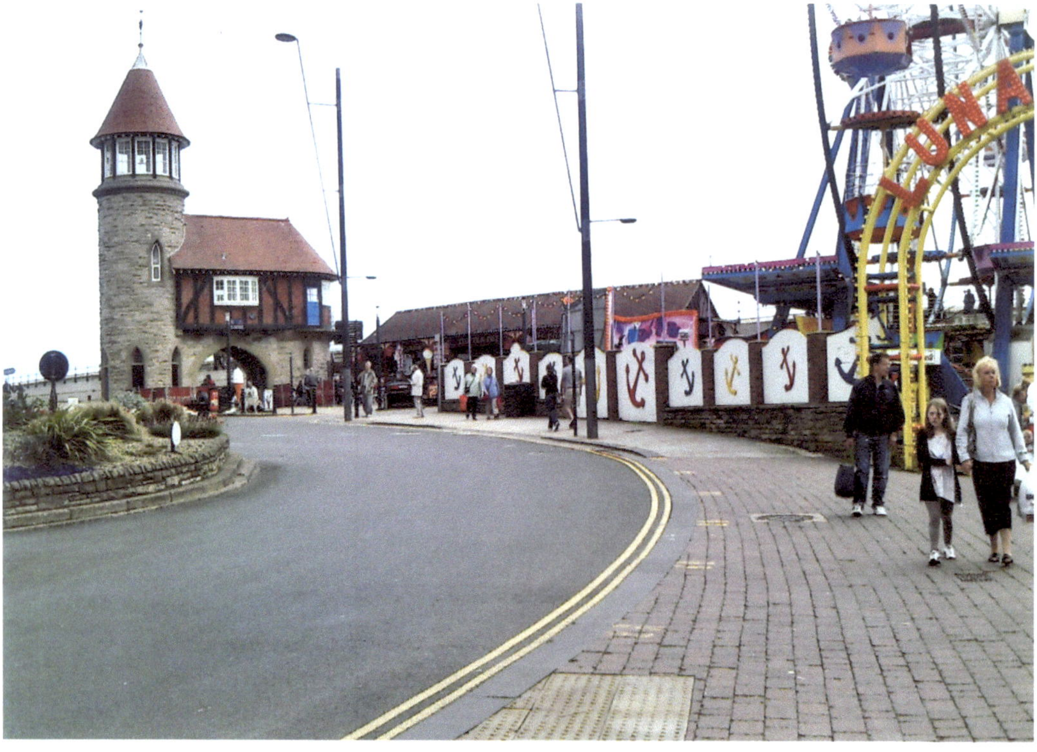

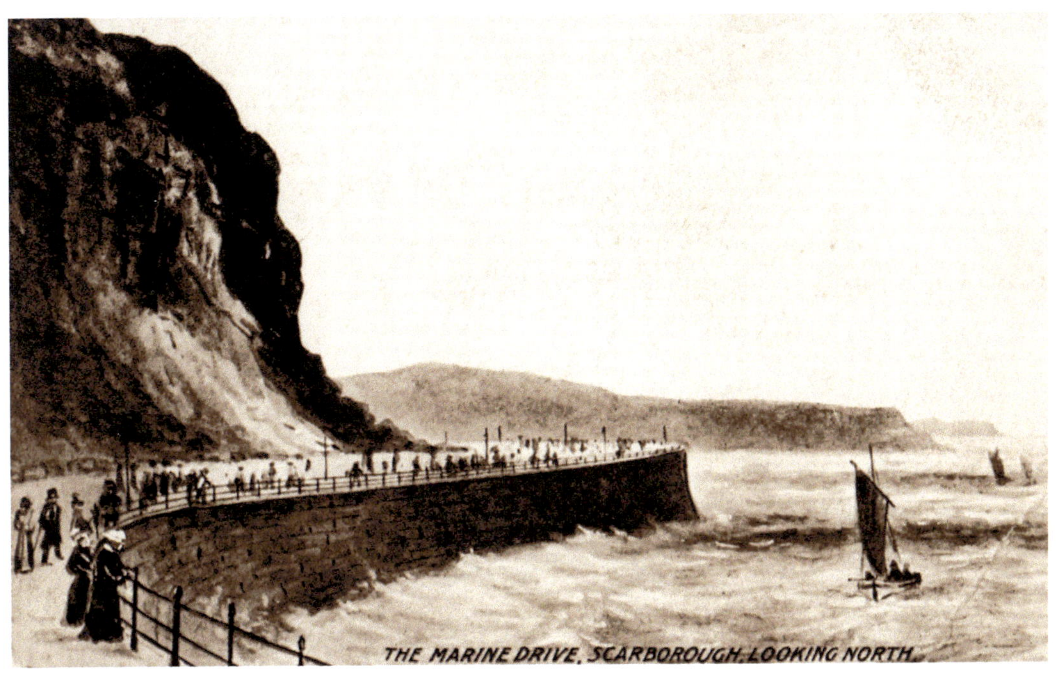

The Marine Drive at the North Bay

This view was taken during the Edwardian period. Visitors are watching yachts in the North Sea. The cliff with the castle on top can be seen to the left. Like the modern picture below, the view is looking north. Marine Drive has been lashed mercilessly during stormy weather and the road has been closed frequently. Indeed, such has been the damage that a new sea wall has recently been built.

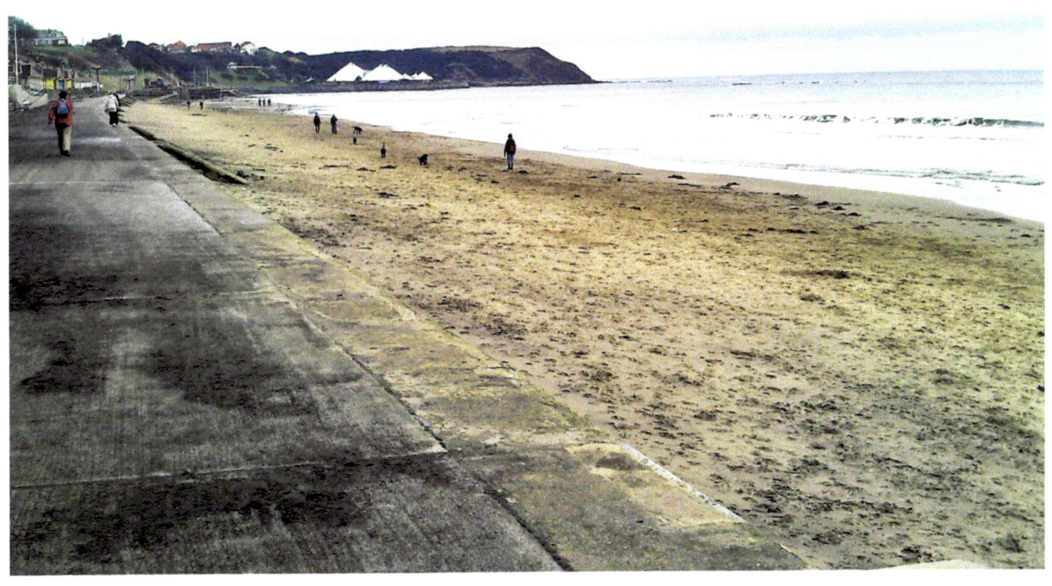

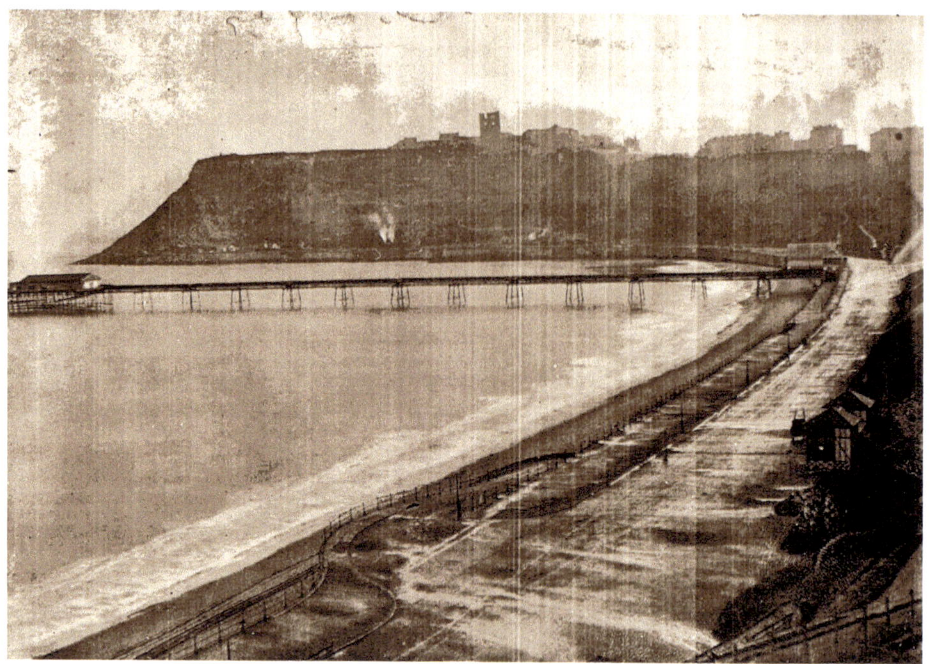

Scarborough's Pier

At one time, Scarborough had a pier, which was built by Eugenius Birch, a well known designer of seaside piers. The pier was completed at a cost of £16,000 in 1869. However, the location was not ideal as this part of the coast suffered badly from storms. Such an event occurred on 8 January 1905 and brought about its demise. It has never been replaced and the lower view shows where it once existed.

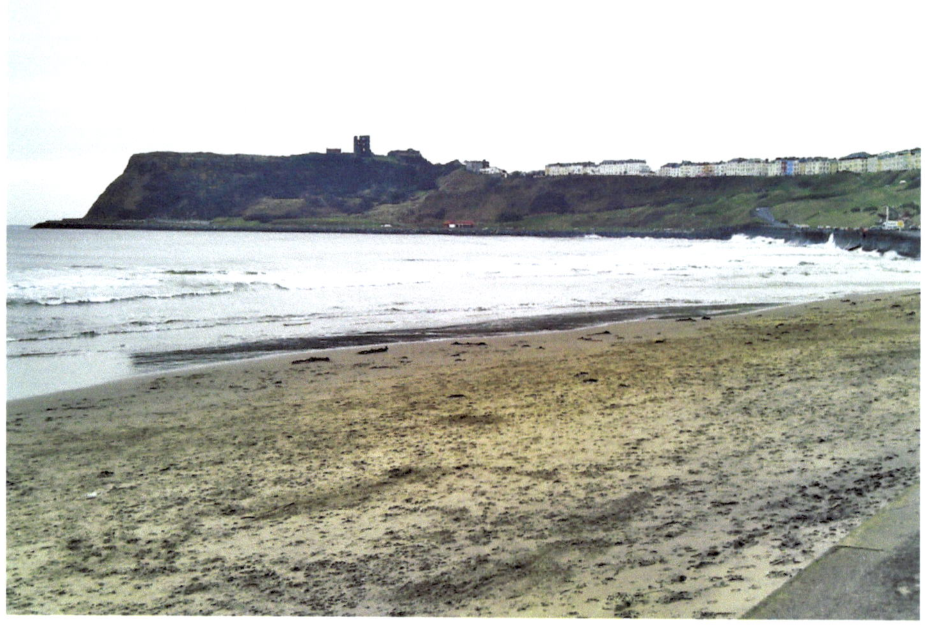

Bathing hut machines,
seaside donkeys and
the pier are in view.
In those days, the
Victorians saw the
seaside as a place to
take in fresh air and
enjoy walks along
the shore, as well as
sea bathing, which
they saw as healthy.
Tanning was viewed
as 'common' and
only people like farm
labourers had tanned
skin. In modern times,
the seaside chalet has
replaced the bathing
machines of the
Victorian period and a
row of these colourful
structures can be seen
at the North Bay shore.

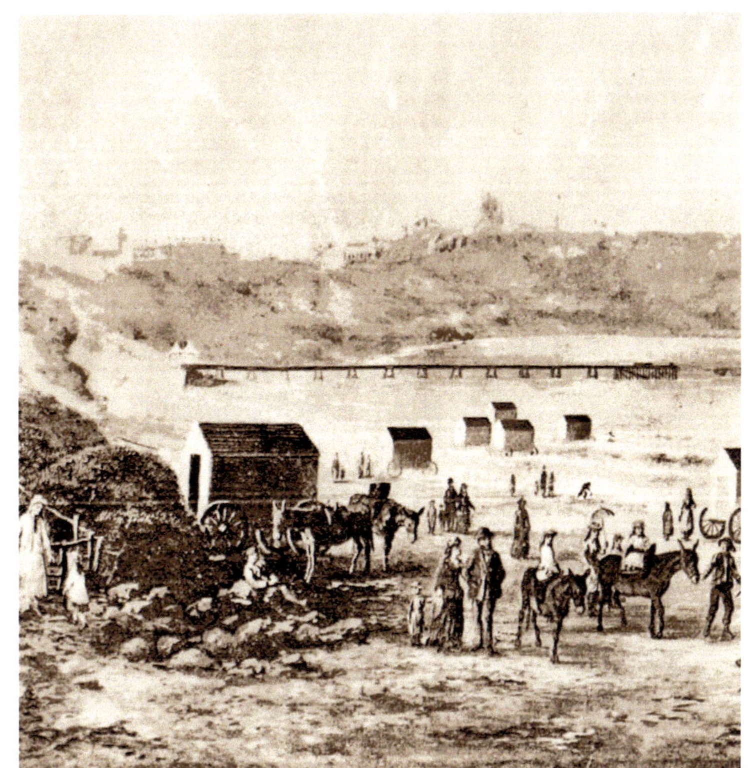

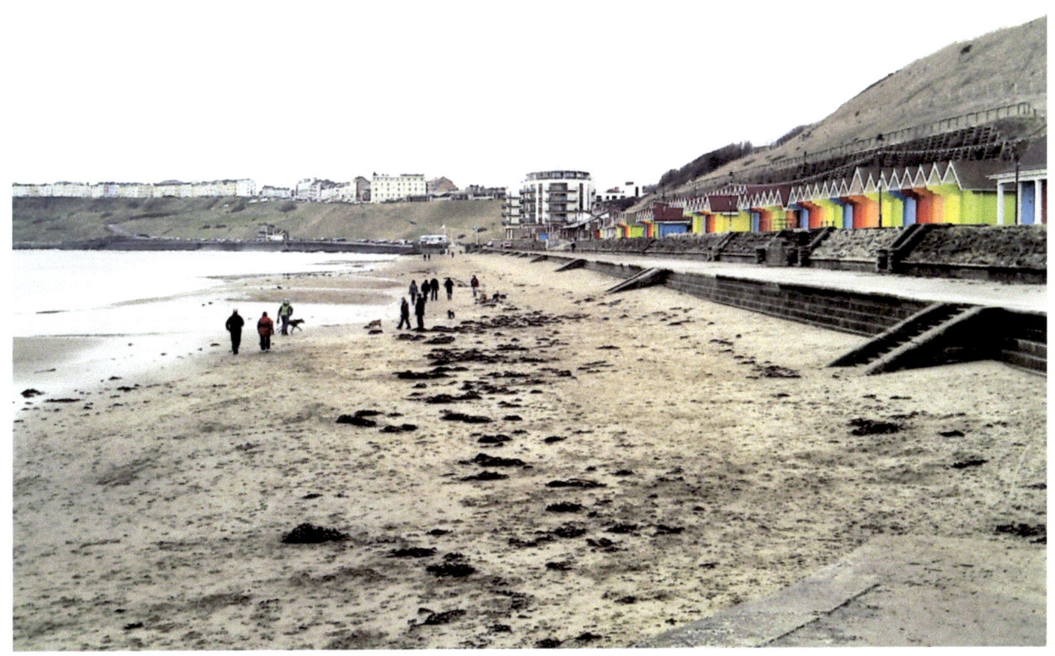

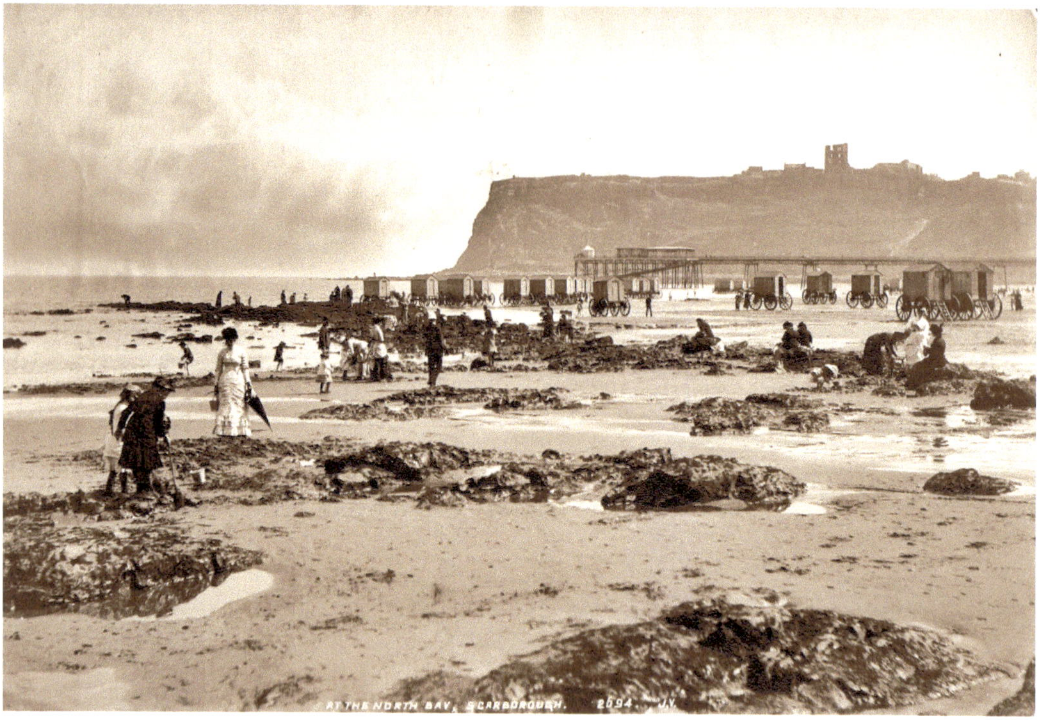

Two Views of the Seashore at North Bay in about 1891

Bathing machines are in profusion along the beach with women, children and men dressed in the Victorian fashion of the day, no swimming trunks, bikinis and swimsuits here. Indeed, the bathing machine was designed to protect female modesty in this period, when ladies were objects of mystery and female legs were not to be seen. It has been said that Scarborougb was the first seaside town to introduce these bathing machines and there is evidence that they were hired by three ladies in 1797. The theatre which can be seen at the end of the pier held Pierrot shows during the summer months, a favourite entertainment of Victorians.

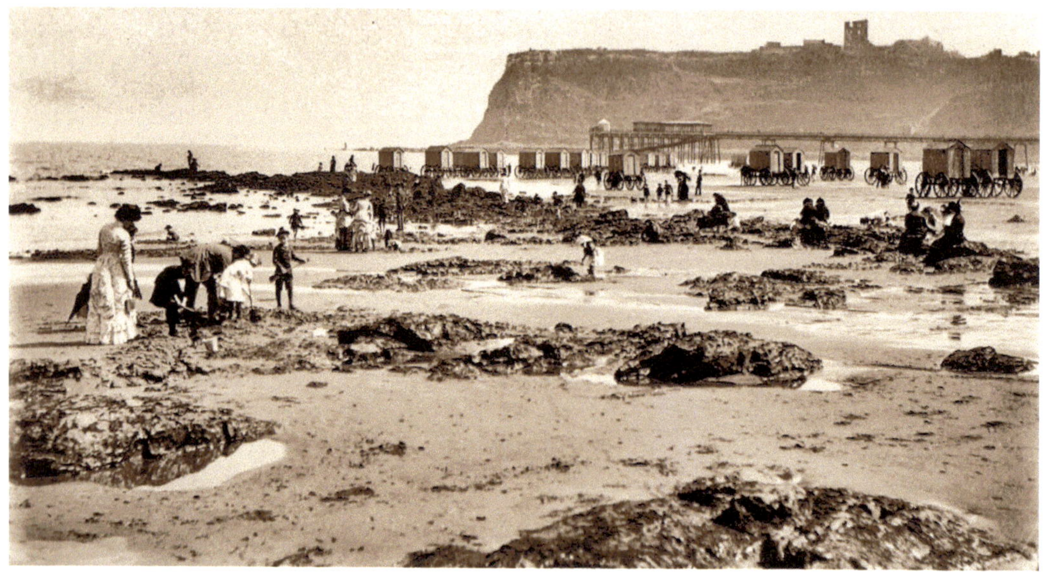

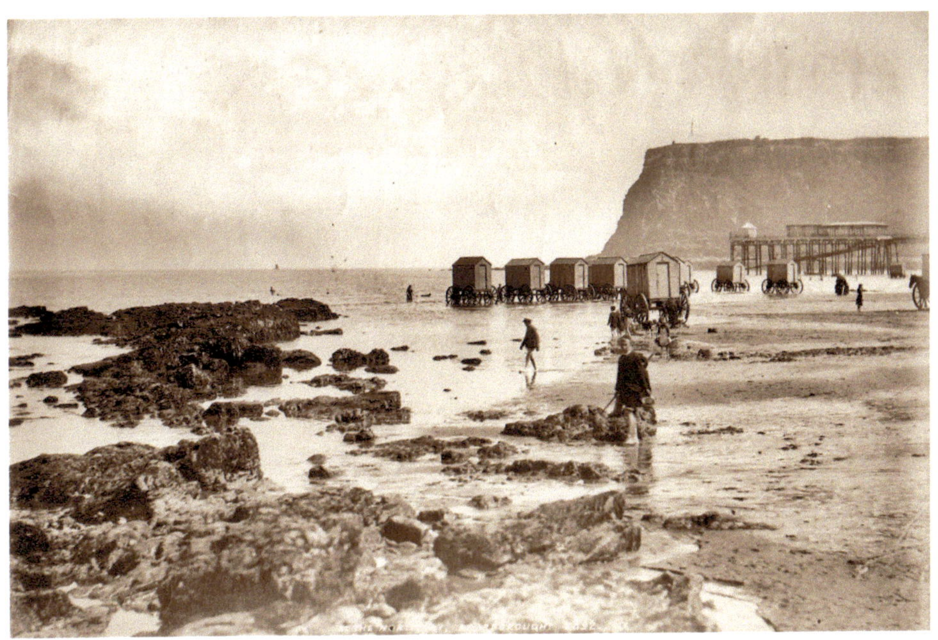

Bathing Machines on North Bay Shore in 1891

They were really changing rooms on wheels, which could be taken down to the sea's edge and allowed women to enter the sea with their modesty protected. The modern view shows their eventual replacements, the seaside chalet. These colourful structures serve a similar purpose, but with extras, like running water, electricity, and facilities for making drinks and storing food. Indeed, many people hire them for the week, the season, or just for the day. Some are even for sale.

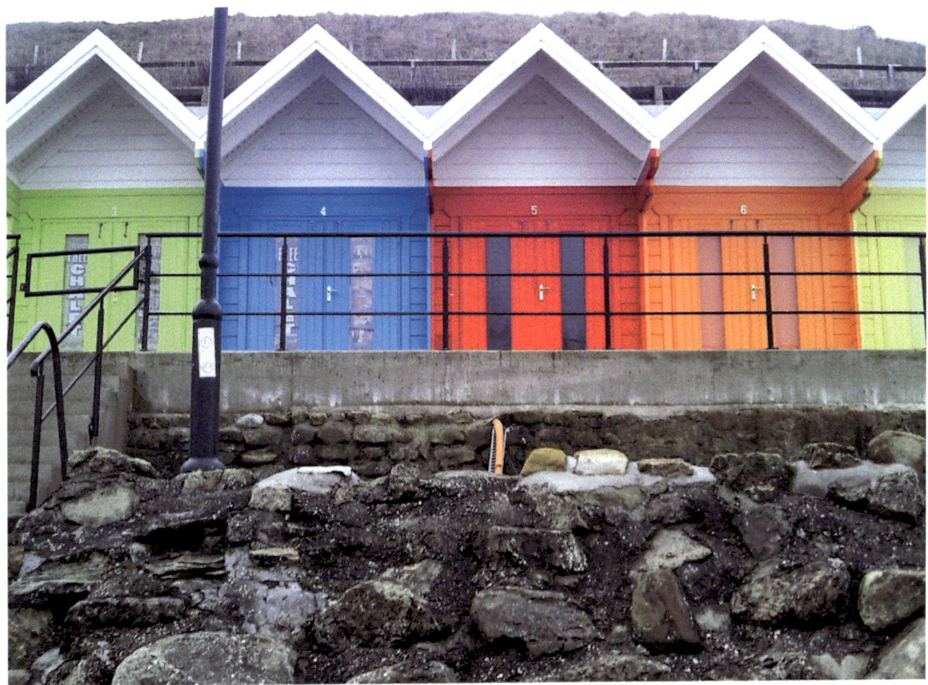

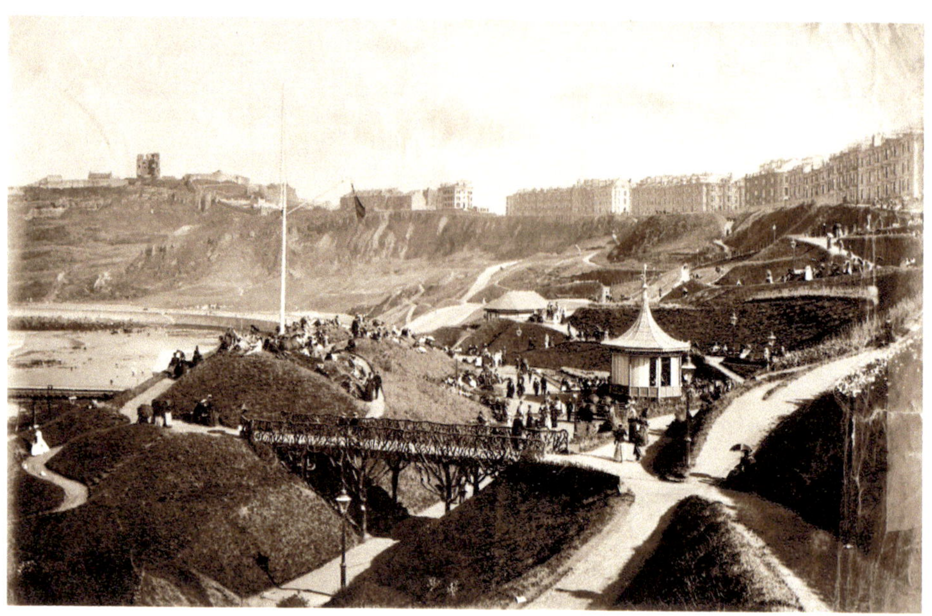

Clarence Gardens

The Victorian holidaymakers enjoyed peace and quiet, along with floral displays, which go hand in hand with their pursuit of healthy fresh air away from the smoky industrial towns from which many Victorians had made their fortunes. Clarence Gardens on North Bay provided such facilities and can be seen here at around 1897. The entrance to the pier was just left of the flagpole. On the top of the cliffs are the hotels and apartments, which provided accommodation in those days. The modern picture shows that most of these buildings still exist and perform similar functions as hotels, although some buildings have been converted into flats and studio apartments, which provide homes for local people.

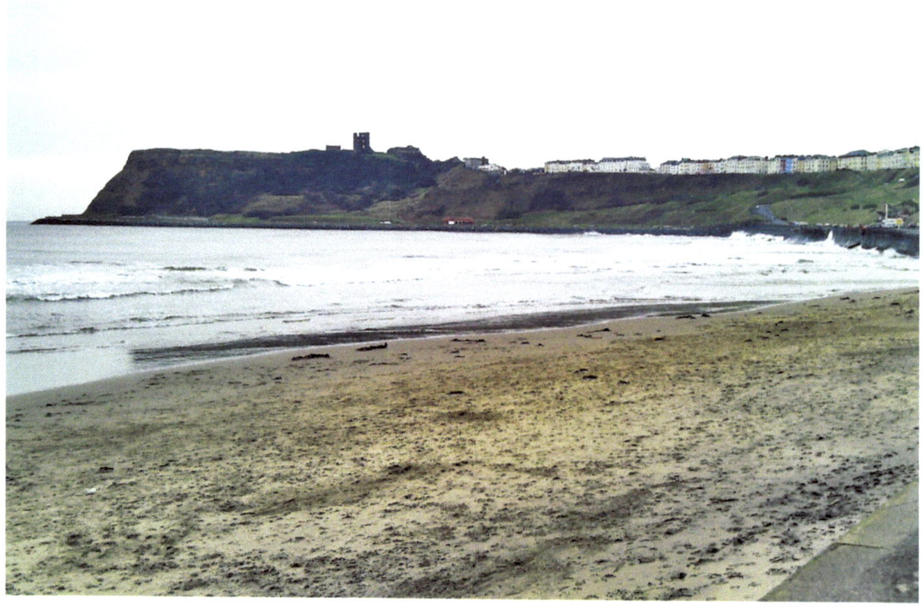

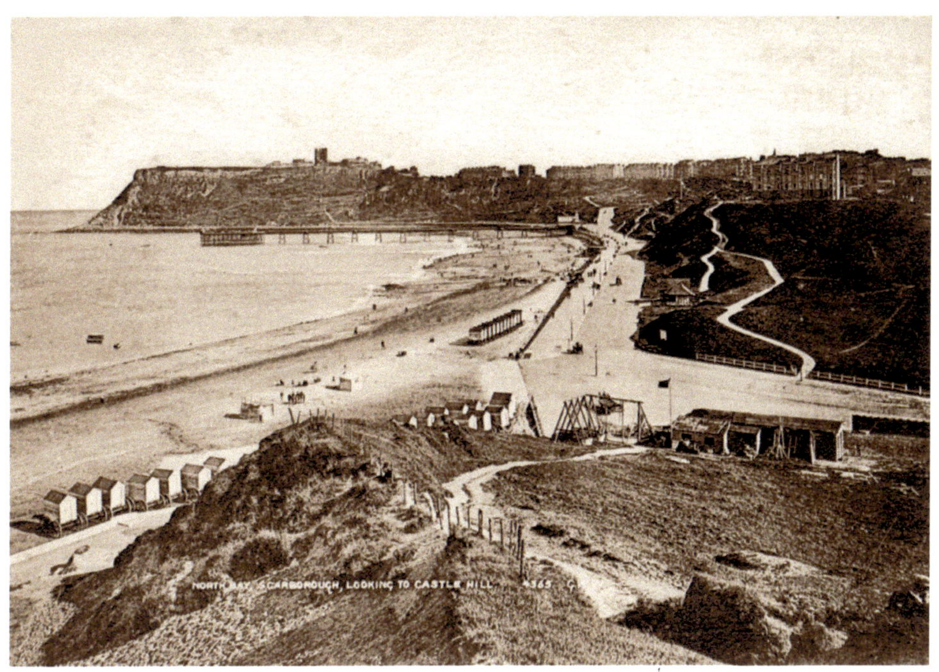

The Shore at North Bay

The area always being a little more refined than the more commercial South Bay, bathing machines are lined up ready for use while people wander along the beach. In the background is the castle, the pier, and the structures along the cliffs. Apart from the buildings on the cliff, all of the Victorian structures have long disappeared and the modern picture shows a much quieter North Bay, although people still enjoy a stroll along the Marine Drive and the beach here as an escape from the South Bay and its busy commercialism.

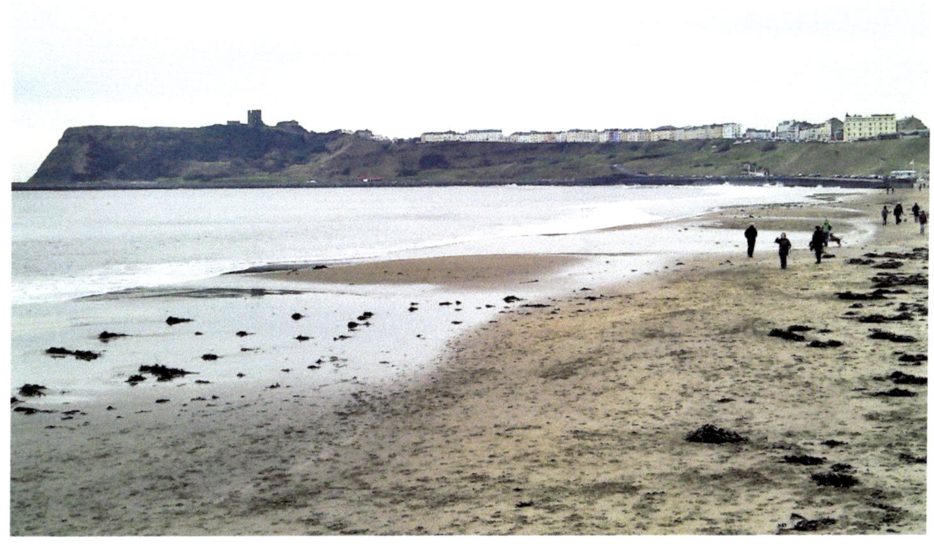

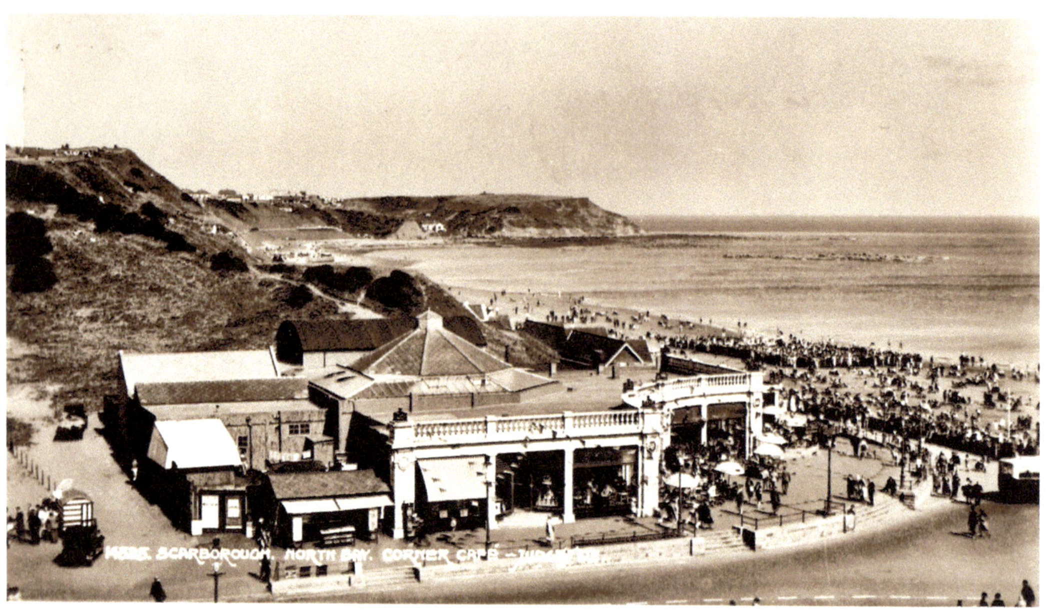

North Bay

The photograph above shows the Corner Café in the 1930s. In an effort to improve facilities in the area, a plan was brought forward to replace the café and structures leading up to Peasholm Park with a modern complex of residential apartments and shops, which can be seen under construction in the mid-2000s. The new building contains modern flats for sale, which give unobstructed views of the bay and castle; a supermarket and café are provided on the ground floor.

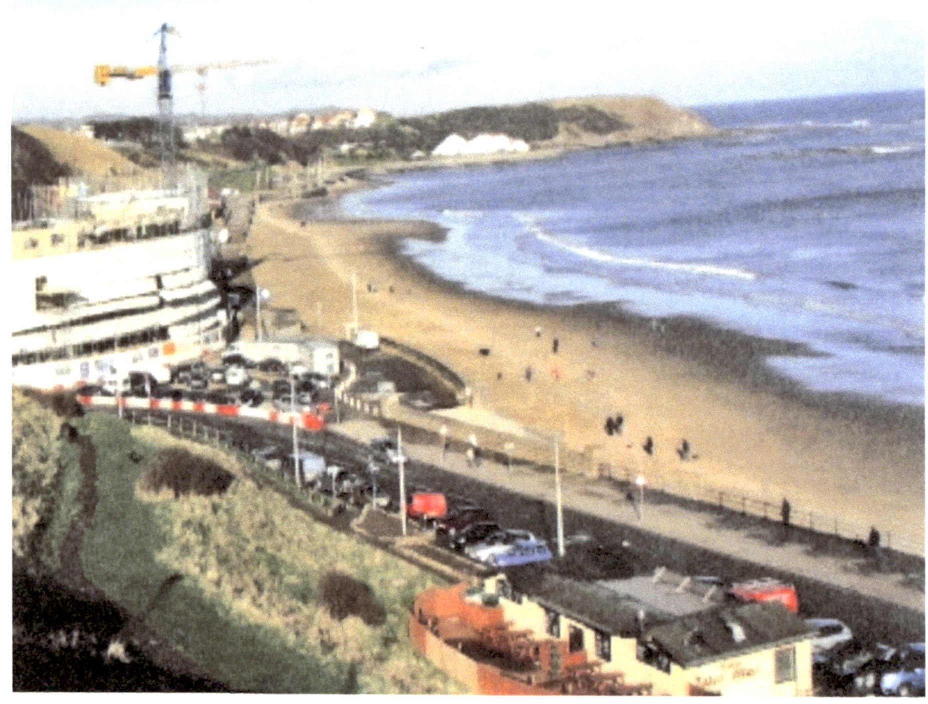

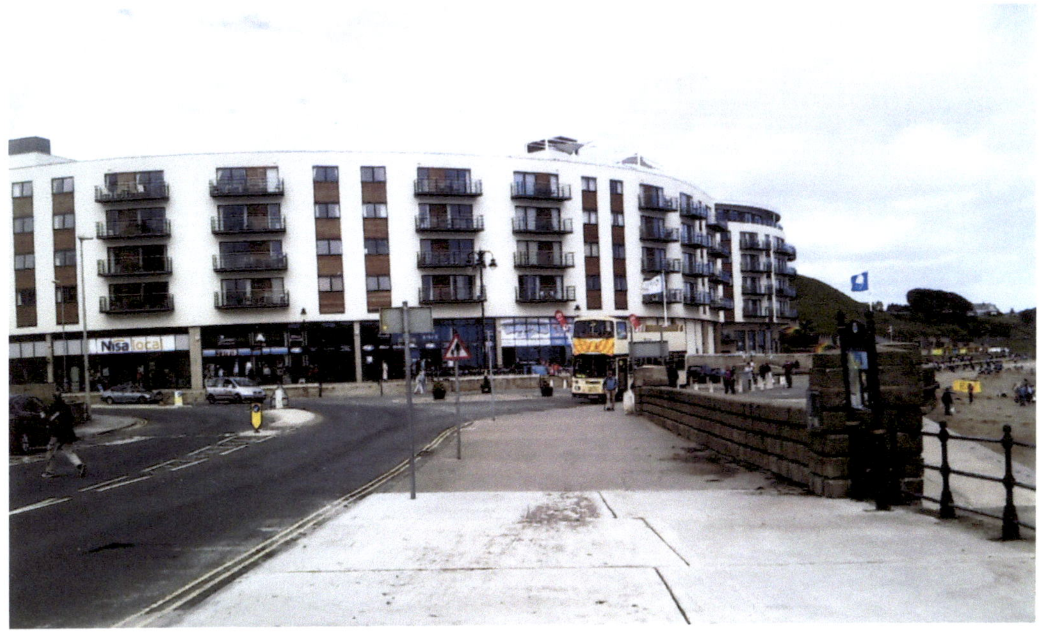

North Bay

The new apartments, with shops and cafés underneath, are seen here during the summer of 2011. The beach appears to be quite busy and North Bay appears to have a Blue Flag award for its water quality. Open-top buses of two operators, Scarborough & District and Suncruisers, both run services along the seafront between North and South Bays. Here, they can be seen at the North Bay terminus at the new apartment building.

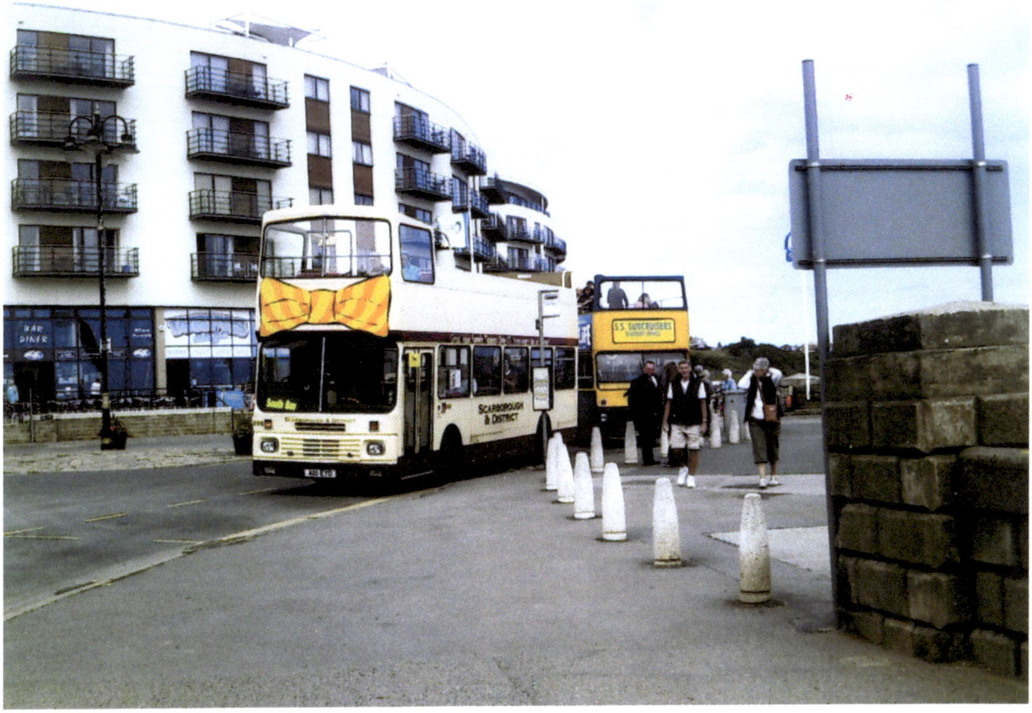

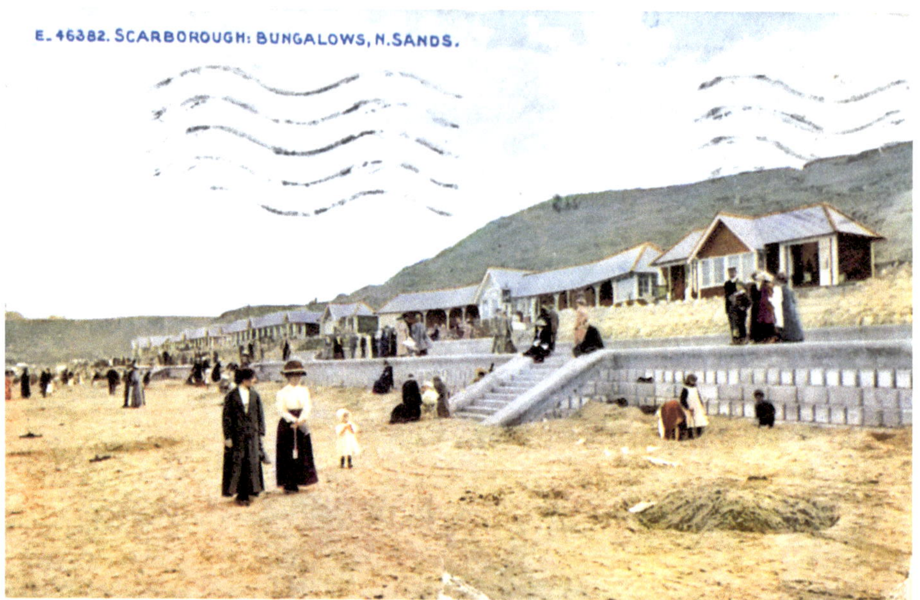

Bathing Facilities

Early replacements for the bathing machines of the Victorian period were wooden bungalows, seen here in this North Bay view of the Edwardian period, just before the First World War. The shore is busy with children of the period building sandcastles (nothing really changes) and parents watching while walking along the beach. Today, the modern chalet provides the facilities needed by holidaymakers and a row of these colourful structures can be seen here.

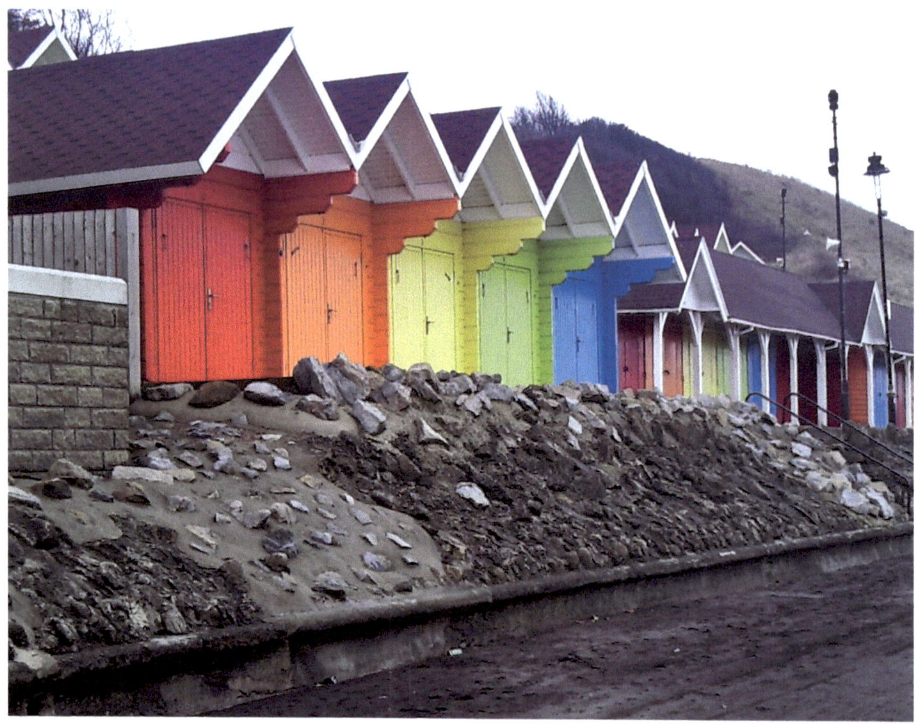

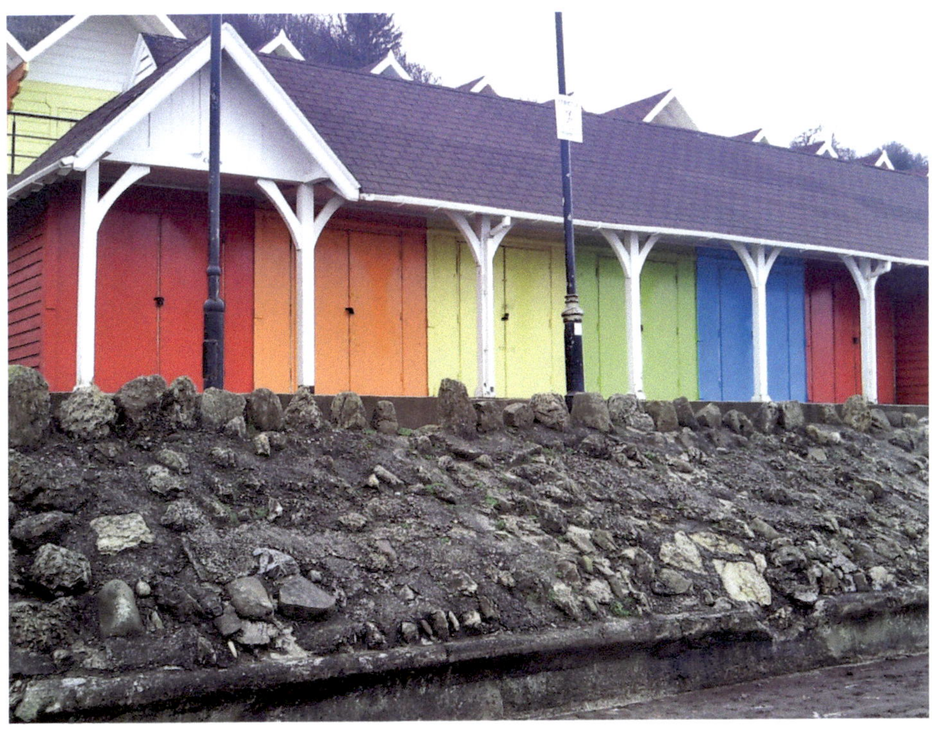

The Chalets

Another view of the chalets at North Bay and a view of the shore at North Bay from these chalets showing that Scarborough's beach here has a blue flag, the sea being very clean here and suitable for bathing.

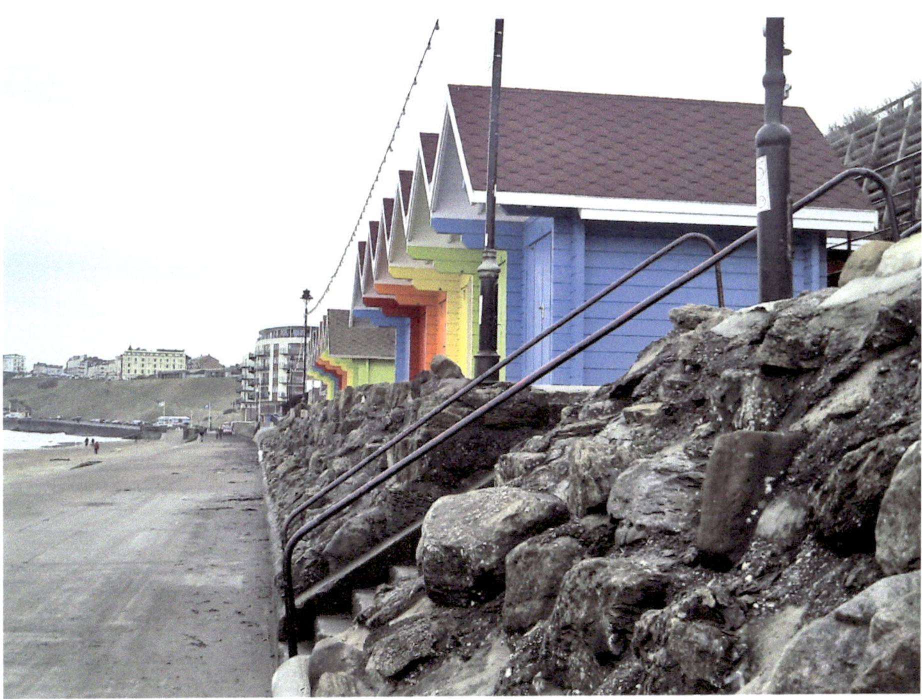

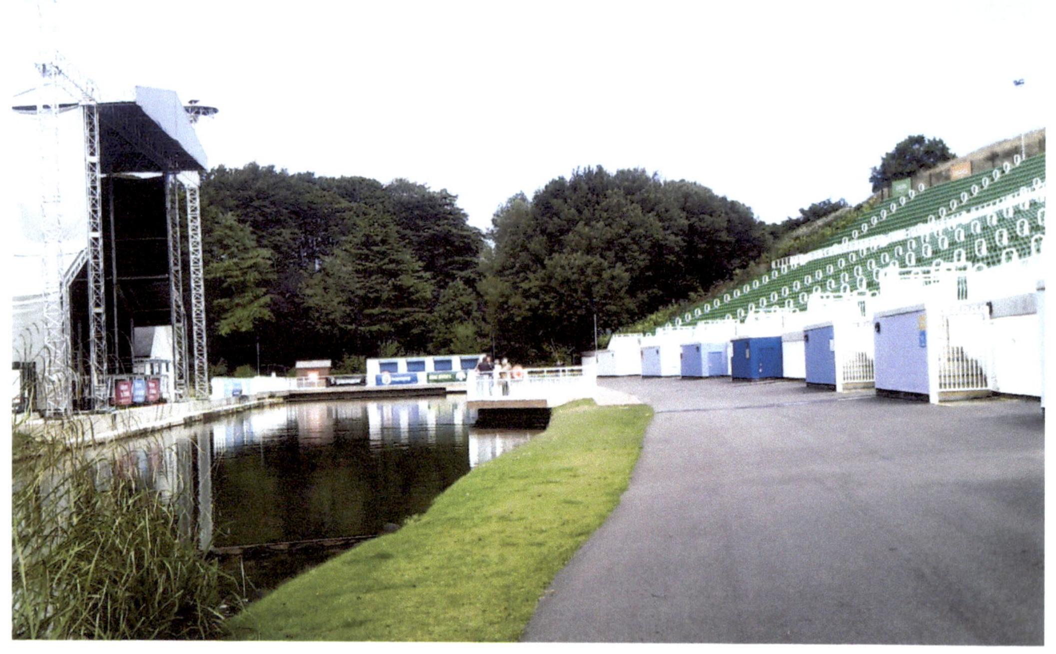

The Outdoor Theatre

The new Open Air Theatre at North Bay. Constructed by Scarborough Council, it replaced one which had closed some years ago. This new theatre was opened in 2011 by the Queen and is seen here in the summer of the same year. Below, the pathway linking North Shore with the Open Air Theatre. The track of the miniature railway is on the left in the wooded area.

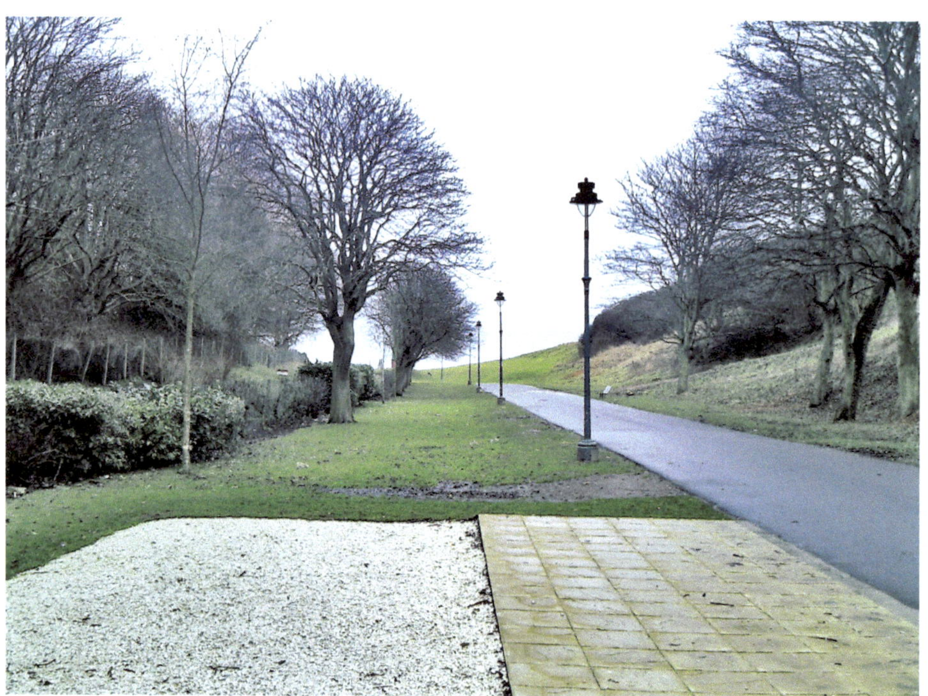

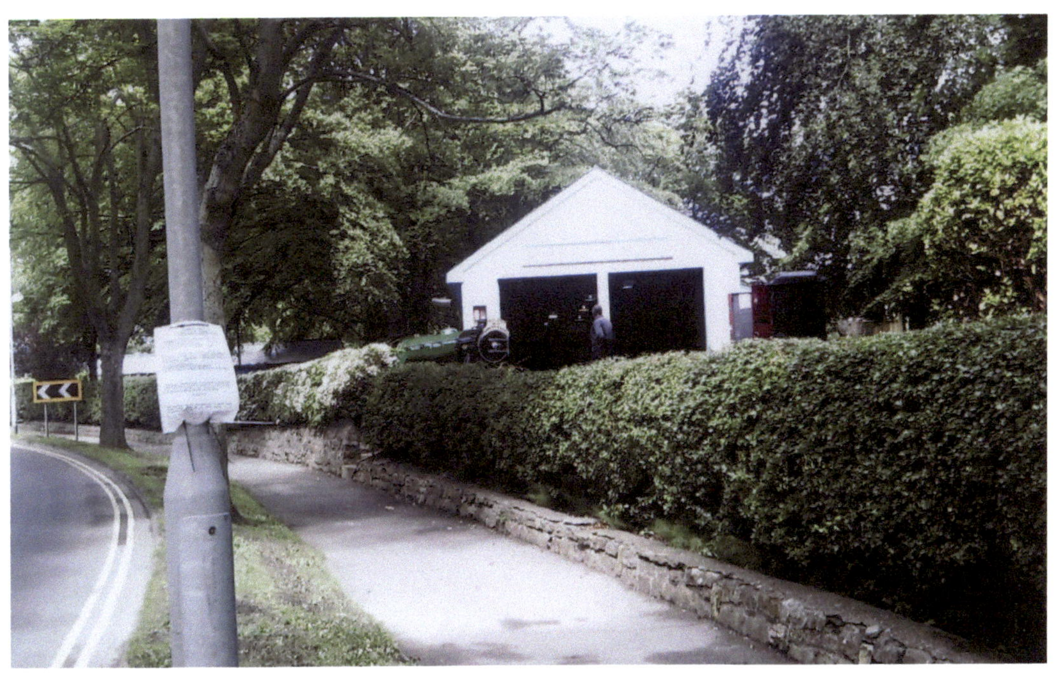

The Miniature Railway

The miniature railway at North Bay, opposite Peasholm Park. This North Bay Railway operates trains between North Bay and Scalby Mills and does good business during the summer. Below, one of the locomotives of the North Bay Railway after arriving at the North Bay station. The locomotive, No. 1932 *Triton*, is electrically powered although it has the appearance of a steam engine and was built by Hudswell-Clark, styled after LNER A1 pacifics.

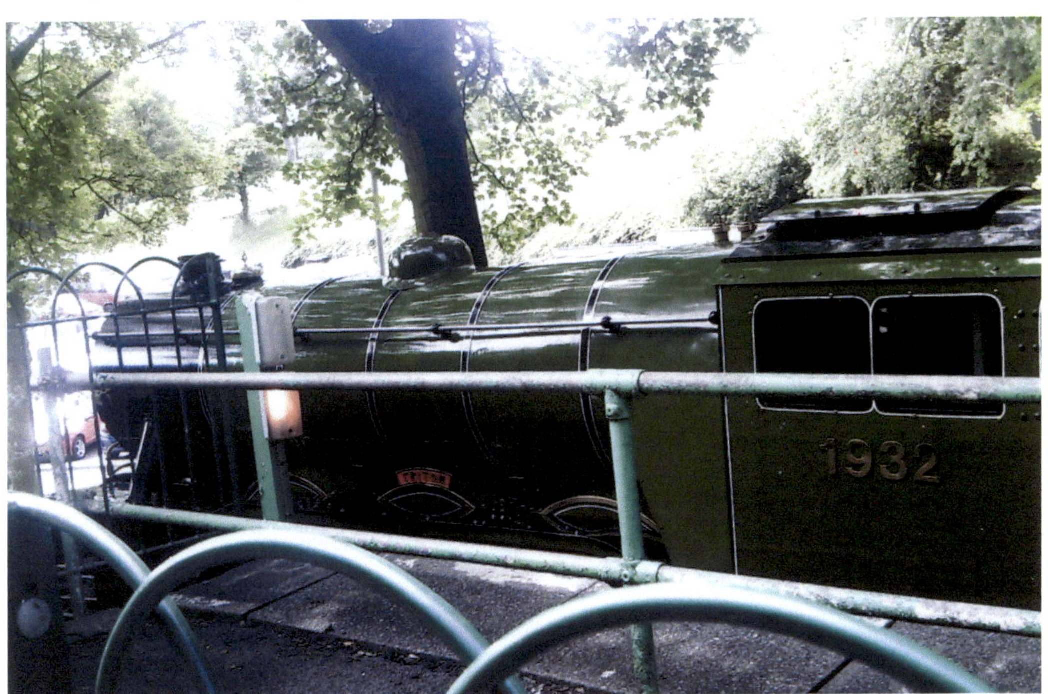

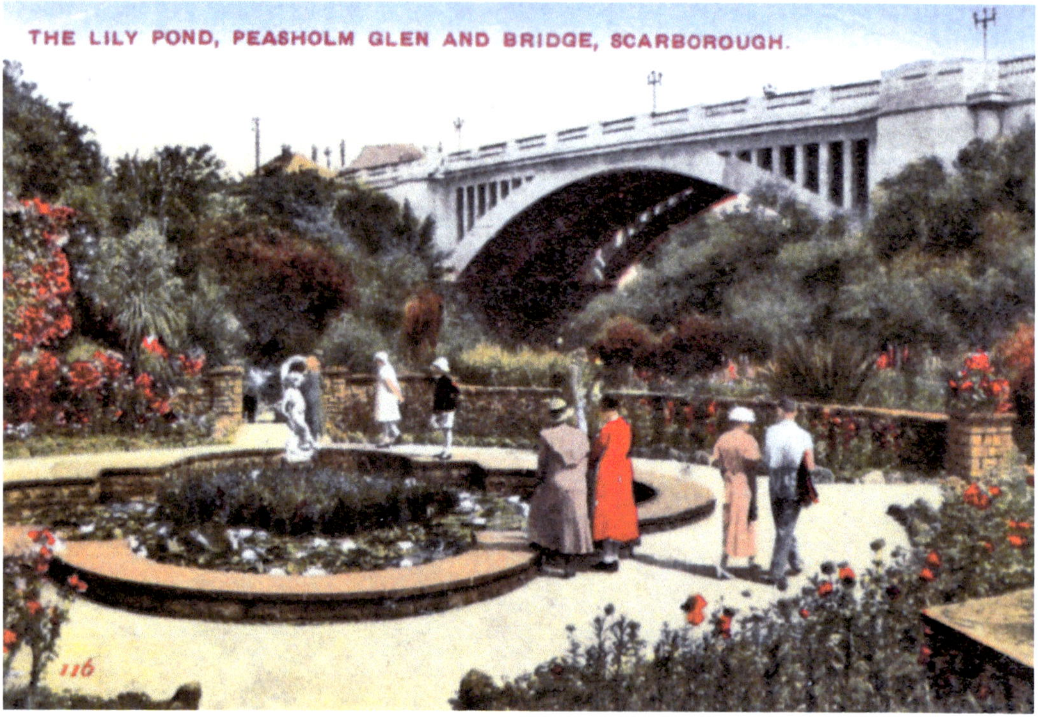

Peasholm Park

Two views of Peasholm Park in the early years of the twentieth century, depicting the Glen with its little lake. Peasholm Park lies at the end of Royal Albert Drive, which also contains the miniature railway, water features and the newly reopened open air theatre.

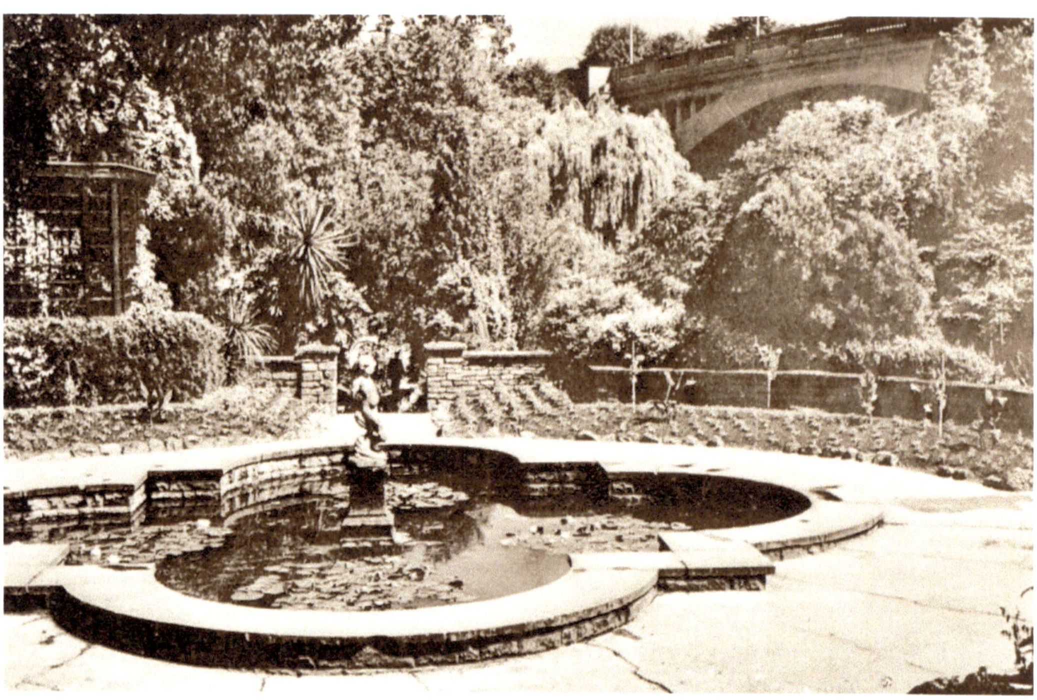

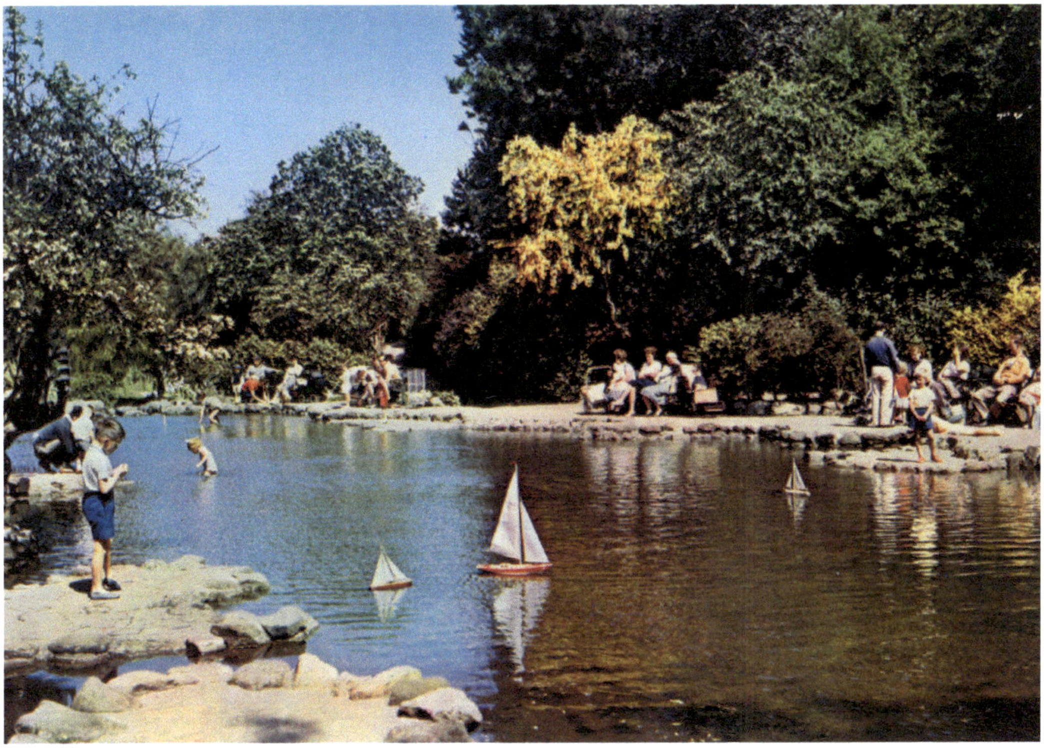

Peasholm Park

The children's boating pool at Peasholm Park in the twentieth century.

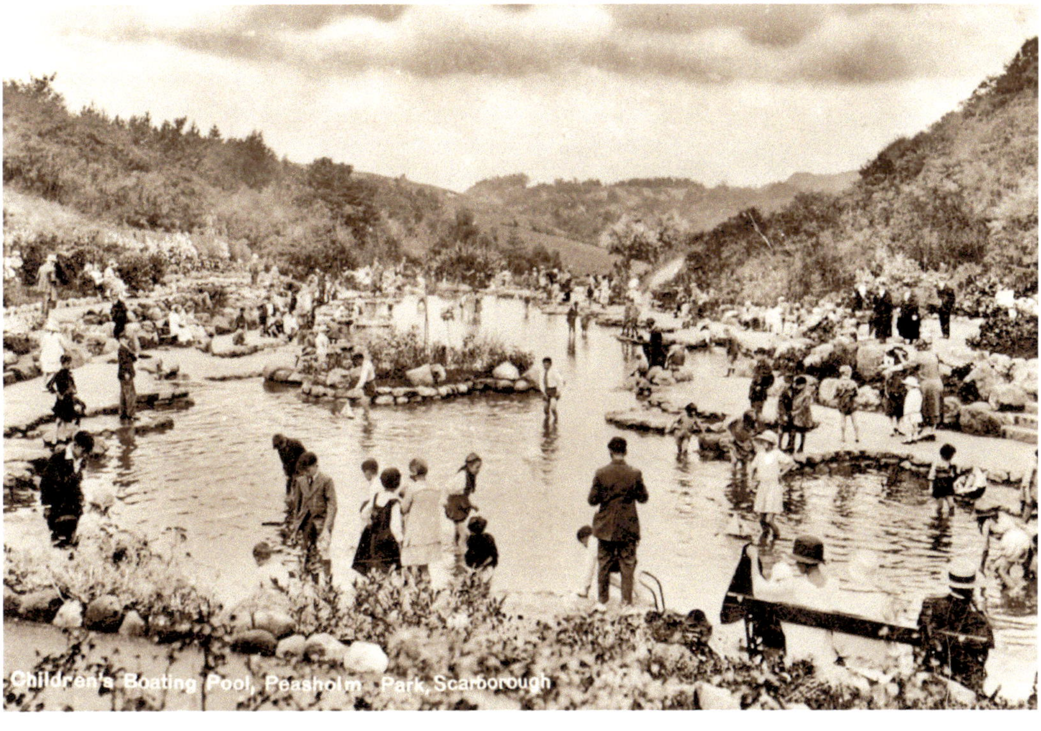

Children's Boating Pool, Peasholm Park, Scarborough

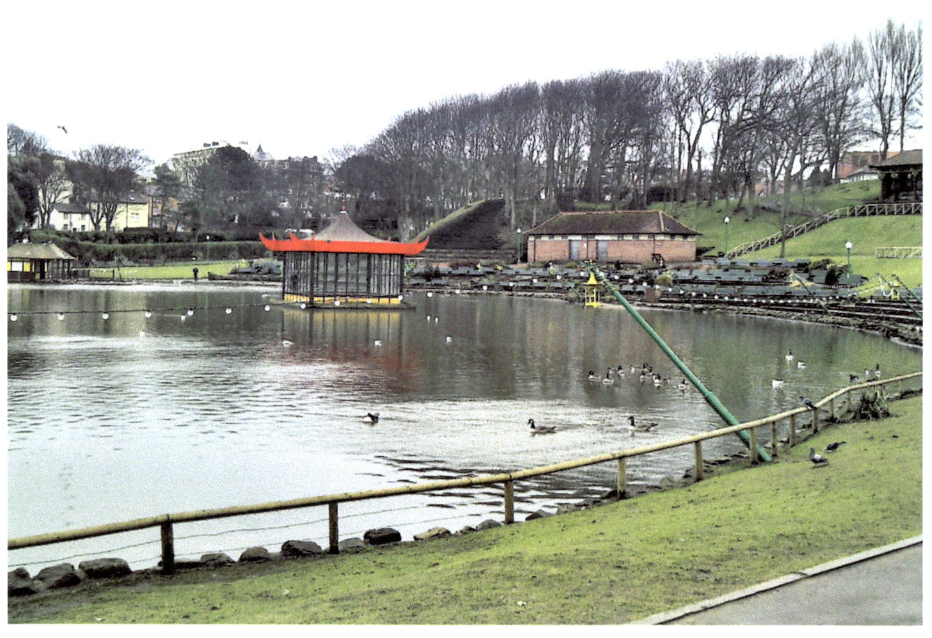

Views of the lake at Peasholm Park with its pagoda in the background and Japanese gardens.

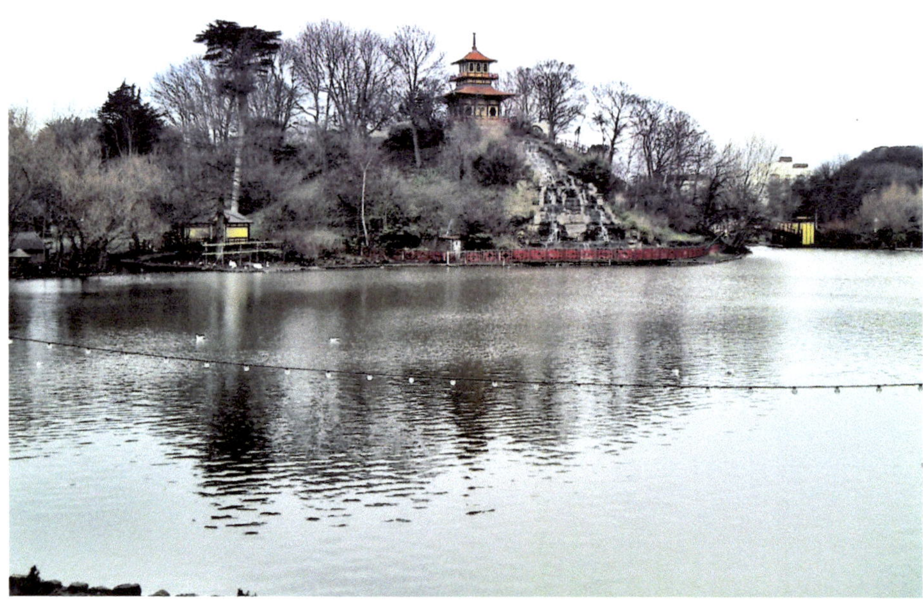

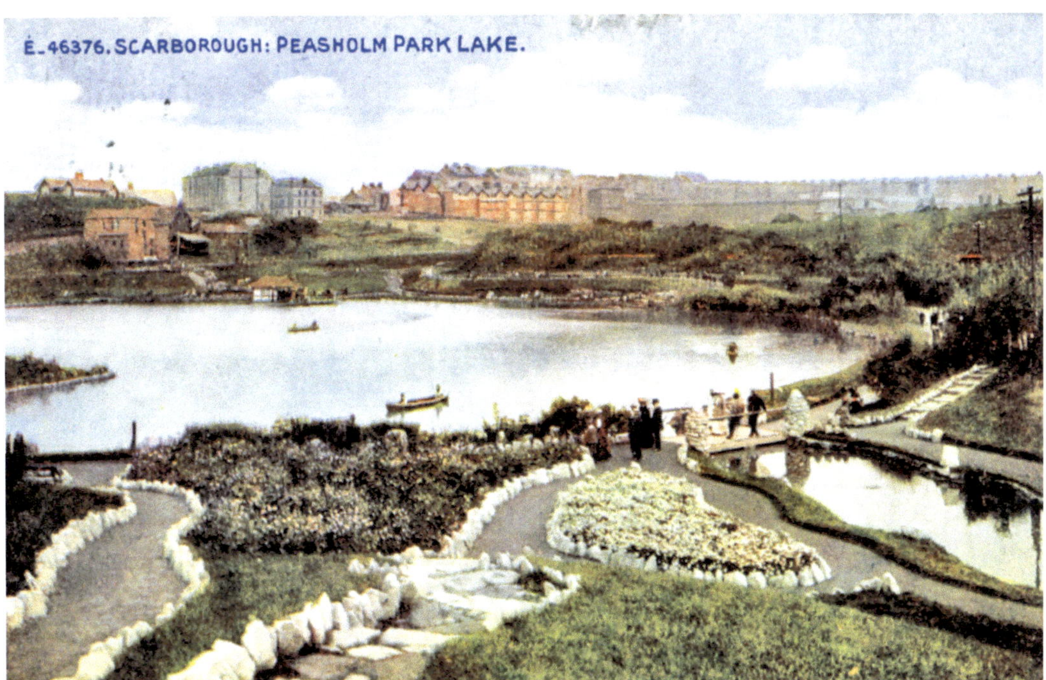

Peasholm Park

The manmade lake at Peasholm Park as it appeared in the early years of the twentieth century. Compare that to the modern day view of 2011, the lake now having Japanese features, complete with lanterns.

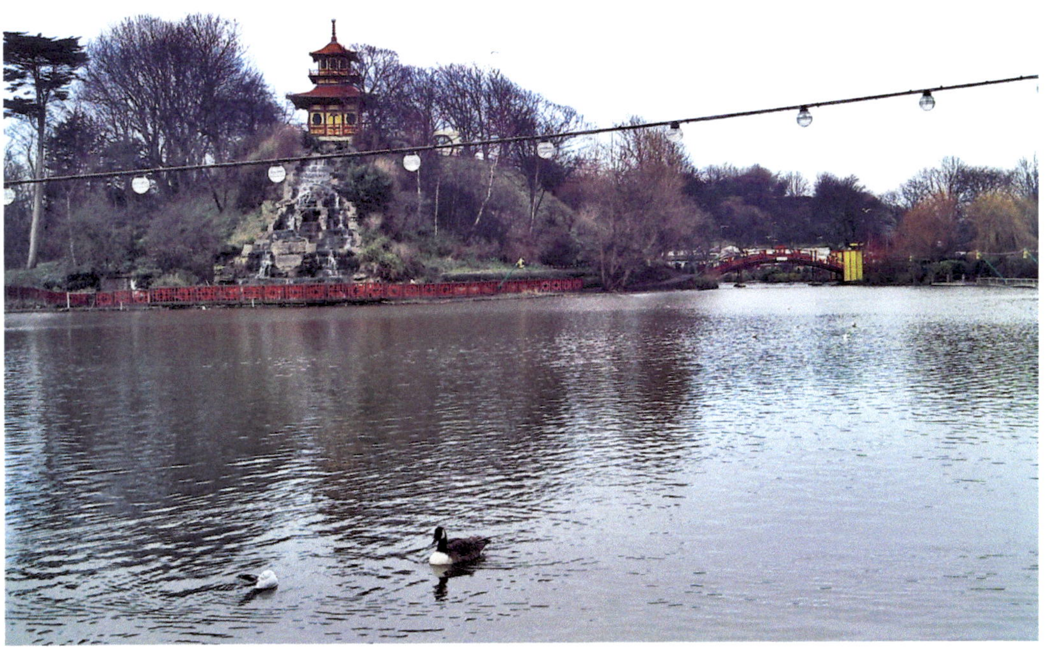

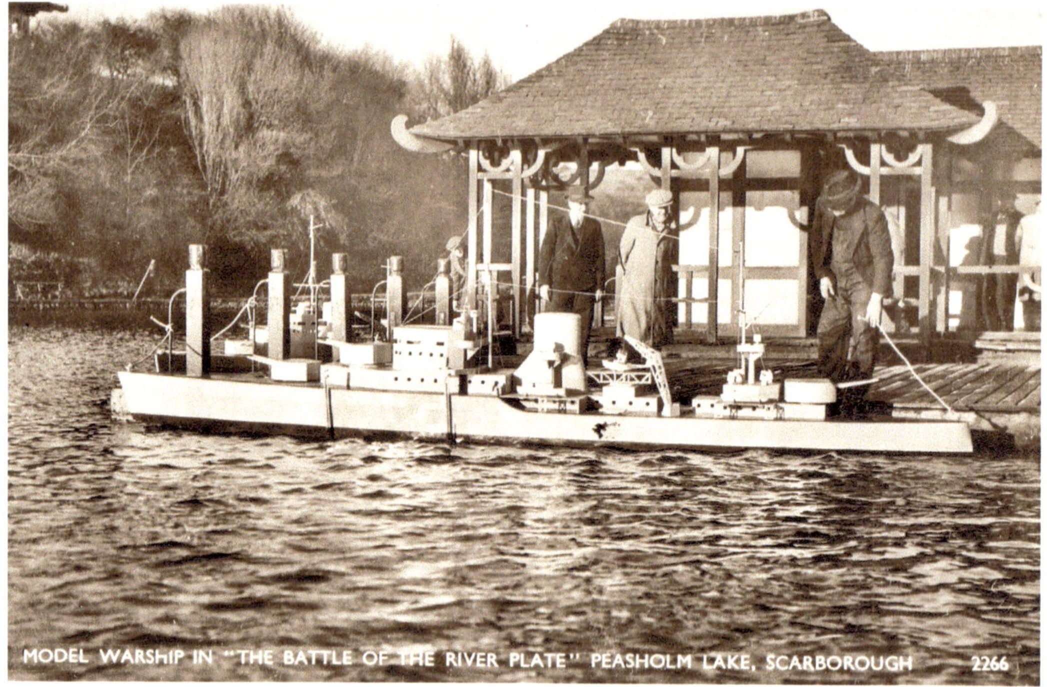

Peasholm Park

The lake at Peasholm Park is often used to give displays of famous sea battles using model ships. These re-enactments can be very realistic and are a feature during summer months. Above, one of the model warships is seen as it prepares for a re-enactment of the famous Battle of the River Plate during the Second World War. Below, the lake at Peasholm Park at the end of the twentieth century, with a view of the same spot in the 1930s as the inset.

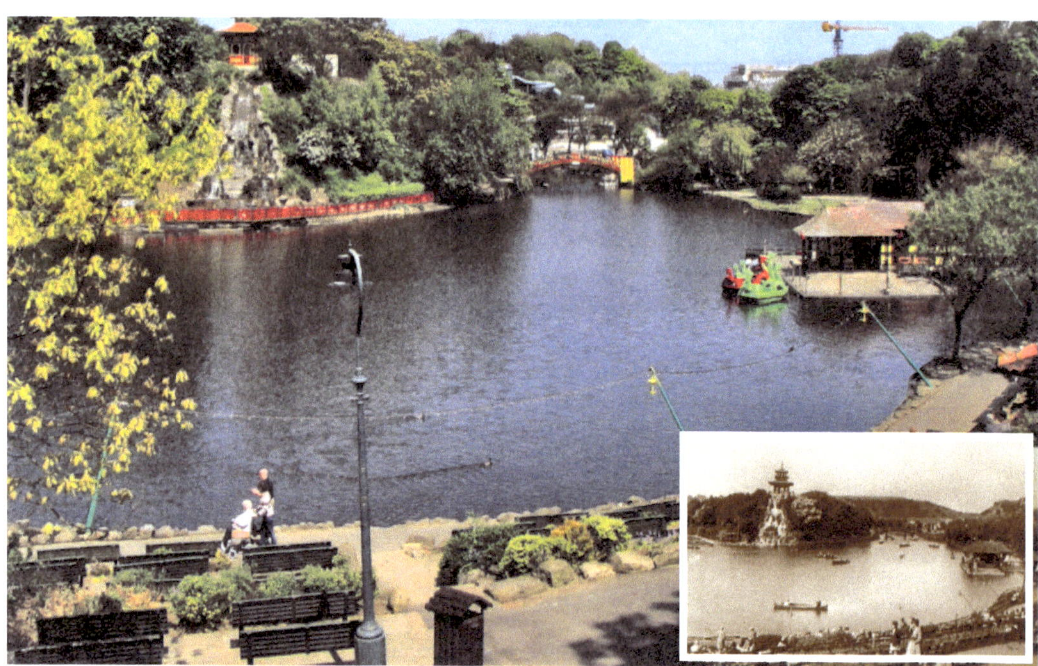

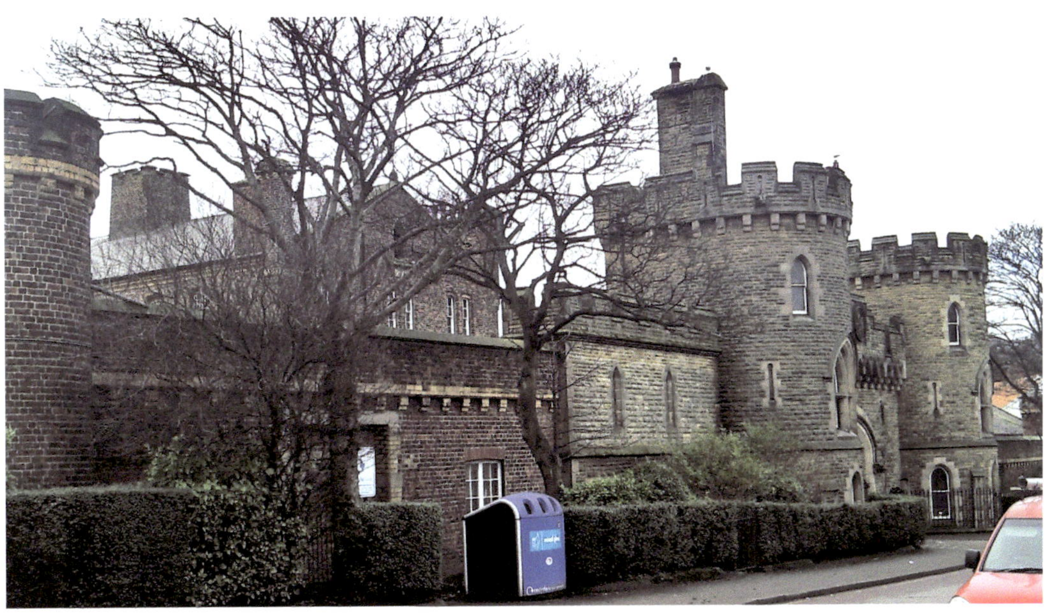

The prison was designed by William Baldwin Stewart and, by May 1865, plans were approved for a prison to accommodate thirty-six male, twelve female and four debtors (debtors still went to prison then) or juveniles. Capacity was later increased to seventy-nine. Work on the new prison started in September 1865 and was to cost £12,000. Only a little over a year later, in October 1866, twenty-two male and twenty-two female prisoners were transferred from Castle Road gaol. It is interesting to note that there were no separate prisons for the two sexes. The prison had thirty-six cells over three floors (twelve to a floor), with six on each side and two-feet-thick whitewashed walls. The new prison was supposed to be escape proof but, within the first week, one prisoner, Scott, scaled the 15-foot wall using an improvised rope. Today, the old prison is used by Scarborough Borough Council and plans have been devised to turn it into a hotel, although concerns have been raised about the conversion of what is a Grade II listed building. Dean Road was also the location of the Scarborough workhouse; so being a criminal or poor in the town meant that a person usually ended up on Dean Road. Below, another view of the lake in Peasholm Park.

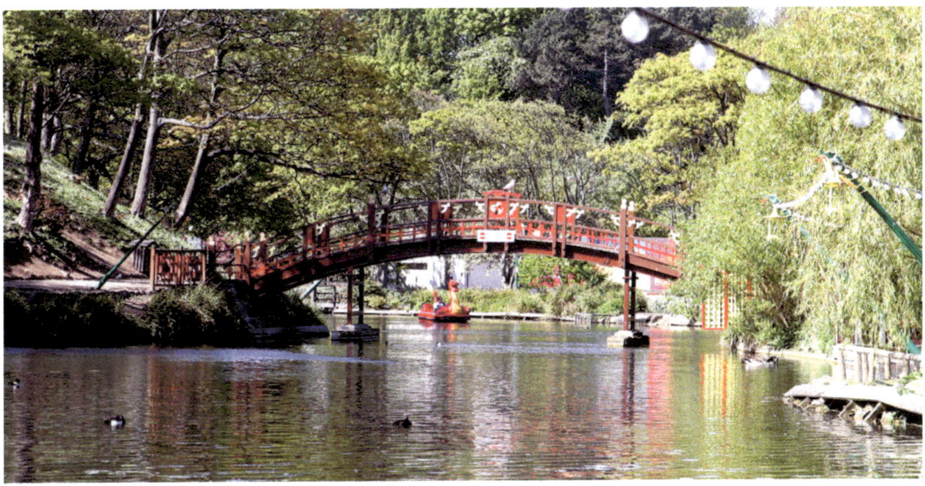

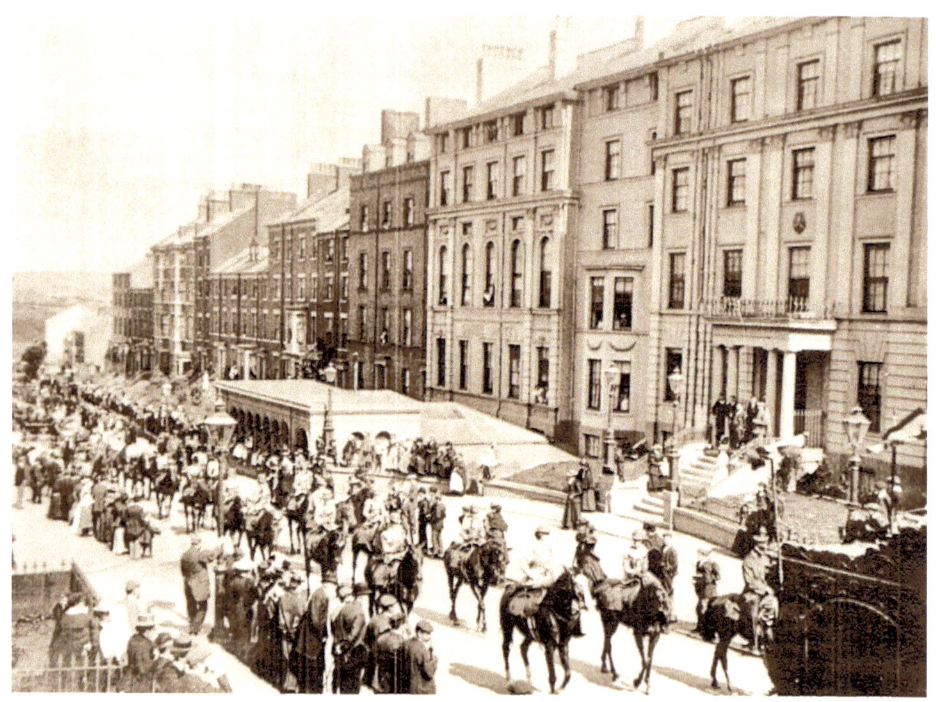

Military Parade

A street coming off the sea front at the turn of the nineteenth–twentieth century, with a military parade passing through. The modern view shows a much quieter street on the North Bay.

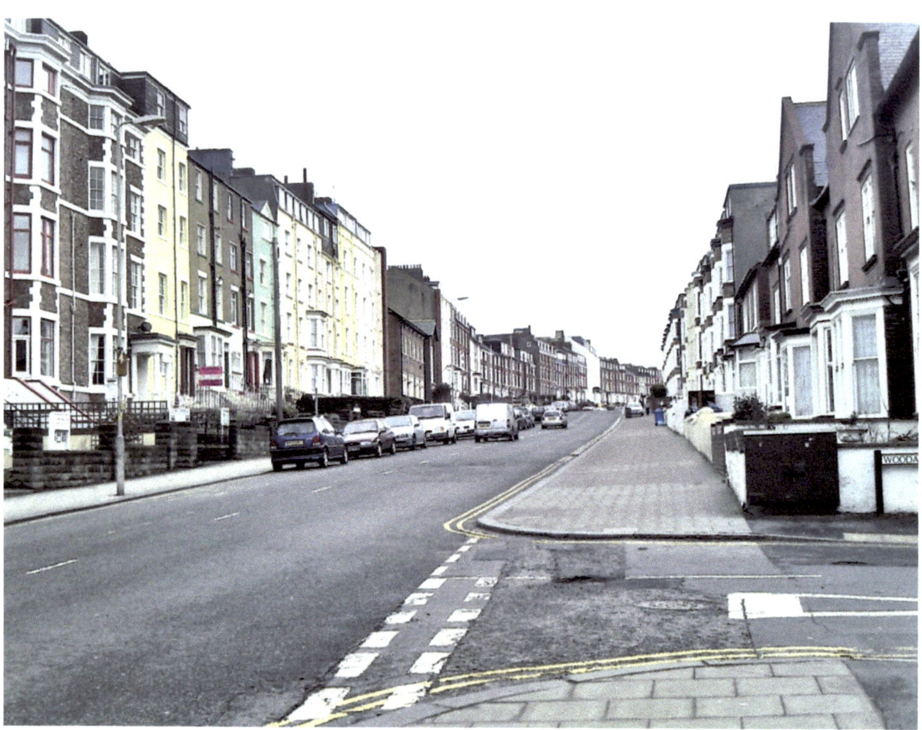

The Old Town

Late eighteenth-century and early nineteenth-century Scarborough at Old Butter Cross with Ye Old Brass Tap Hotel in view on Low Conduit Street. The old town here, close to the castle, still has steep roadways down to the seafront as can be seen here. Below, another view of late eighteenth-century Scarborough with St Mary's church at the top of the hill. Again, roads and paths are steep here.

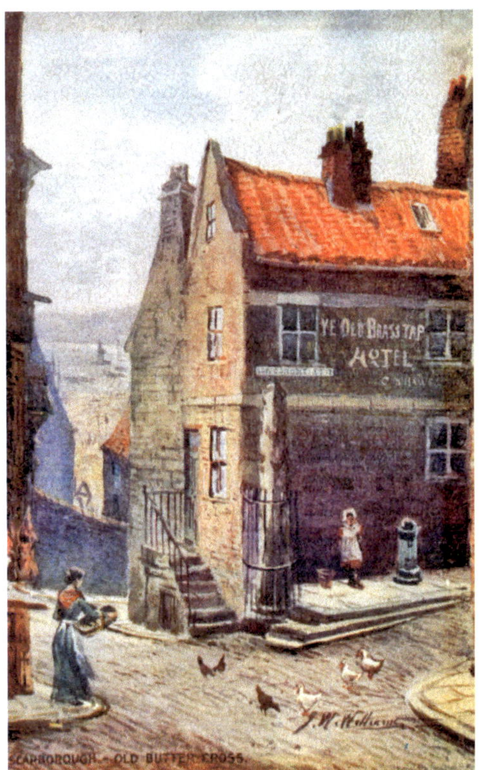

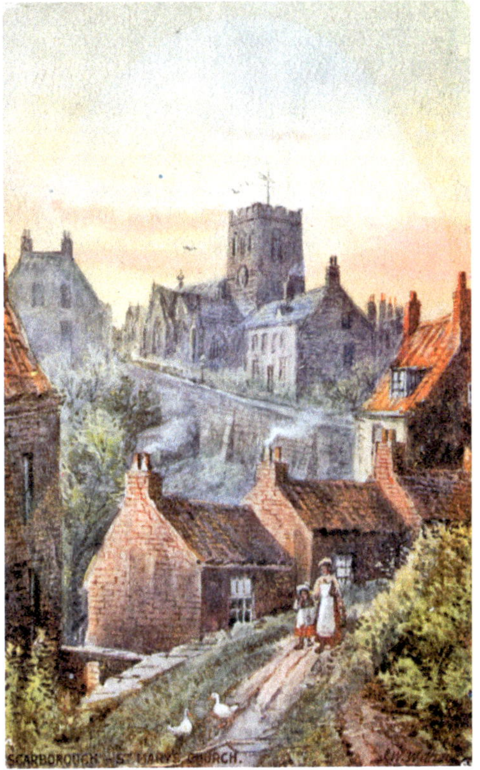

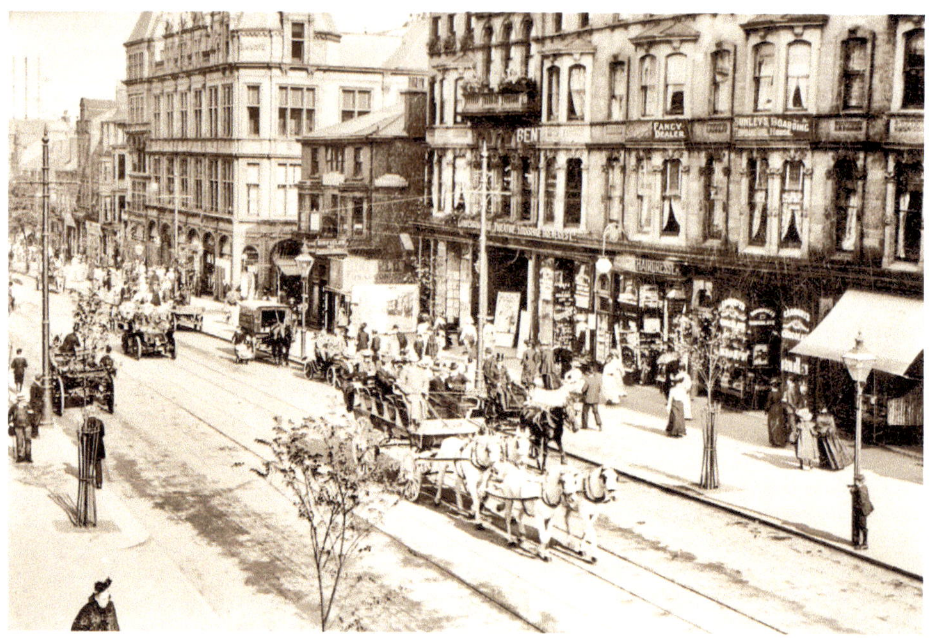

Westborough Road

The main shopping street on the south side Scarborough, known as Westborough, is seen here during the Edwardian period with horse-drawn charabancs carrying passengers through the town. It is noted that virtually all transport in this period was horse-drawn. The shops here advertise some products which are still familiar today, like Cadbury's chocolate. Just behind the charabanc is a tobacconist's shop, definitely unfamiliar today. Nowadays Westborough is pedestrianised, as can be seen in the lower picture, and the Brunswick Shopping Centre, which can be seen on the right, has recently been built, replacing shops on the right of the old picture.

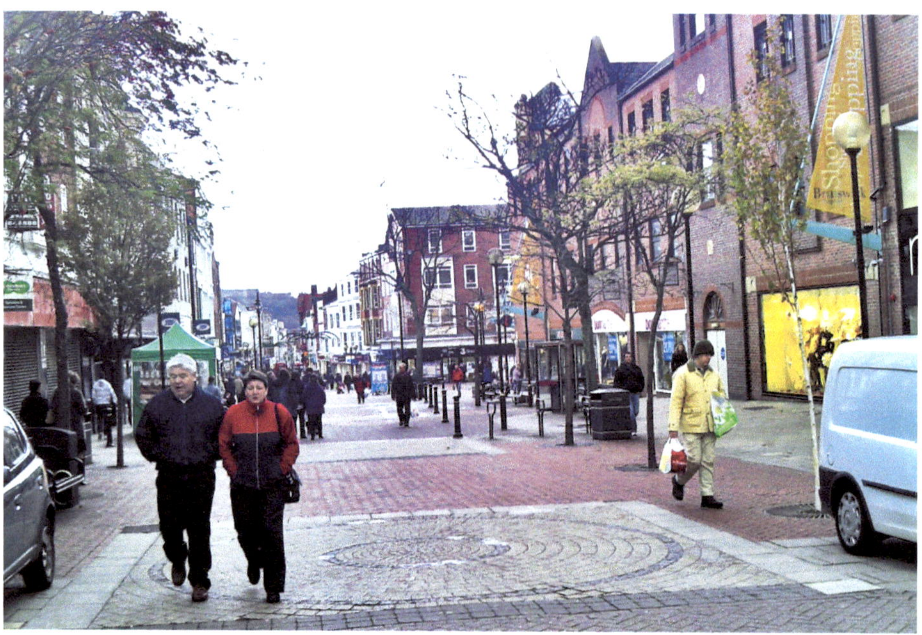

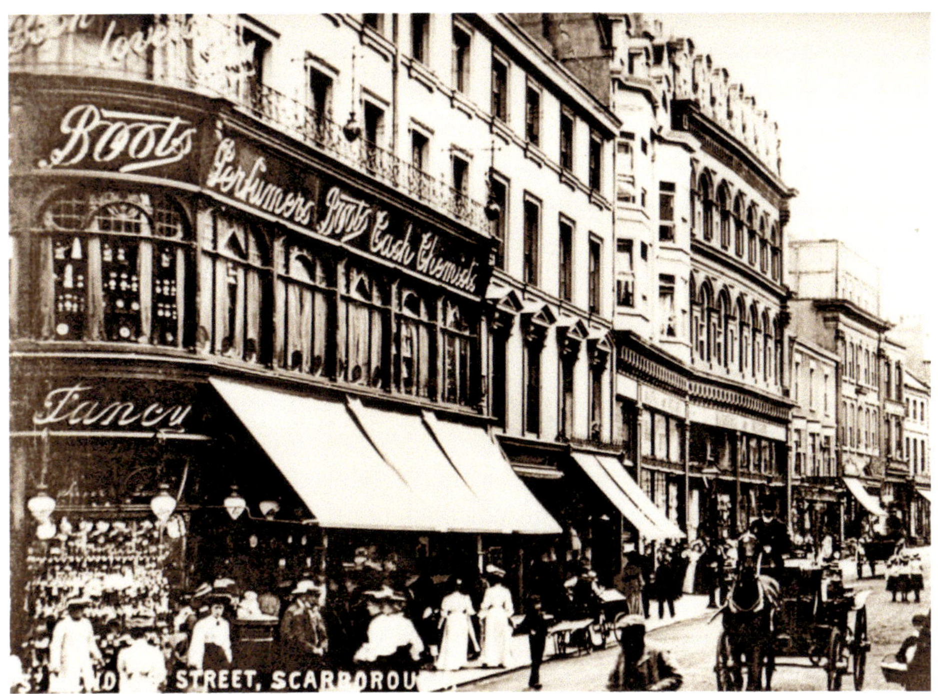

St Thomas Street

St Thomas Street links Westborough with North Marine Road, showing its shops as they appeared in Edwardian times. In the forefront is Boots the chemist with its splendid window display. Boots still has a presence in the town with its store on Westborough, opposite the Brunswick Shopping Centre. Below is St Thomas Street in 2011.

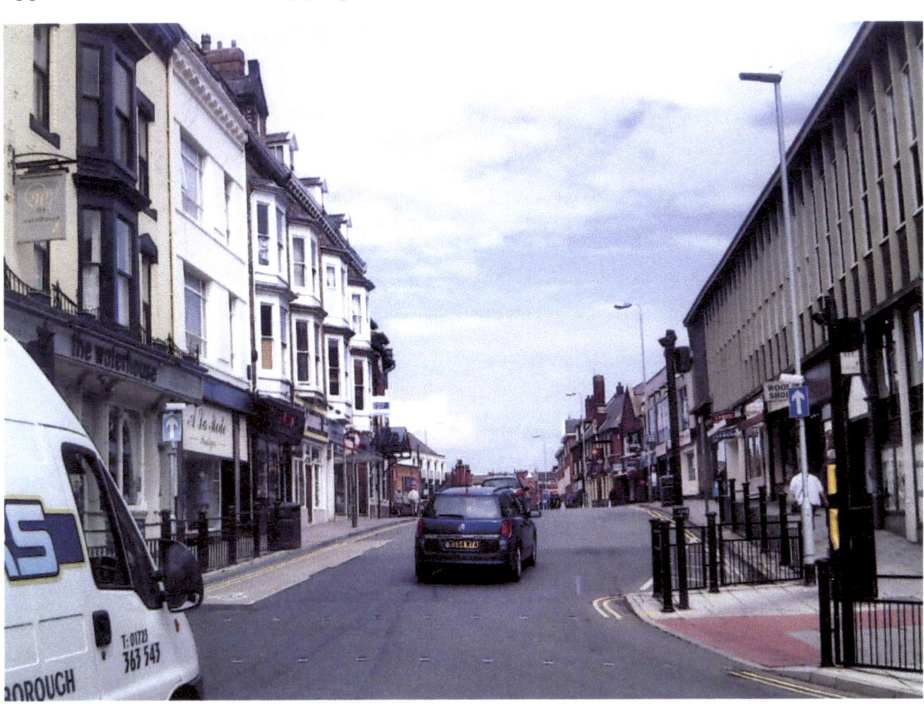

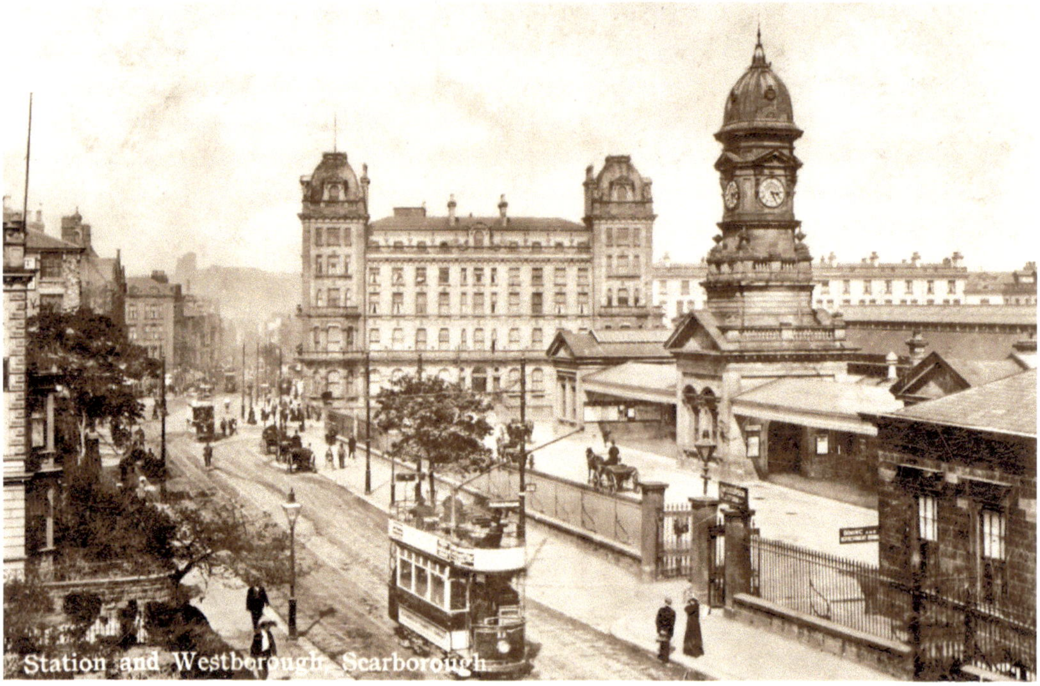

The Railway Station

Above is a view of the railway station exterior and Westborough during the Edwardian period, seen here with an open top tram on a service to Falsgrave. Below, Scarborough railway station looking from Westborough in 2011.

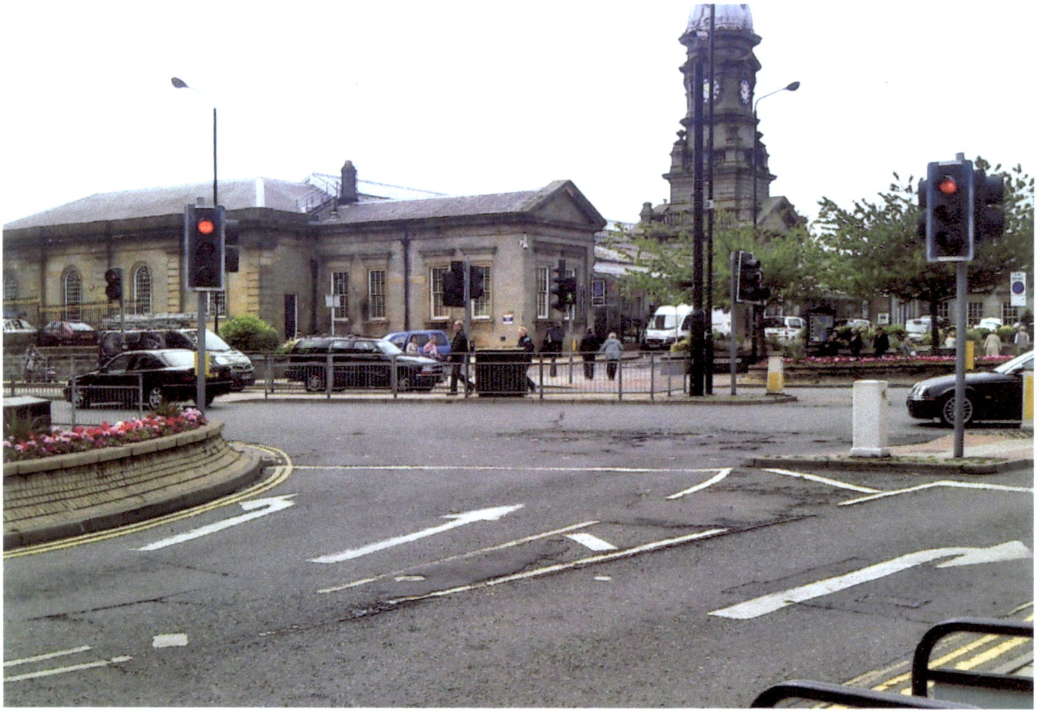

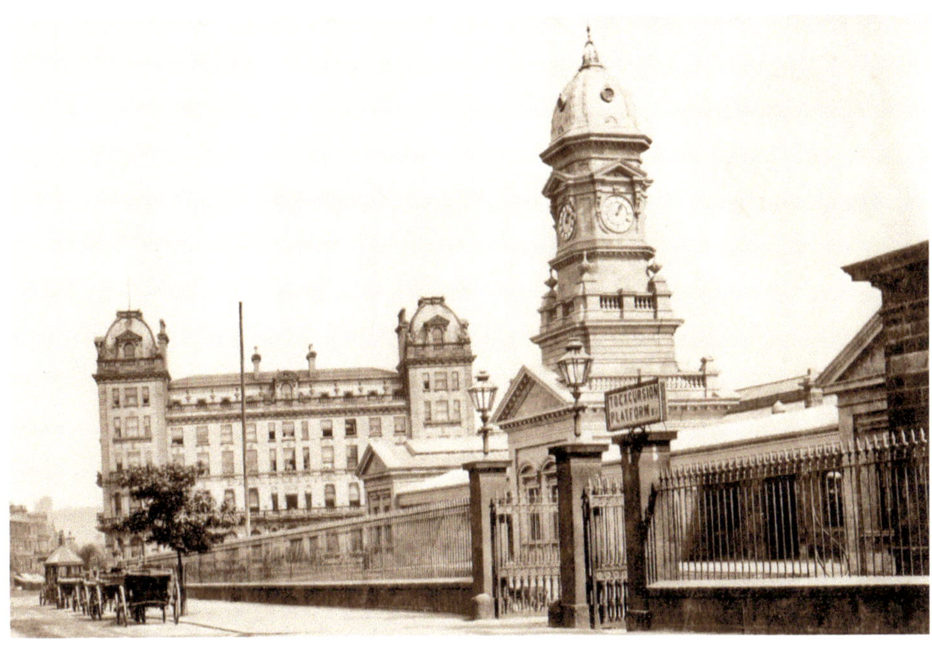

The Railway Station

The clock at Scarborough station, built by Potts of Leeds, is still a prominent landmark. Official opening of the station took place on Monday 7 July 1845, when a train of thirty-five coaches brought a large party to Scarborough at around 1.35 p.m. After festivities, the train left Scarborough at 3.45 p.m. and the station was left to deal with the many millions of passengers who would use it as a holiday destination or to conduct business locally. Below, 'For King and Country', a troop of soldiers, watched by many locals, wait to depart for foreign soil and are being blessed by local clergy. It must have been some event; the soldiers were probably off to South Africa to fight in the Boer War.

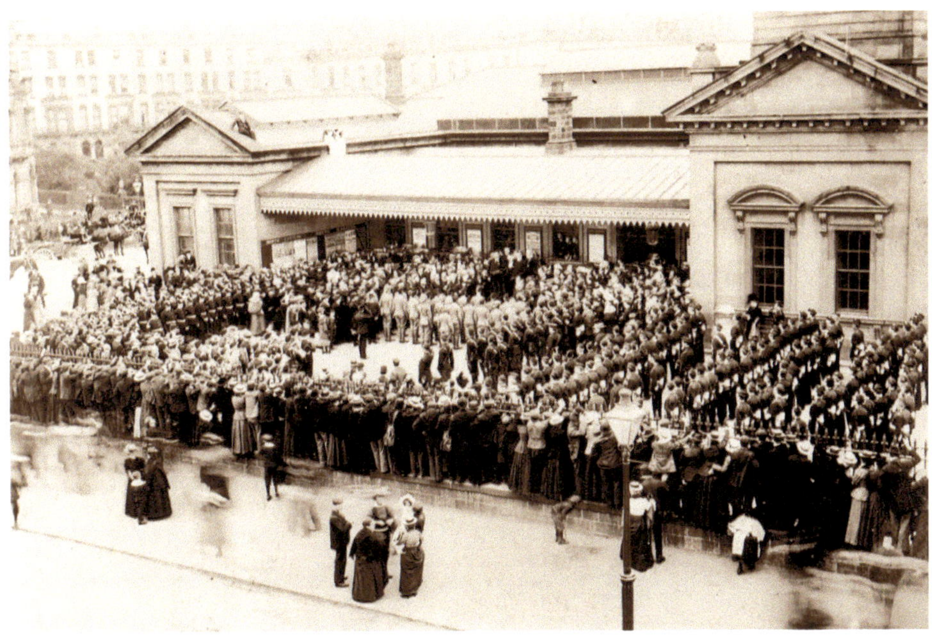

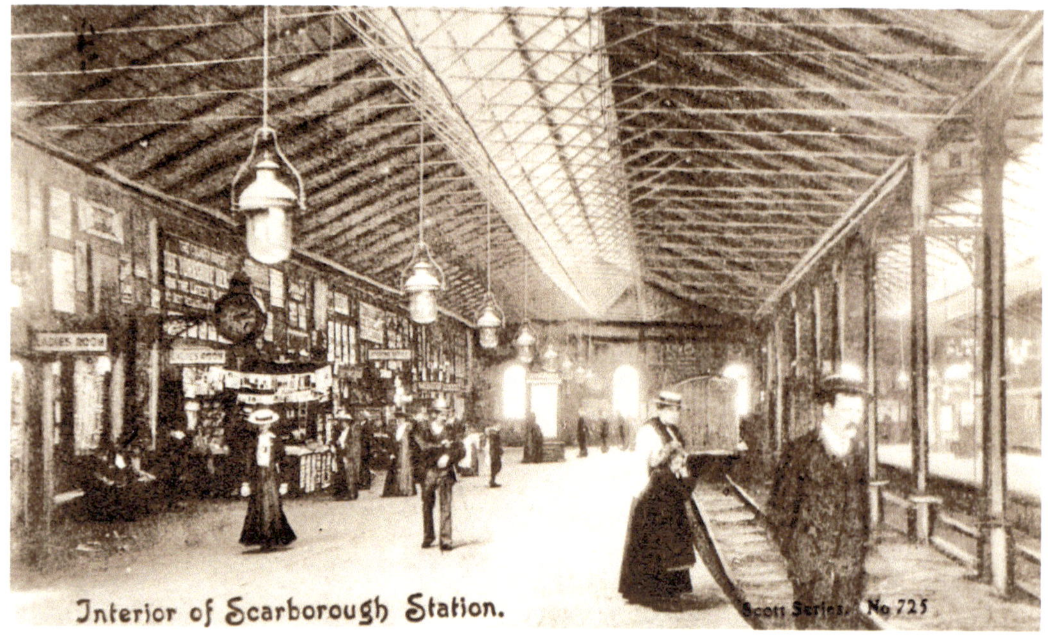

The Railway Station

Interior of Scarborough station in the early twentieth century and a simpler layout today as traffic has significantly declined with closure of so many branches during the 1960s. The station was designed by the York and North Midland Railway architect, George Andrews, and contained all the facilities expected for the nineteenth-century railway traveller, many of which have since disappeared. The old kiosks and ornate gas lamps have disappeared, although a café still exists on the main platform. The station was transferred to North Eastern Railway ownership in the 1850s, thence becoming part of the London and North Eastern Railway in 1923. From 1948, the LNER here became part of British Railways North-Eastern Region when nationalised and then became owned by Railtrack at privatisation. It is now part of Network Rail.

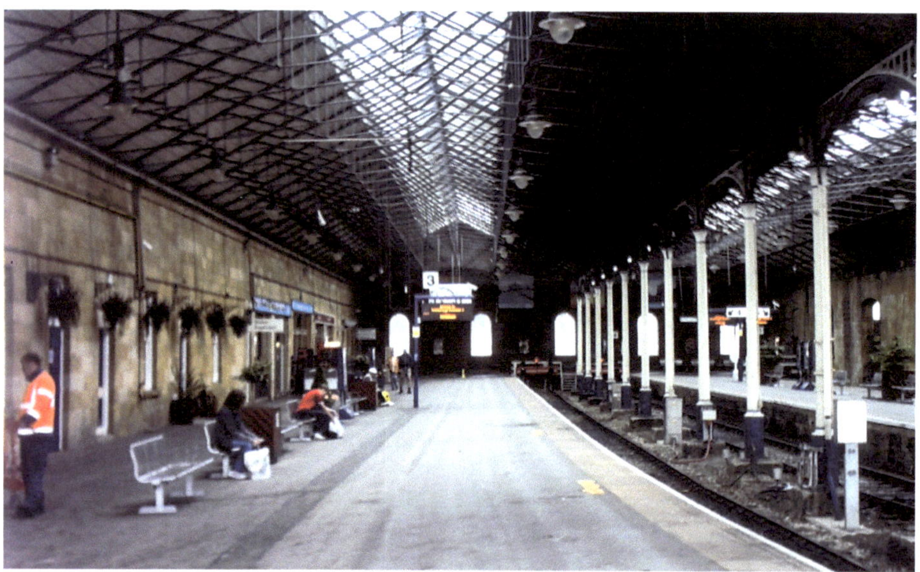

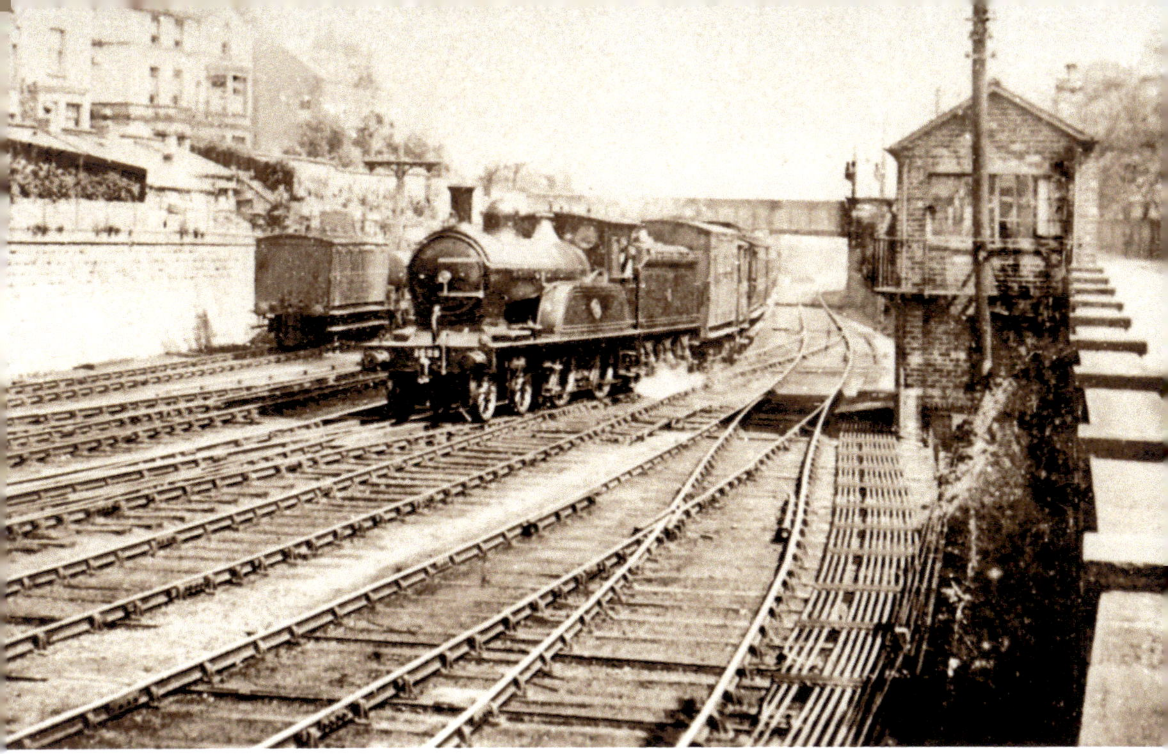

The Railway Station

A passenger train arrives at Scarborough in North Eastern Railway days with 4-4-0 locomotive No. 1629, built in 1893, at its head. Below is a 1930s view of Scarborough station, with the *Scarborough Flyer* train departing for York. Nearest is a steam railmotor train, favoured by the LNER as they were relatively cheap to run on local branch lines, about to depart for Whitby.

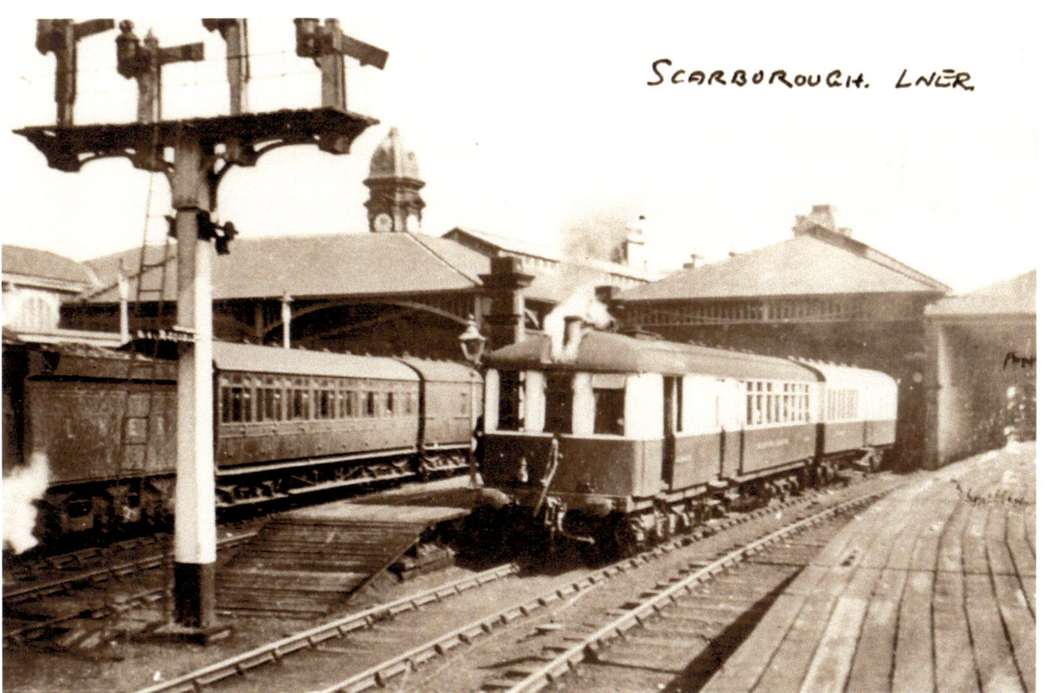

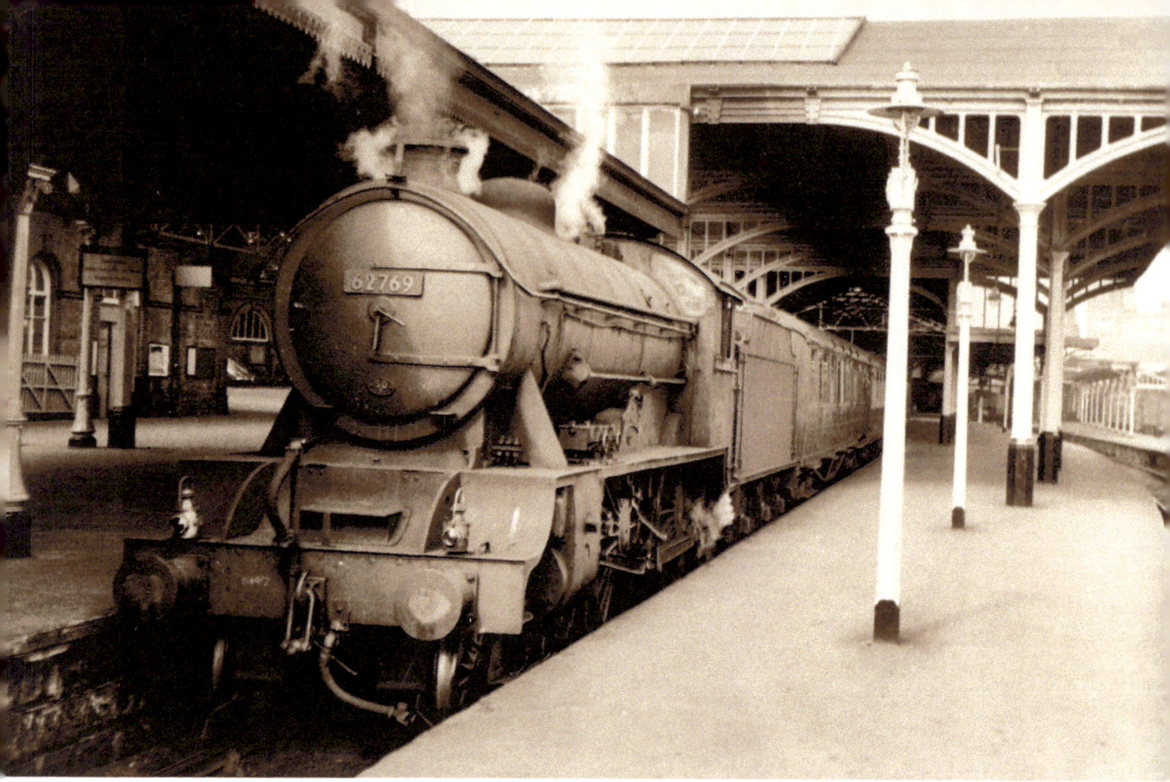

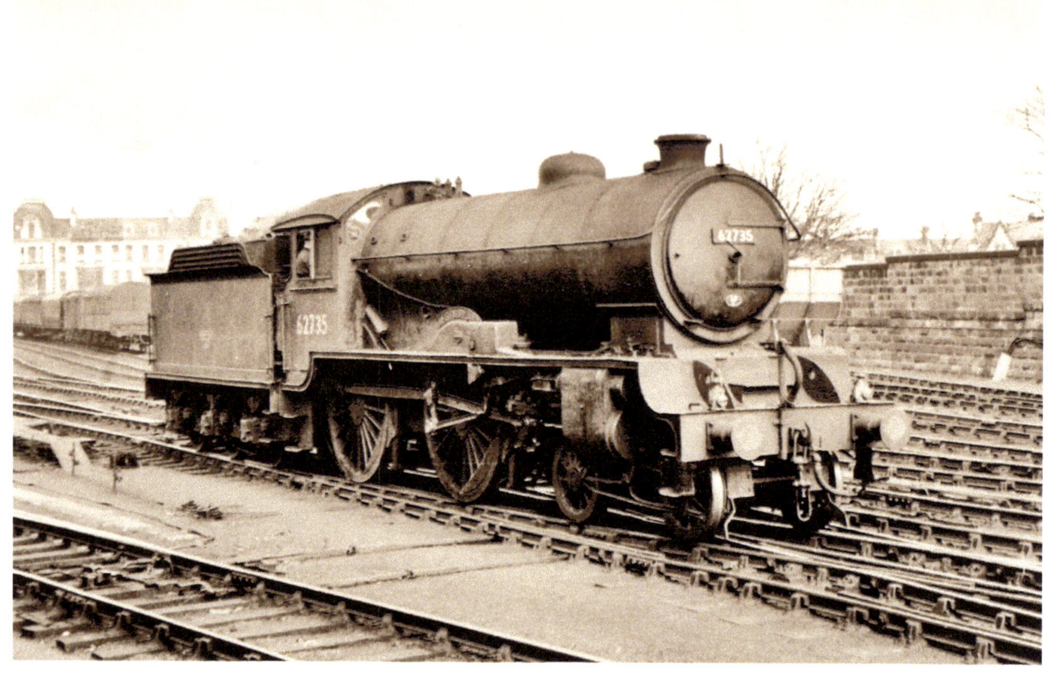

The Railway Station

Waiting at Scarborough station on 30 April 1958 is ex LNER D49 4-4-0 No. 62769 *The Oakley* with a passenger train for York. Another D49 4-4-0 No. 62735 *Westmorland* awaits its turn of duty at Scarborough station on the same day.

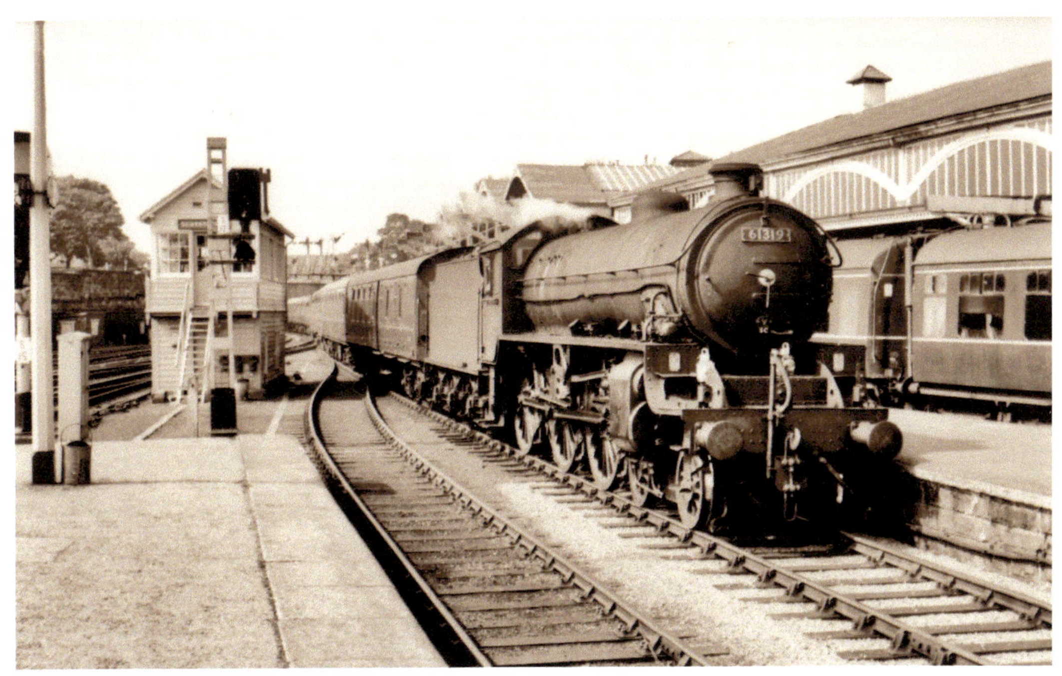

The Railway Station

As main line steam traction went into decline, BR B1 4-6-0 No. 61319 is seen approaching the buffers at Scarborough station with a train of empty coaches in the summer of 1965. These coaches were, probably, forming an excursion train, which will return to the West Riding later in the day. As steam declined, new diesel trains were introduced on many local services, an example of which waits at Scarborough station during the summer of 1965.

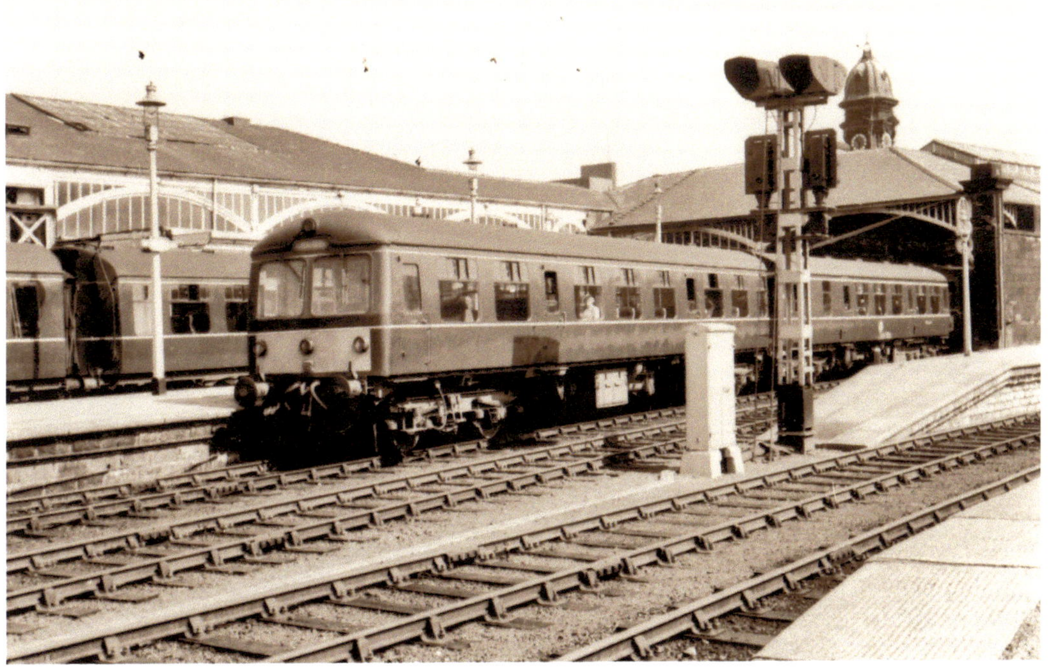

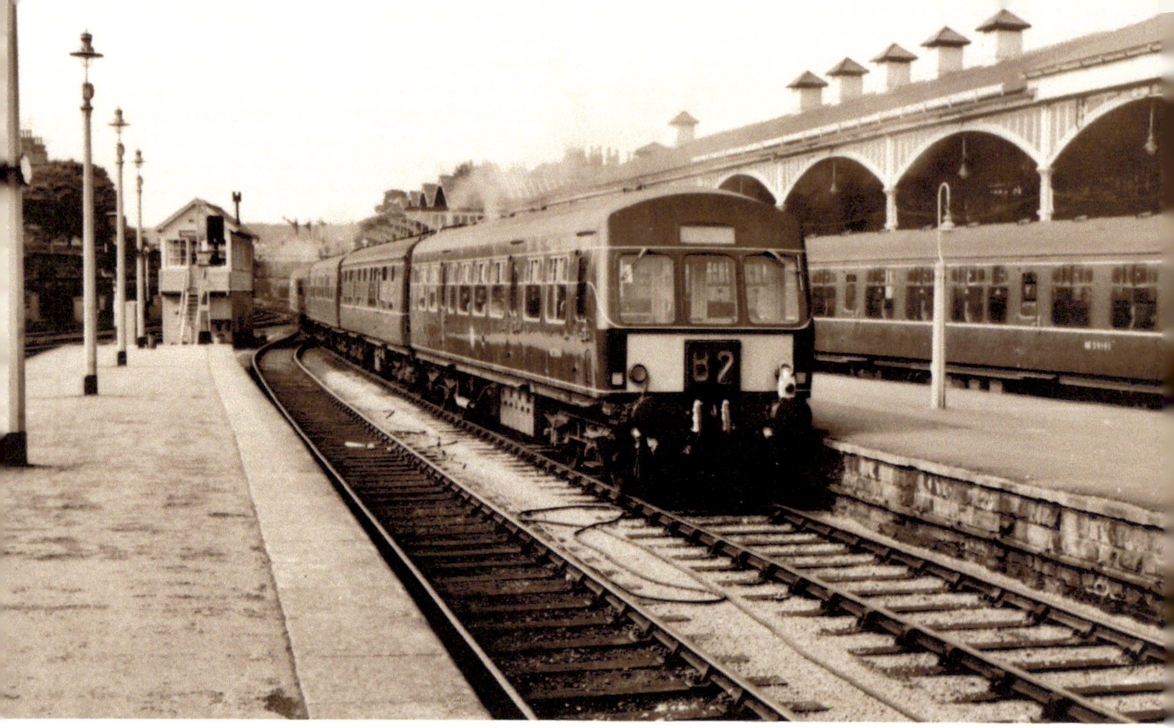

The Railway Station

Departing from Scarborough station is a diesel multiple unit train in the summer of 1965. It was hoped that the introduction of such trains would prolong the life of local branches, but this was not to be and rationalisation of services made Scarborough station very much quieter than it had been in the past. Introduction of diesel trains meant that remaining steam engines were left with menial tasks. Here 81 4-6-0 No. 61319 is on shunting duties at Scarborough station, something of a come-down for an express engine.

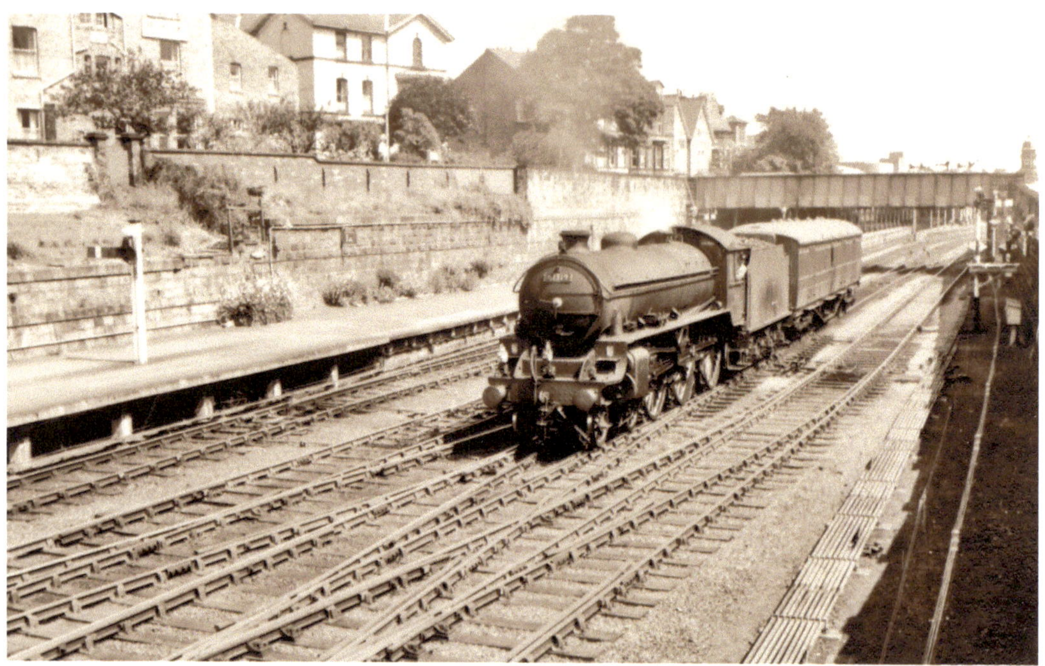

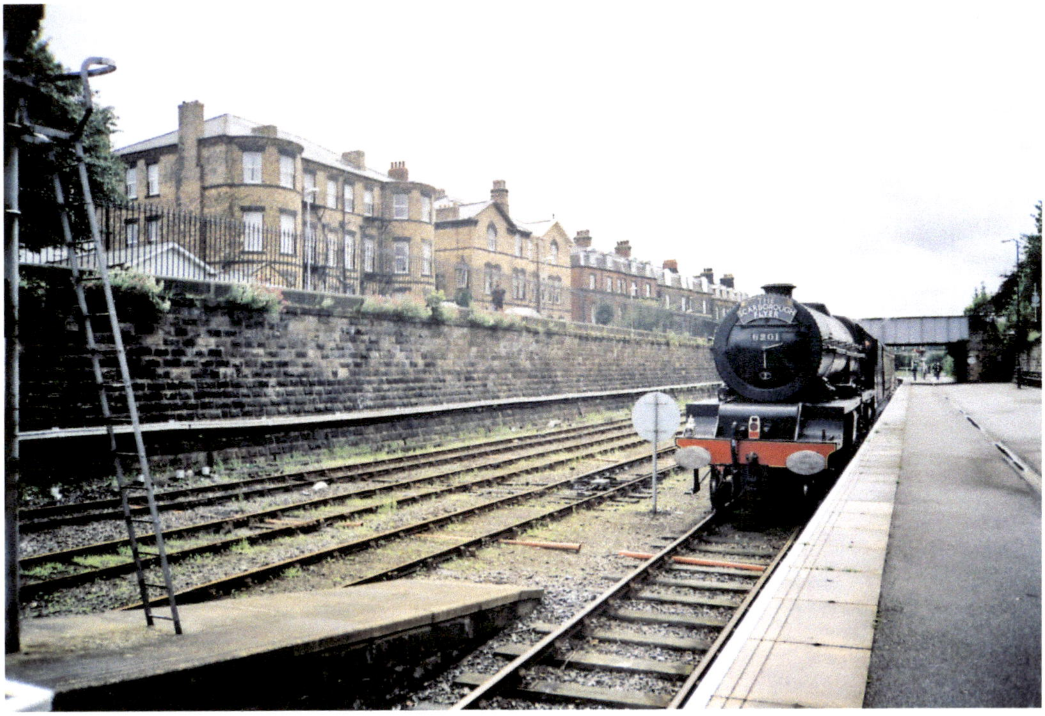

The Railway Station

Steam traction returned to Scarborough in the 1980s as special excursions were run between here and York, which brought new tourists to the seaside town. Here, in 2007, is ex-LMS Princess-Royal class pacific No. 6201 *Princess Elizabeth* on such an excursion. She is being coaled and watered before being turned on the turntable near Seamer Road at the site of what was once the locomotive shed.

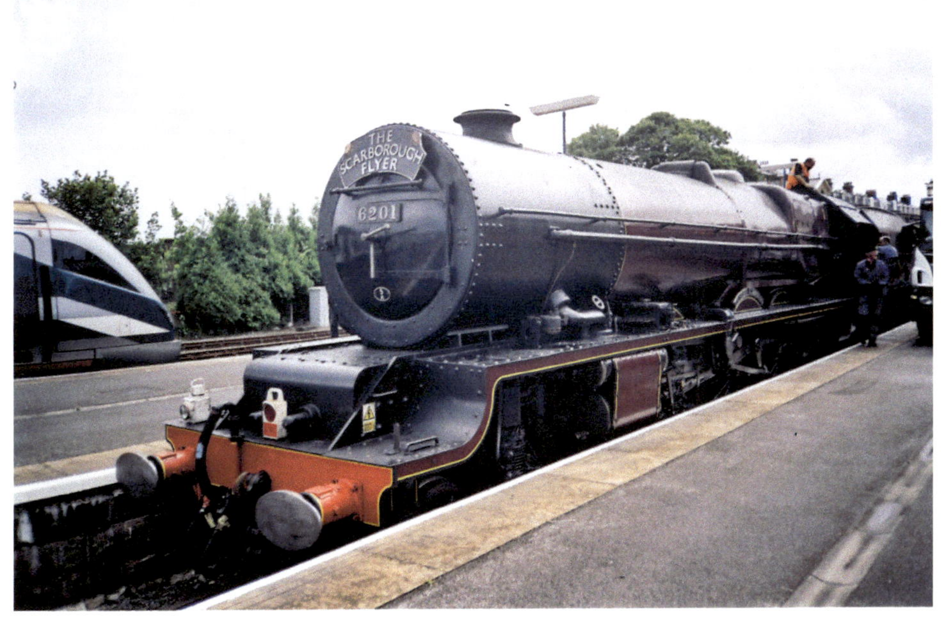

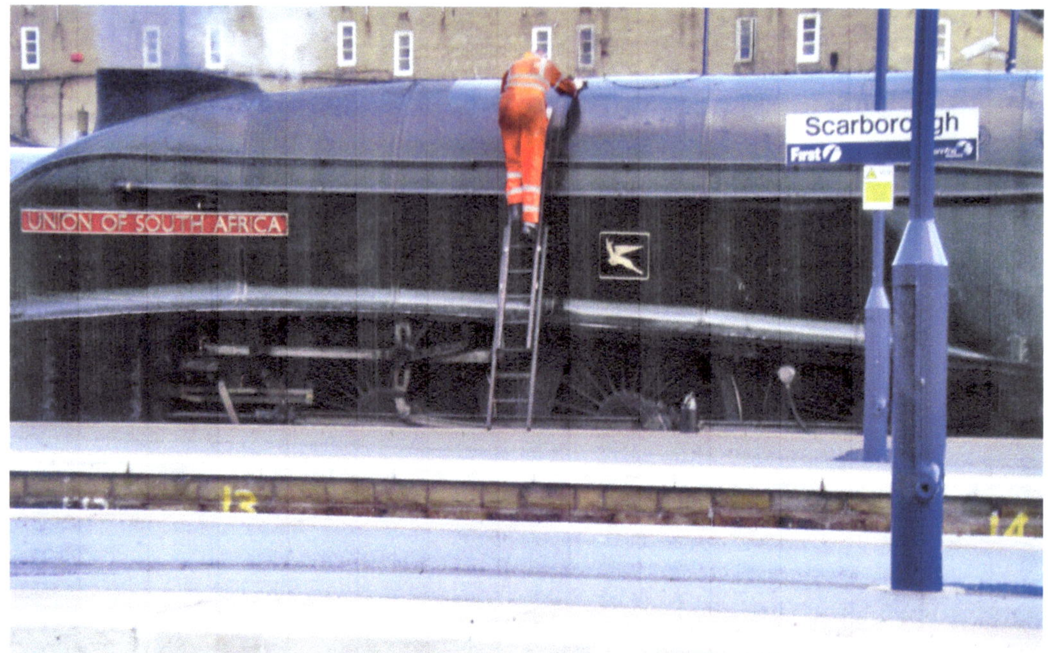

The Railway Station

Having just arrived in Scarborough from York, ex-LNER A4 pacific No. 60009 *Union of South Africa* is being cleaned before running to the turntable. Running under the road bridge at the end of Scarborough station ex-LMS 'Jubilee' 4-6-0 No. 5690 *Leander* reverses its train to Seamer Road, where the engine will be turned and the whole train will then come back to the station ready to return to York. These steam specials continue to run to Scarborough during the summer months.

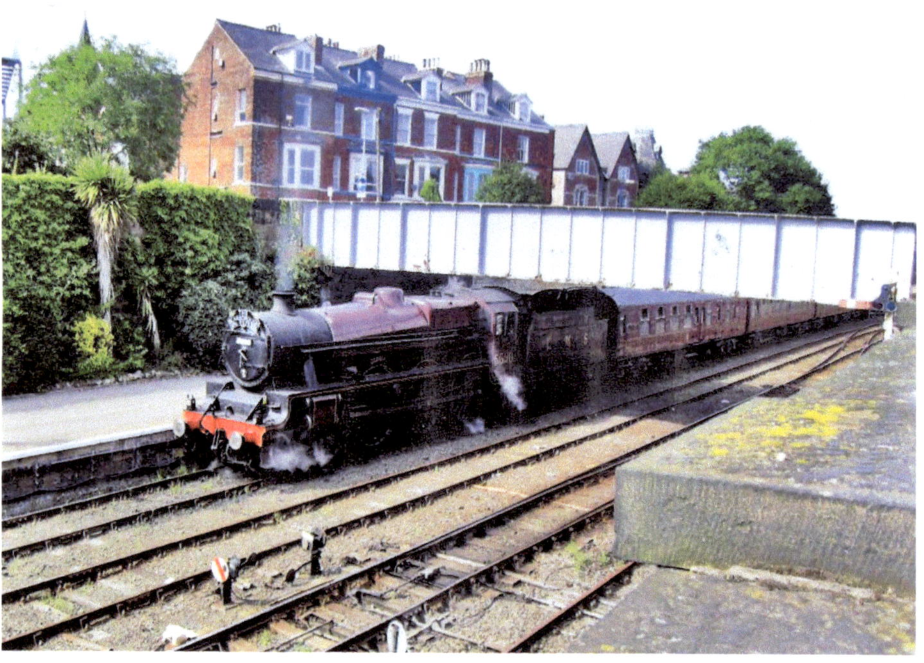

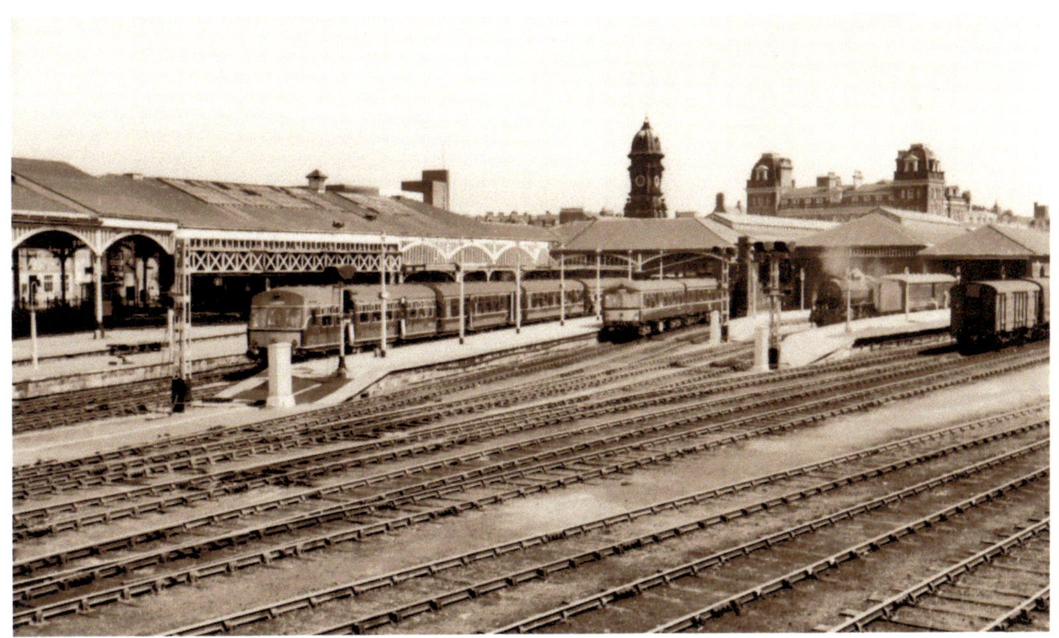

The Railway Station

A general view of Scarborough station during the summer of 1965, with both steam and diesel traction engines in sight. As the modern picture of 2010 shows, the station has been substantially rationalised and most of the canopies in the 1960s view have been demolished. There is, also, far less traffic with only a 'Northern Rail' DMU in view on the left and the main station itself is empty. Gone are the days of railway excursions, which used to make the station very busy during the summer months. Also closure of much of the railway network in the 1960s has done much to reduce the amount of traffic using the station as people prefer to come to the resort by car and then wonder why the roads are always congested.

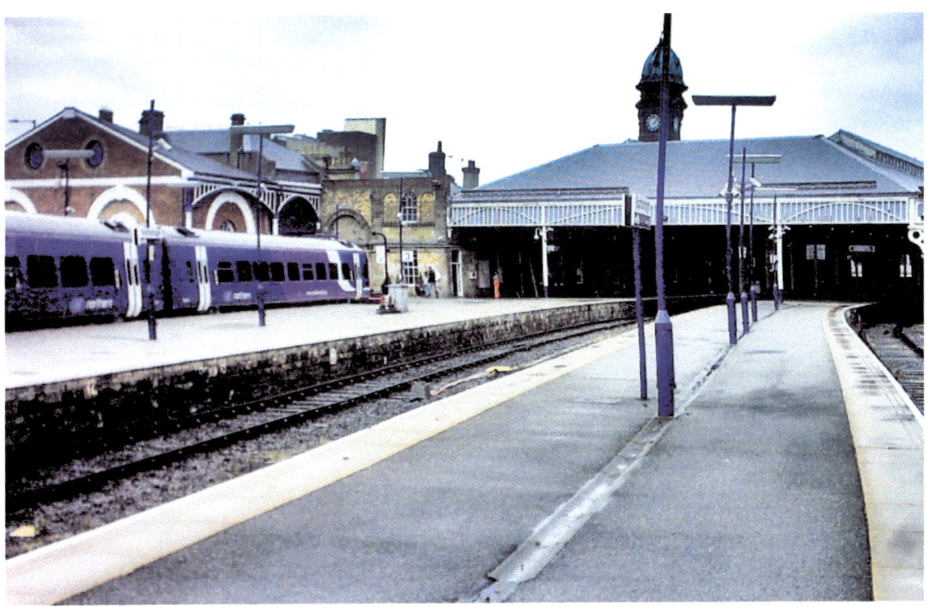

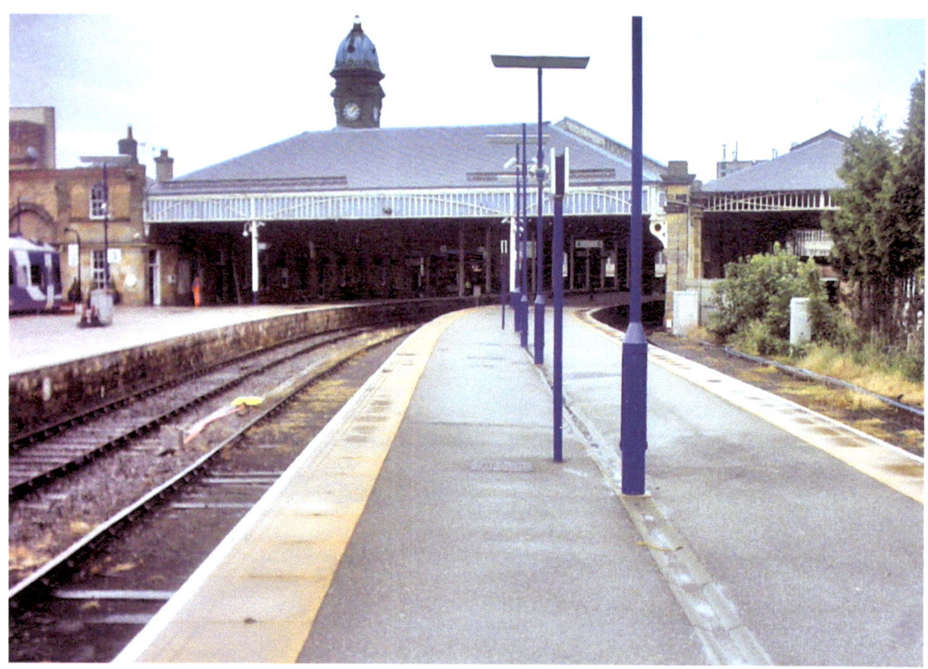

The Railway Station

General views of Scarborough station in June 2010. As can be seen, the station has been reduced somewhat and buildings on the far right of the picture have been abandoned and all track on the right of the platform has been removed. The signal gantry in the lower picture has been demolished and removed to the North Yorkshire Moors Railway at Pickering, where it was installed to control its steam trains operating there.

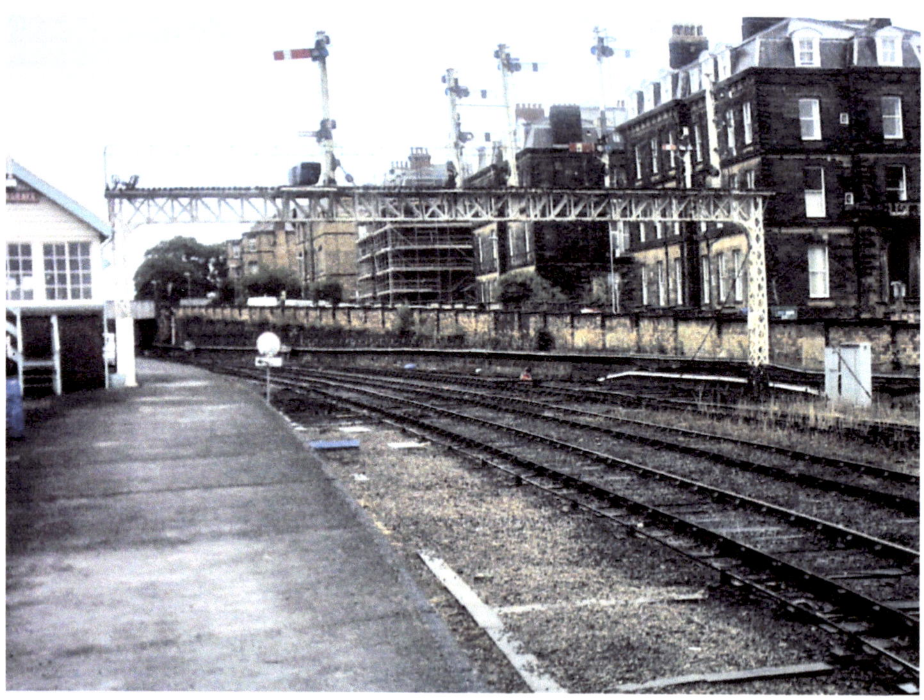

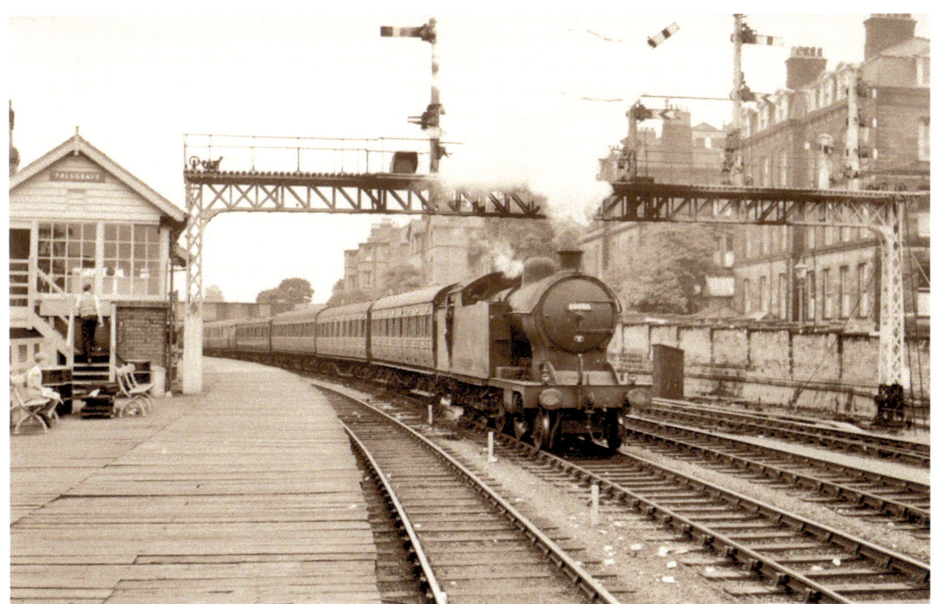

Falsgrave Signalbox

Ex-LNER A8 class 4-6-2 tank engine No. 69886 is seen passing Falsgrave signalbox with an empty stock train on 29 July 1955. In view is the signal gantry, signalbox and wooden platform, which served excursion trains at Scarborough. Behind the signalbox and out of view is the tunnel which formed the start of the line to Whitby. In 2010, the signalbox had fallen out of use, but it is a listed building and remains *in situ*. The track here has been rationalised and the platform is now out of use. The signal gantry would be removed in a few months time. A new building, constructed in connection with re-signalling at the station, can be seen behind the platform and is the reason why the signal gantry is to disappear. The new building hides the now blocked up tunnel of the Whitby branch, which actually closed in 1963, and was one of the reasons why traffic declined at Scarborough.

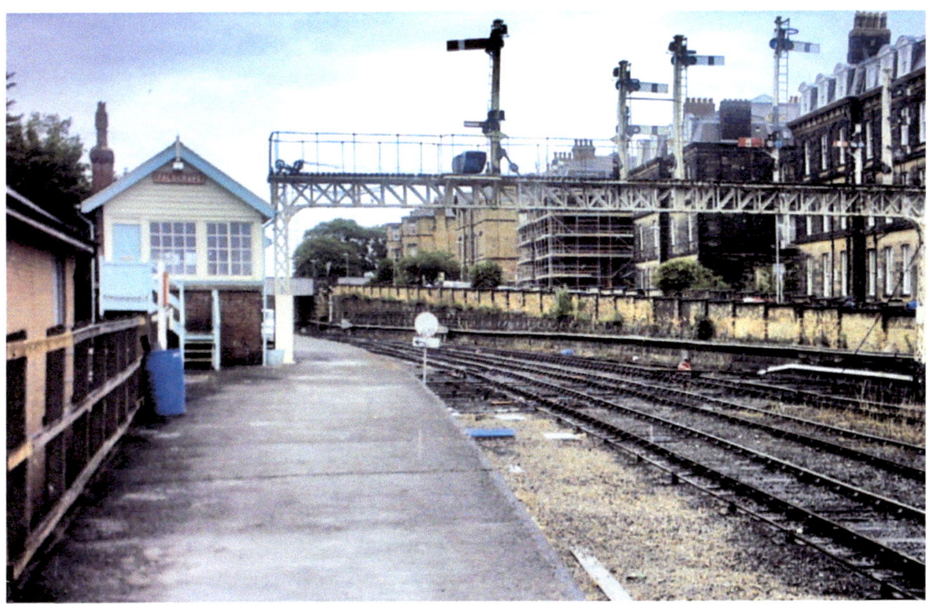

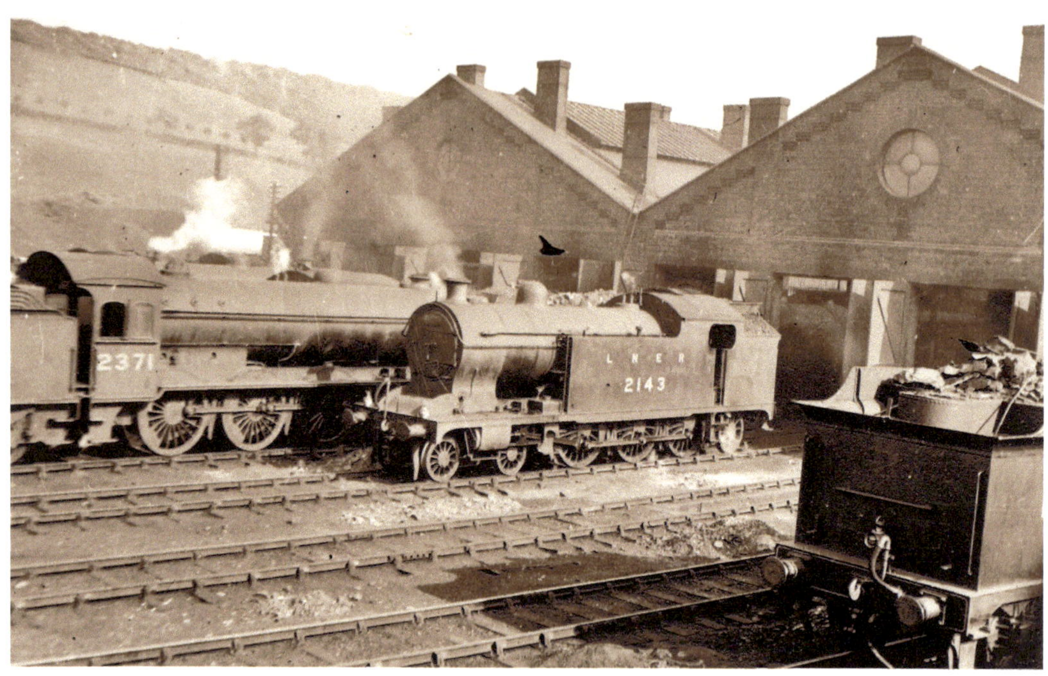

The Railway

To provide locomotives for services out of Scarborough, the railway companies provided a locoshed here, seen as it was in the 1930s when under LNER ownership. In view are an A8 4-6-2T and an LNER 816 4-6-0. Below is the locoshed on 2 June 1963, just after it was closed. In the background is the gasworks at Seamer Road, which itself has disappeared with the arrival of natural gas. Between the shed and the gasworks can be seen the gantry for the main line into Scarborough station.

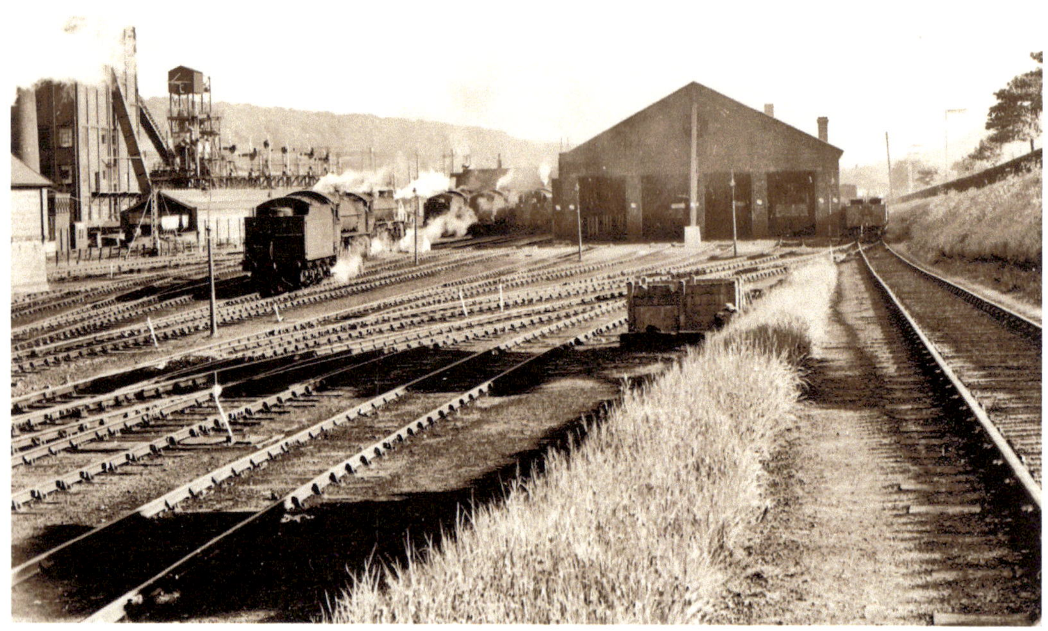

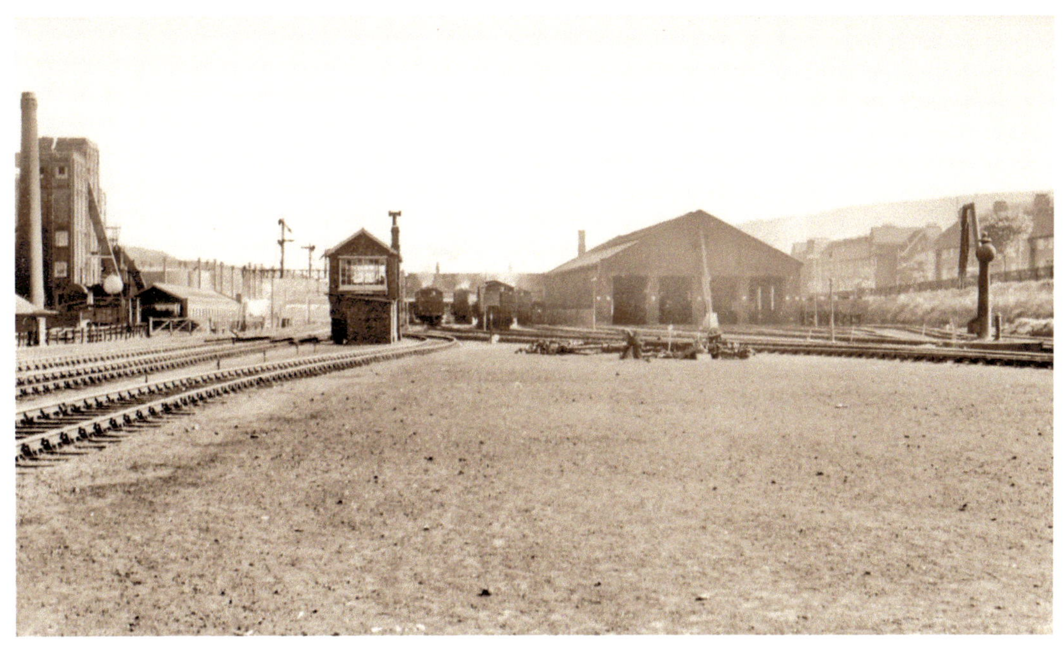

The Engine Shed

The engine shed at Scarborough with Seamer Road visible on the right. It is around this point that the turntable is situated to turn steam engines operating between here and York. Modern traction, in the form of a diesel locomotive, is seen on shed at Scarborough on 2 June 1963. An express can be seen passing the shed as it heads towards Scarborough. Nowadays, small diesel units operate from Scarborough to York, Manchester and Liverpool, operated by Trans-Pennine Express every hour. In addition, there are Northern Rail trains to Hull, Sheffield and Doncaster, via Filey, running every two or three hours – such is the railway service these days, a shadow of what they once were.

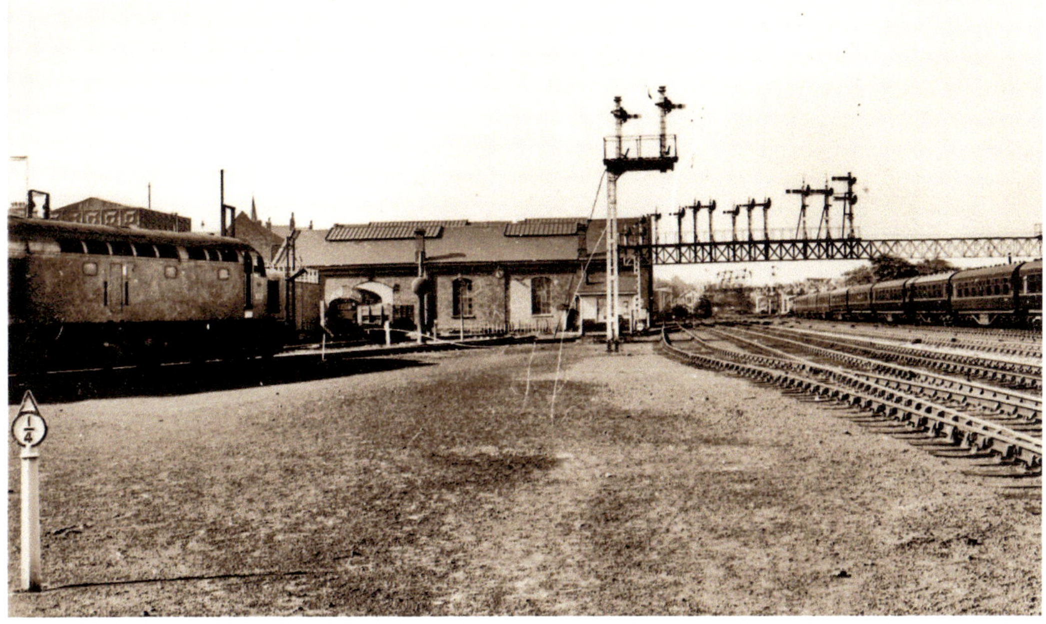

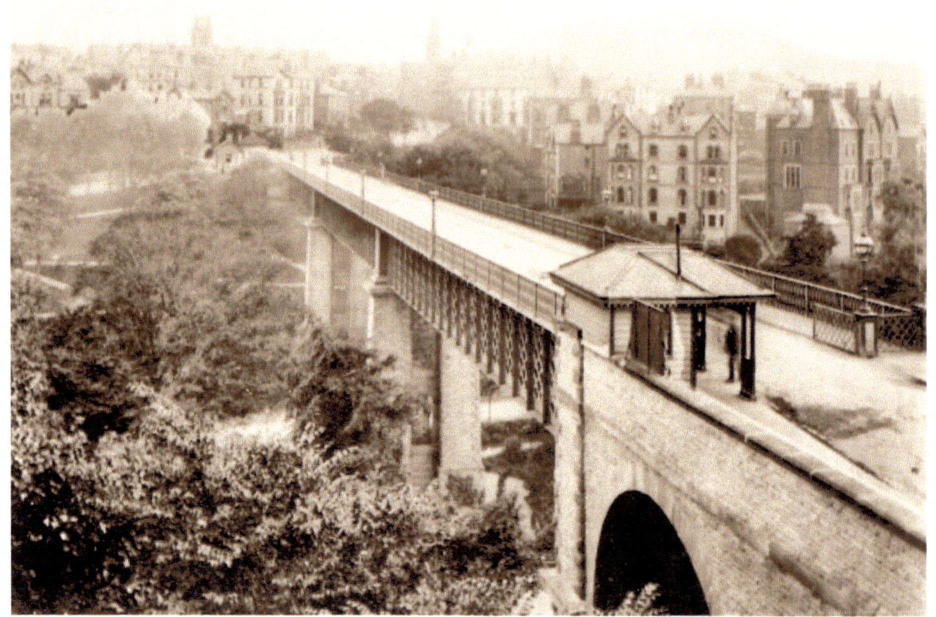

Valley Bridge

Valley Bridge crosses the deep Valley Road and links Scarborough with the main road to Bridlington. The bridge was originally built to cross the River Ouse at York, but found its way to the seaside instead. Toll booths occupy the entrance to the bridge when it was first opened to be replaced by traffic lights in recent years, which control the junction of Valley Bridge with Ramshill Road and Beaumont Road.

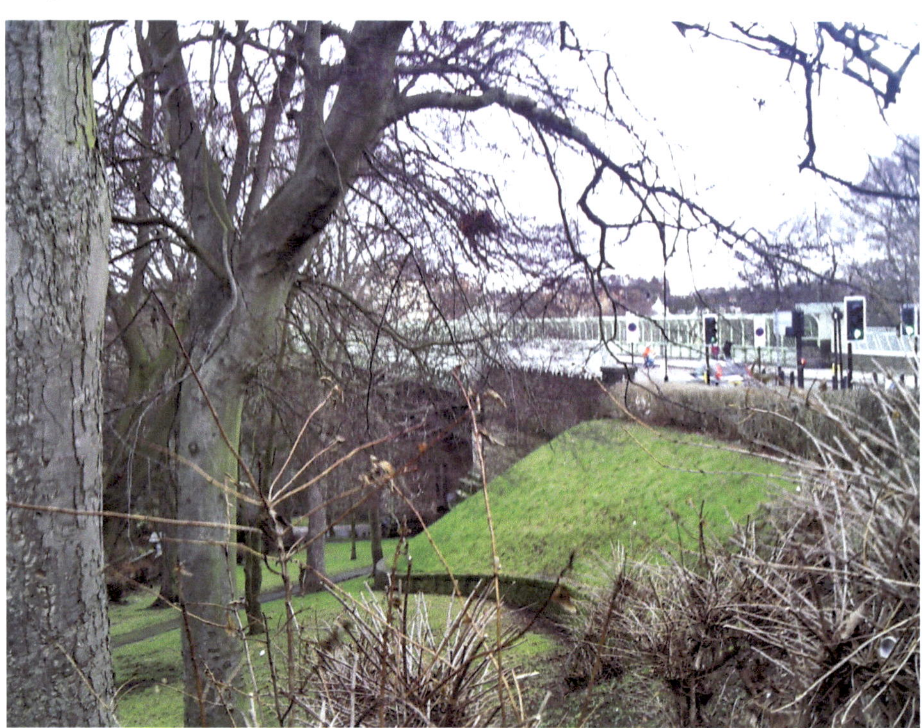

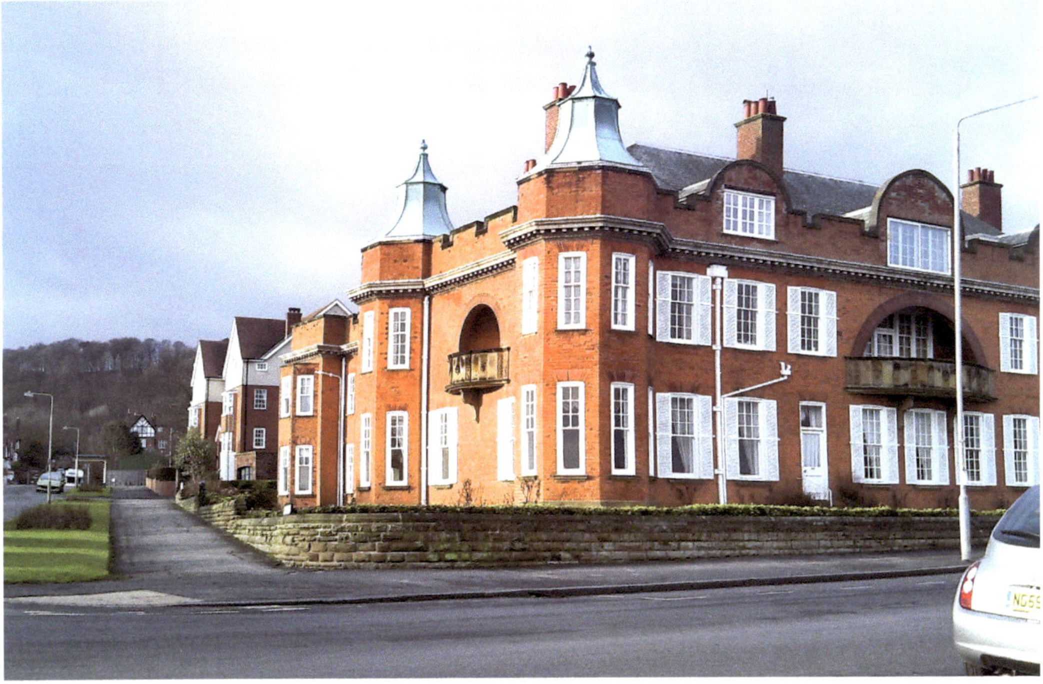

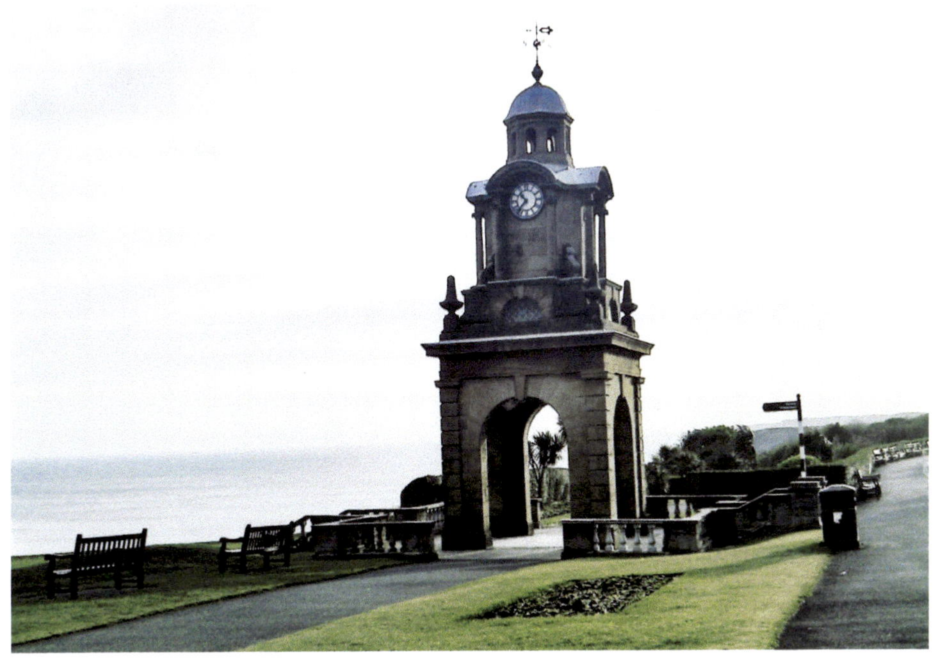

The Royal

At the far end of The Esplanade and the junction of Holbeck Road is the house which found fame as the location for the ITV series, *The Royal*, about life in a 1950s hospital. It was a spin-off from another series filmed locally, *Heartbeat*, and the two programmes were often interlinked. Opposite *The Royal* was the clock tower, still very much in use, seen here looking out towards the sea.

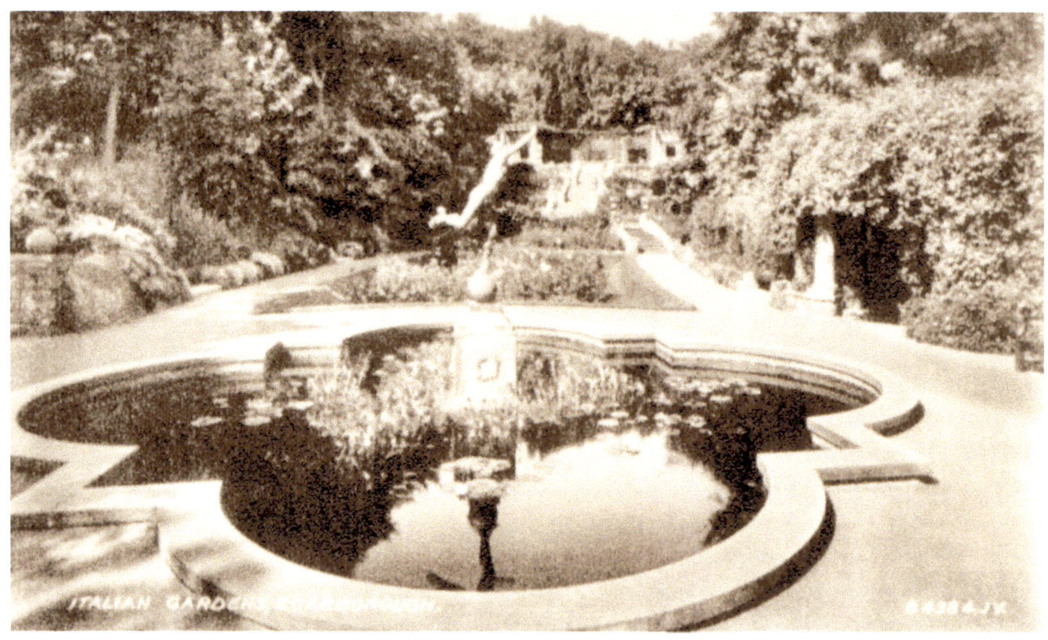

The Italian Garden

Down from The Esplanade and heading towards the rocky seashore lies the Italian Garden, established in the early years of the twentieth century. Very little has changed over the years as can be seen when comparing the Edwardian view and the 2011 picture. Further along the coast once lay the Holbeck Hotel, which gained national fame when it collapsed into the sea due to coastal erosion in 1995 and was broadcast on both BBC and ITV news. Erosion continues to be a problem here, and bungalows between Scarborough and Cayton Bay are under threat of disappearing into the sea. Indeed, a couple have been demolished in an effort to prevent further erosion here.

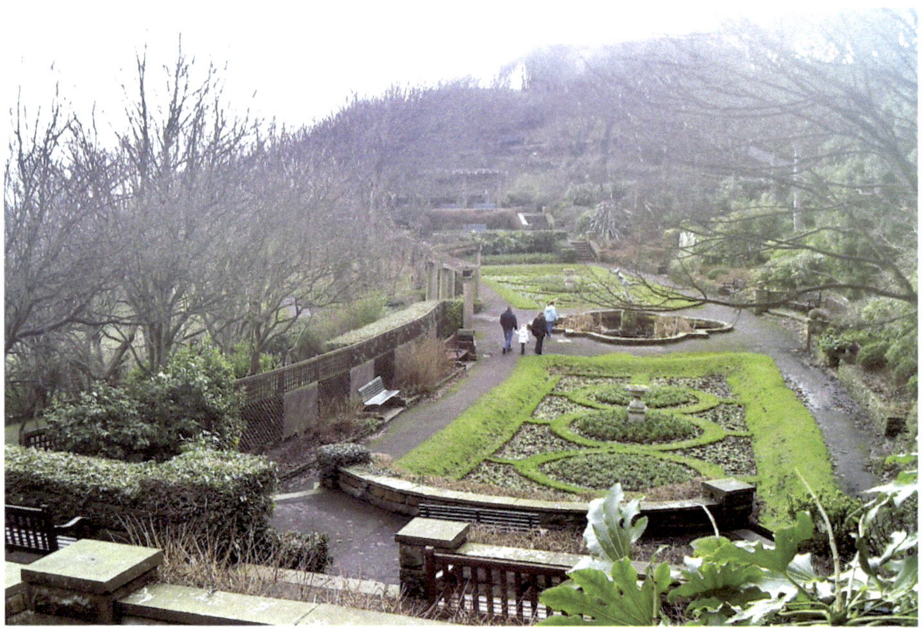

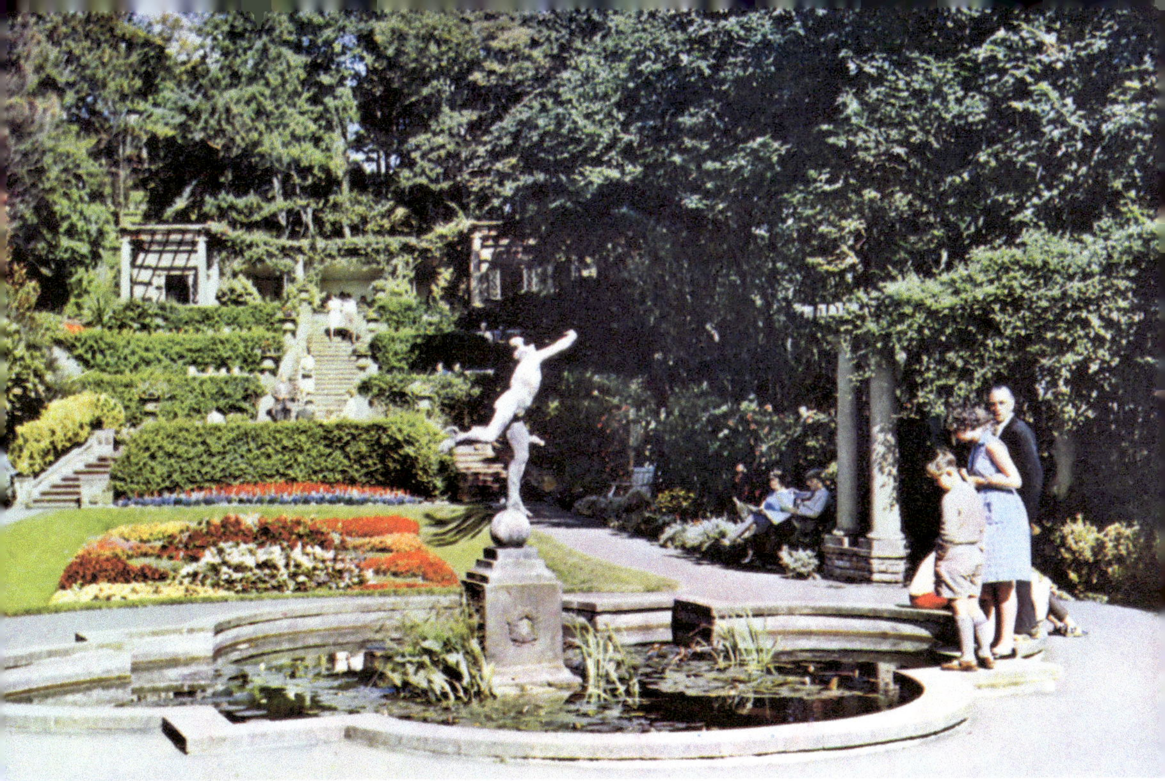

The Italian Garden
Two views of the Italian Garden as it appeared in the 1950s.

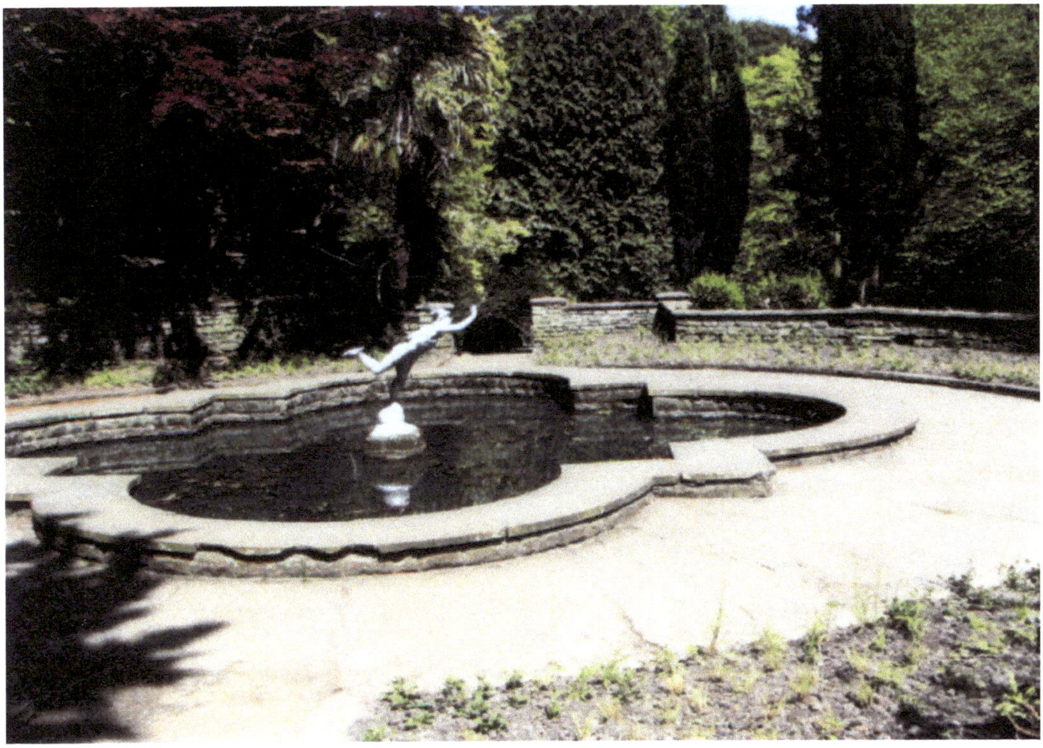

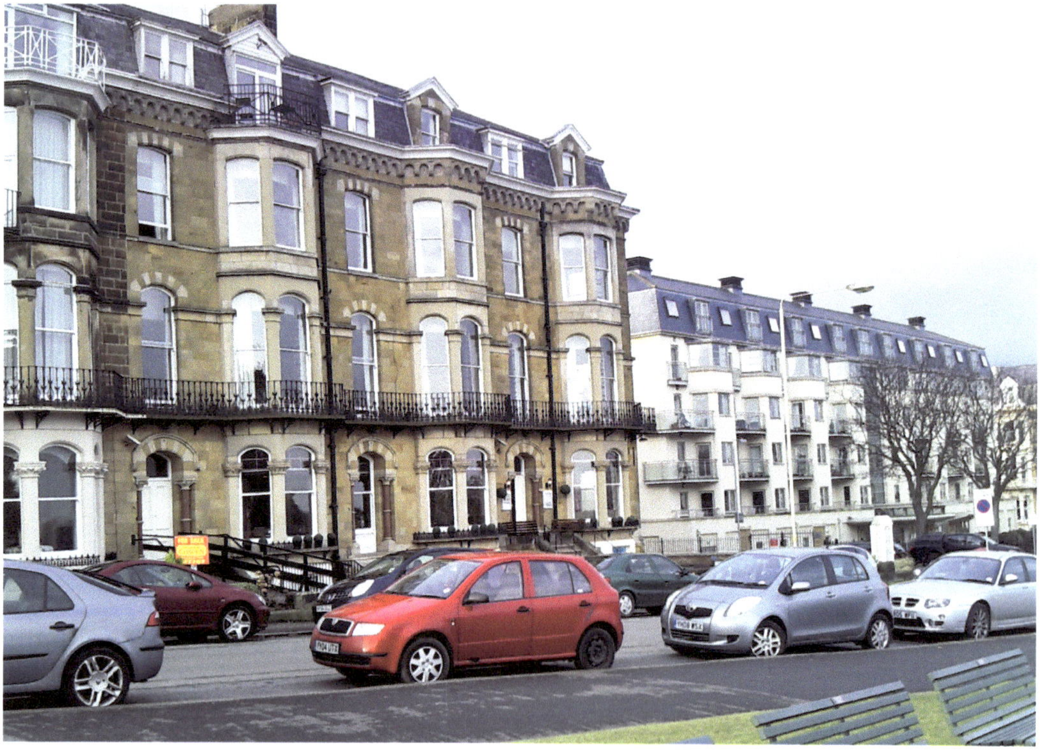

The Ambassador Hotel

Along The Esplanade from the Italian Garden lies the Ambassador Hotel, which is situated on the corner of The Esplanade and Avenue Victoria, the latter running up to Filey Road and the university.

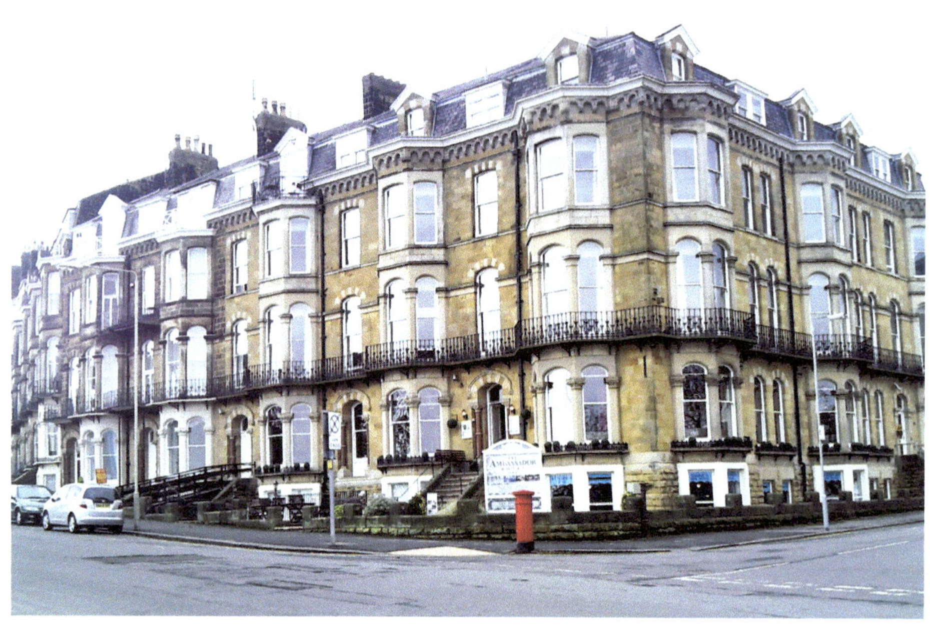

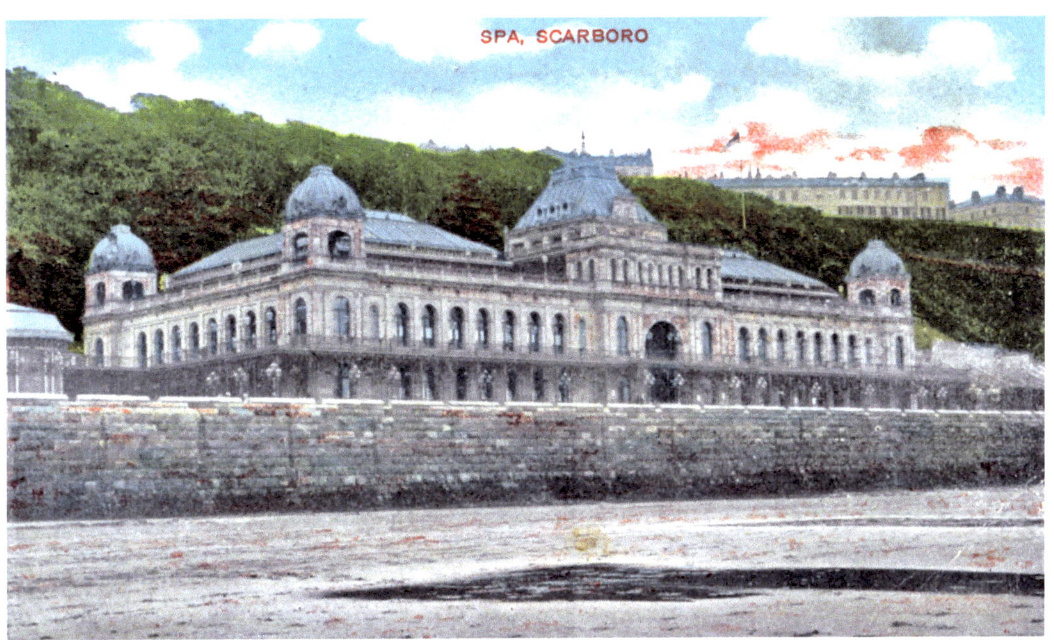

Scarborough Spa

The original Scarborough Spa complex was built in the 1850s, to a Joseph Paxton design. This original building did not survive, however, due to a fire in 1876, and the whole area was totally rebuilt. The new complex lasted for nearly a century until substantial refurbishment took place, which is seen from The Esplanade in the lower picture. The Spa complex held events, often catering for Christmas parties. In earlier days, the Palm Court Orchestra would play here and the modern Spa Orchestra still entertains during the summer tourist season.

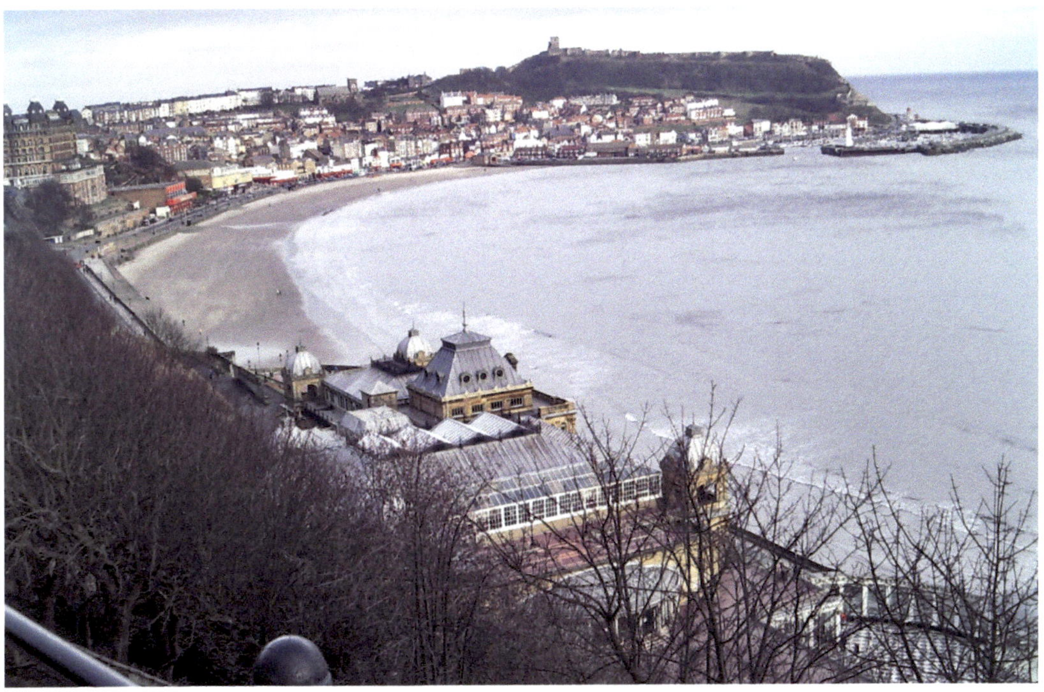

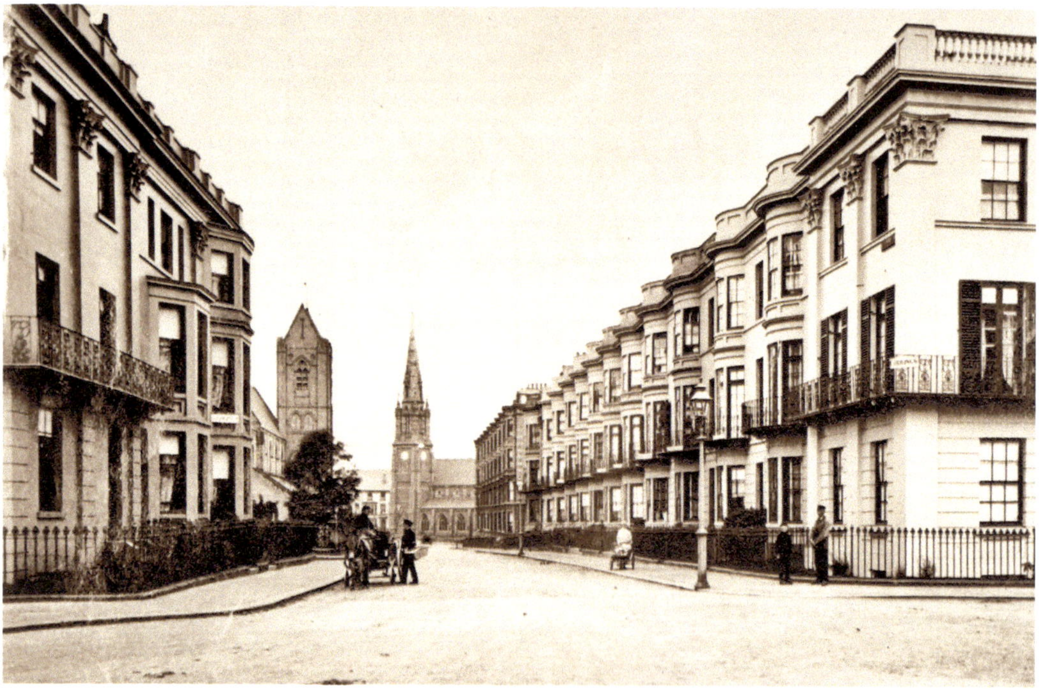

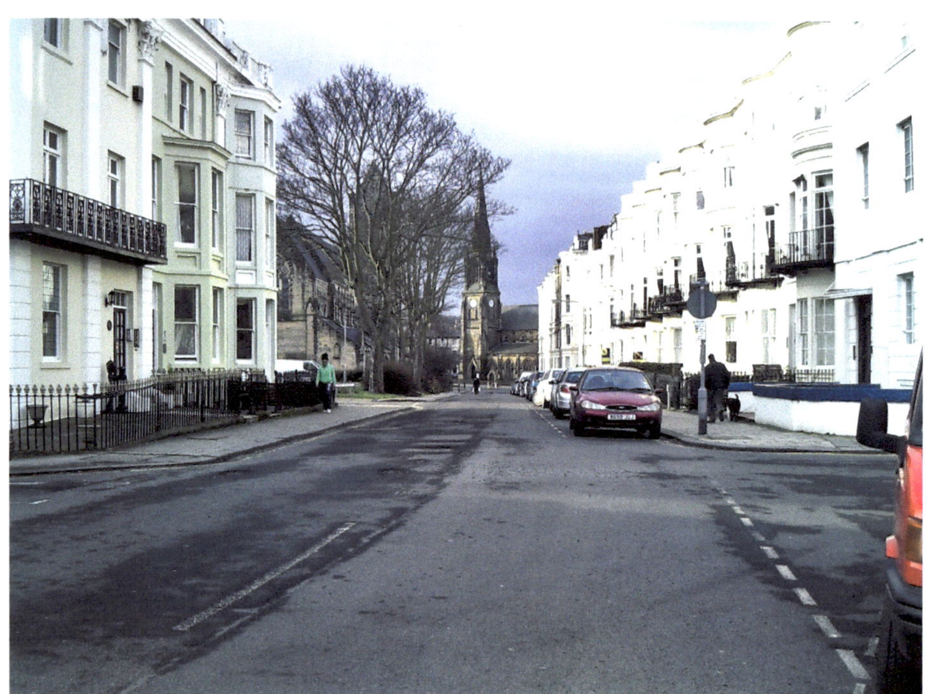

Albion Road

Albion Road connects Valley Road Bridge with The Esplanade. As the two pictures show, the substantial buildings remain and are kept in immaculate condition. Nowadays, the area between the buildings on the left and the church beyond is now taken up with a 'pay and display' car park.

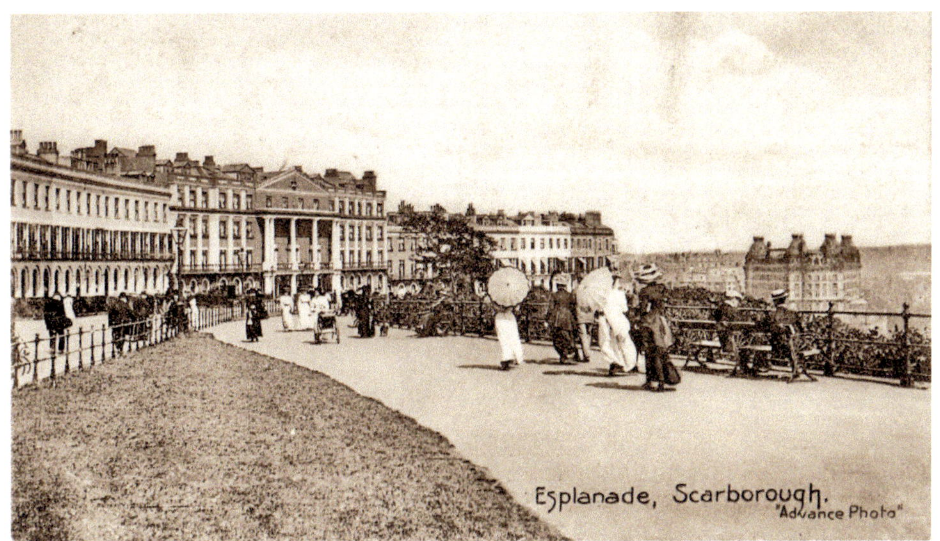

The Esplanade

The Esplanade during the Edwardian period. Women stroll along in the fashions of the day, which must have been heavy and cumbersome, and using parasols to shade from the sun, as tanning was certainly not approved of at this time. Male fashions of suit, peaked caps and straw boaters are seen being worn by gentlemen sitting on the bench on the right and admiring the sea views. In the right background is the famous Grand Hotel, while the Crown Hotel (now known as The Crown Spa Hotel) features in the centre background, flanked by terraces of apartments and smaller hotels. The Crown Hotel was served by a cliff railway, the first of its kind in England when opened in 1875, which linked it to the Spa complex and saved visitors a climb of 224 steps. The Crown Hotel was opened in 1844 and extensively advertised itself, bringing in thousands of visitors from all over the world, which would establish Scarborough as a major destination on the European tour. As tourism developed, hotels here and throughout the town benefitted from this booming industry, which was often served by the nearby railway.

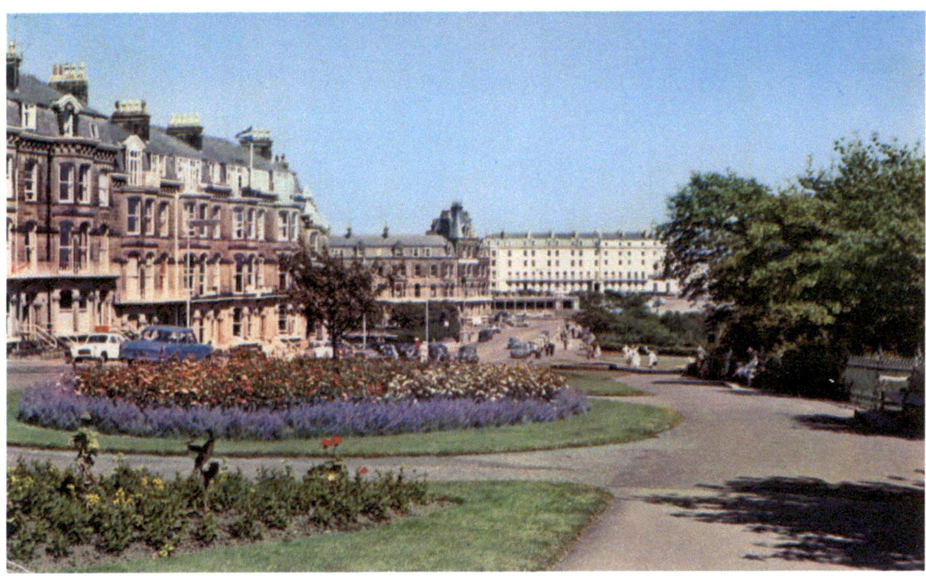

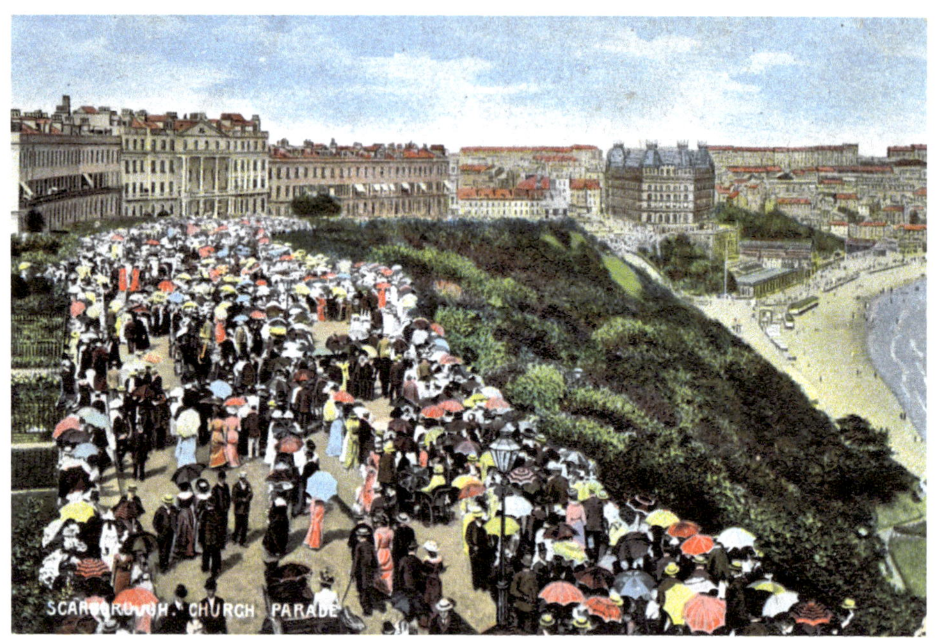

Church Parade

The Esplanade, Crown Hotel and terraces on a busy summer Sunday as visitors and locals alike promenade at the Church Parade. In the background are the South Bay and its attractions, with the Grand Hotel above, as they appeared in the early twentieth century. As was the fashion at the time, ladies used parasols and would have been rather hot wearing, as they did, heavy clothing and corsetry underneath. In the far background is the southern side of Scarborough and its old town. Below, a 2011 view of the Crown Spa Hotel, which is still a high class venue and often hosts conferences during the winter, although there are many guests who visit during the winter months.

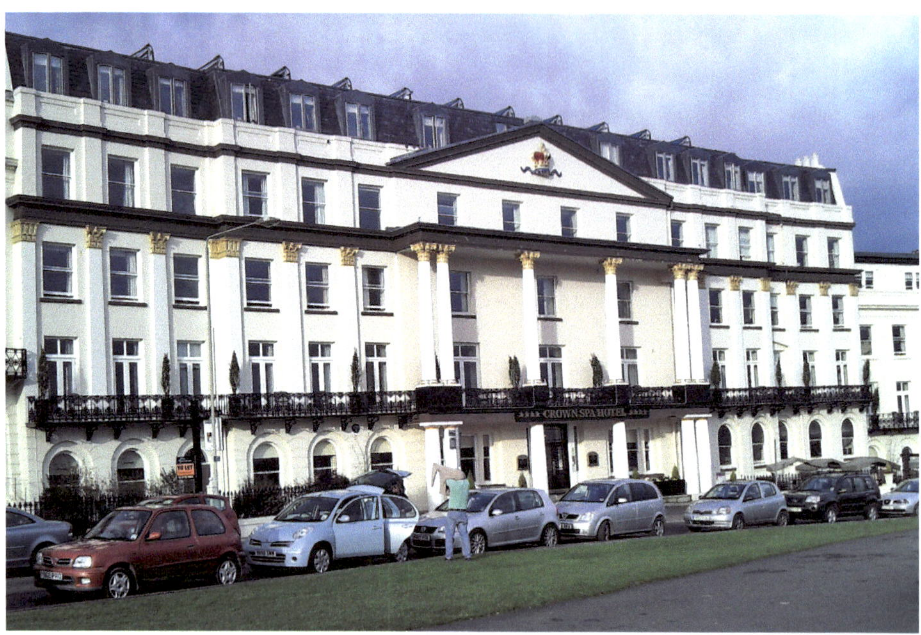

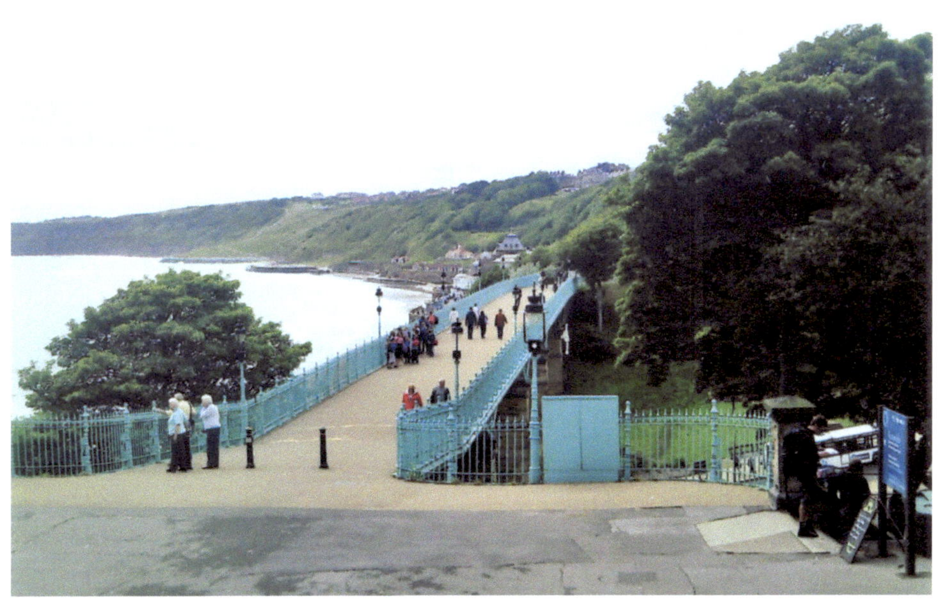

The Grand Hotel

The footbridge linking the Grand Hotel with The Esplanade. Just in view below the bridge is the Spa complex. Below, the Grand Hotel from the end of The Esplanade with views of the footbridge. The bridge links South Bay with The Esplanade. The bay and the town are visible in the background with the castle providing a backdrop. This scene in January 2011 shows how quiet the town can be in the winter months, although there are still visitors around.

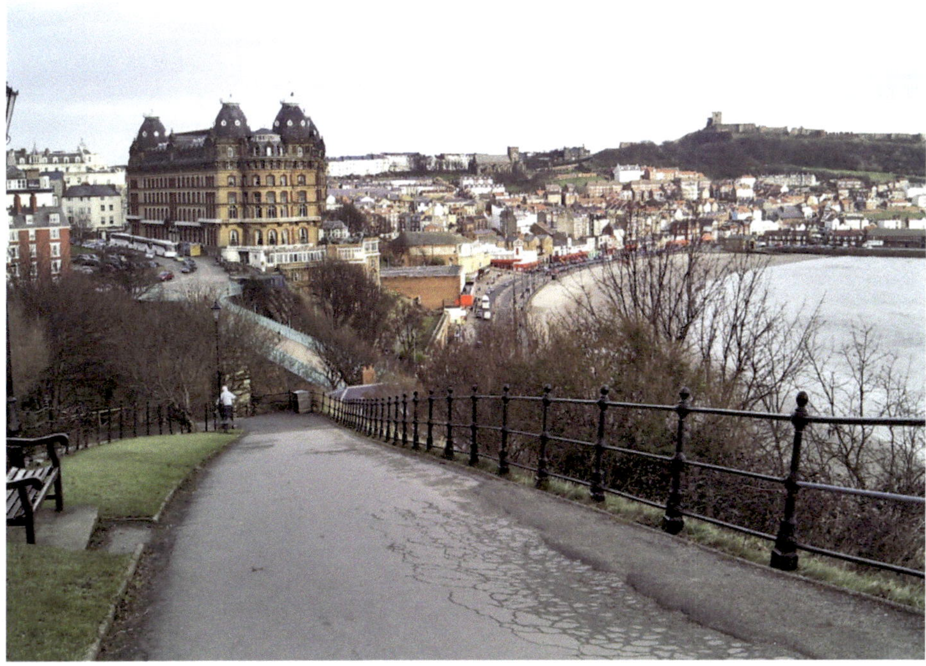

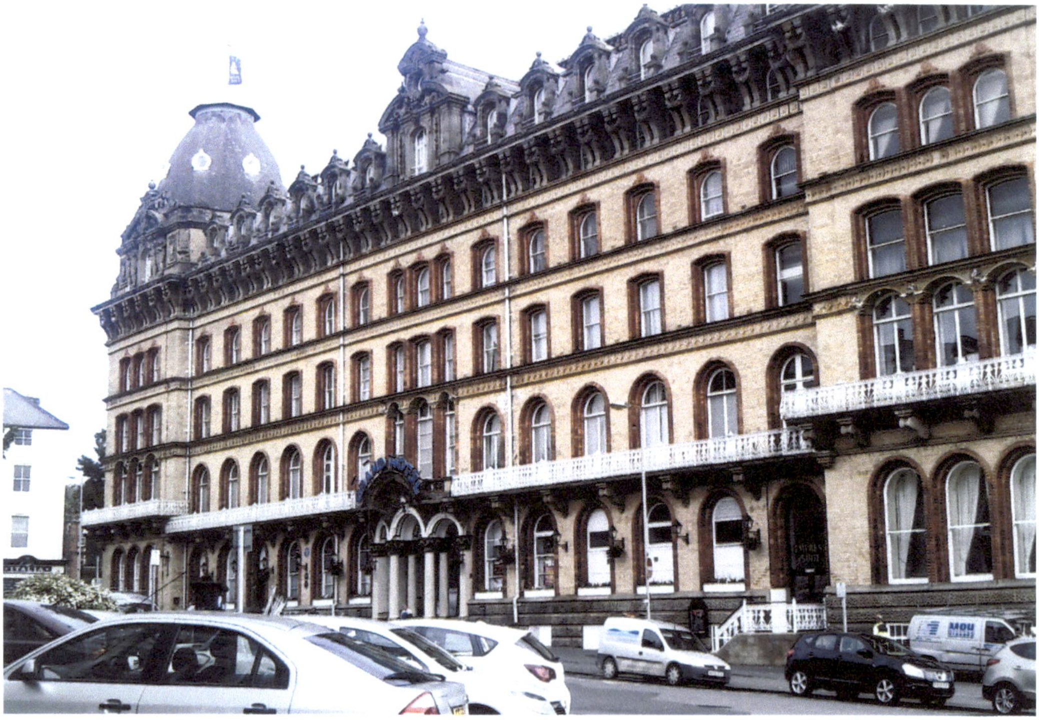

The Grand Hotel

The Grand Hotel in the summer of 2011. Below, is a view of the interior of the Grand Hotel with its grand staircase seen at around Christmas time when the hotel hosts 'Turkey and Tinsel' events. Demonstrated here is yet another way of descending the staircase.

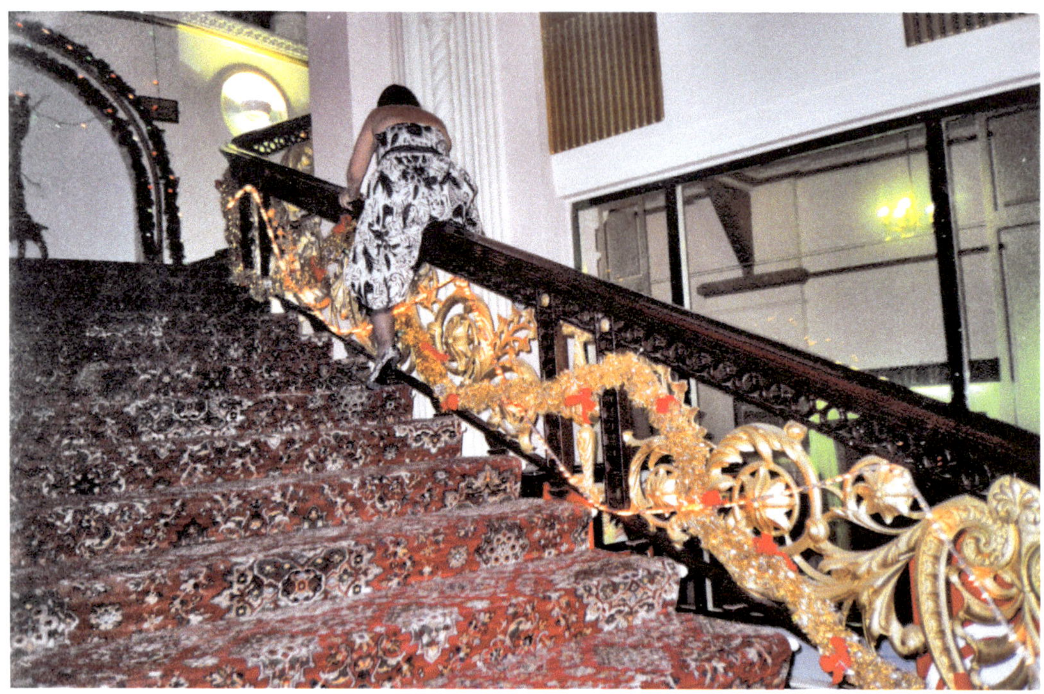

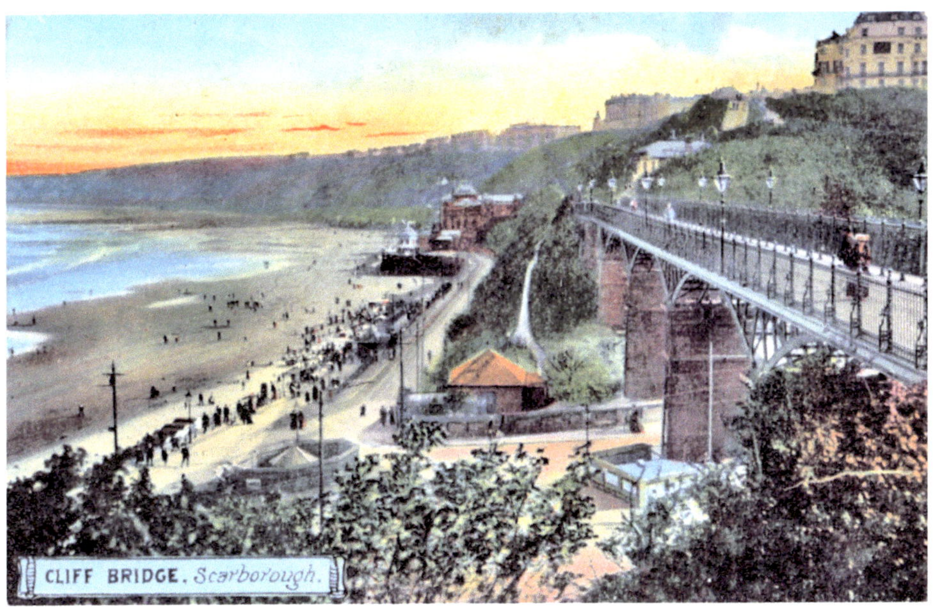

The Esplanade

Looking towards The Esplanade from South Bay in the early twentieth century. The buildings on The Esplanade can be seen above the Cliff Bridge, which links the bay with The Esplanade. The pathway to The Esplanade is visible to the left of Cliff Bridge and the Spa complex is also visible in the distance. There are several people on the beach, while others are wandering along the bridge. The structure at the junction of the road has disappeared and been replaced by a road roundabout which contains public toilets. Below is a very busy summer day in the 1950s at south bay. Overshadowed by the castle, the beach and promenade is packed with visitors, some will have come on day excursions by train or coach, the private car not yet as common as it would become; seen by the lack of vehicles on the road between the shore and the south bay buildings, only a couple of cars and a bus can be seen in this view, the background is the harbour and the lighthouse.

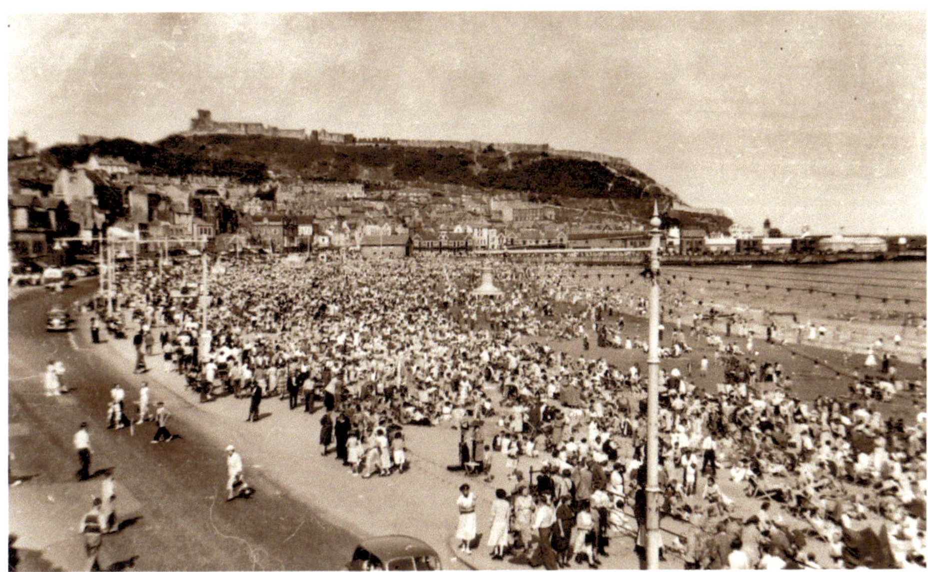

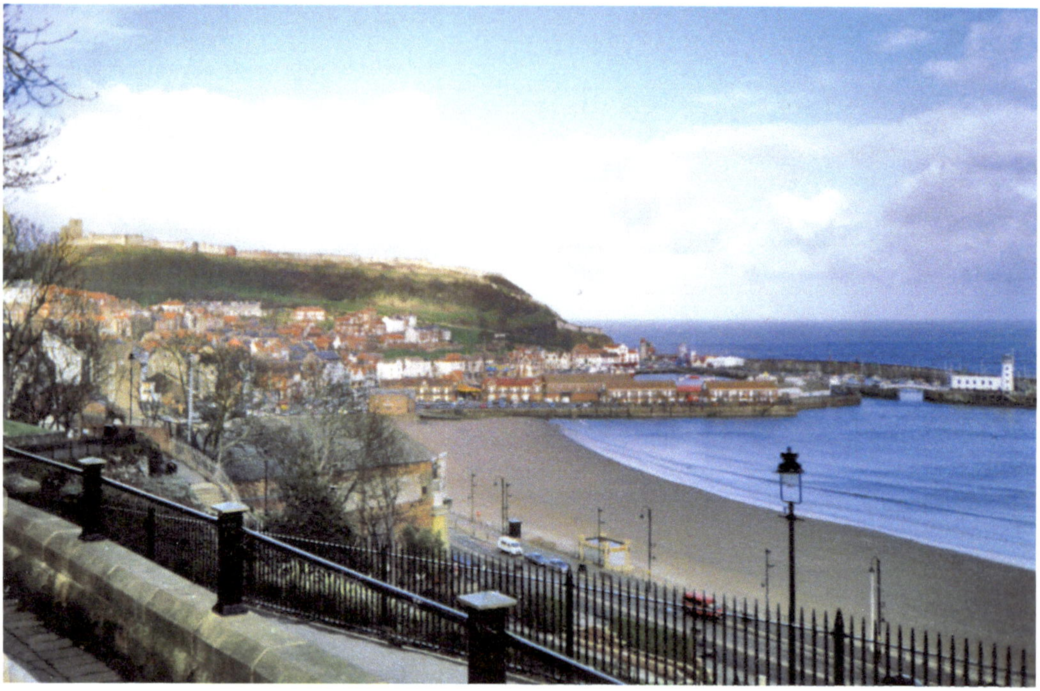

South Bay

Views of South Bay from the council offices on St Nicholas Street. The top view shows the harbour and lighthouse in 2004, while the one below gives a similar view in 2011.

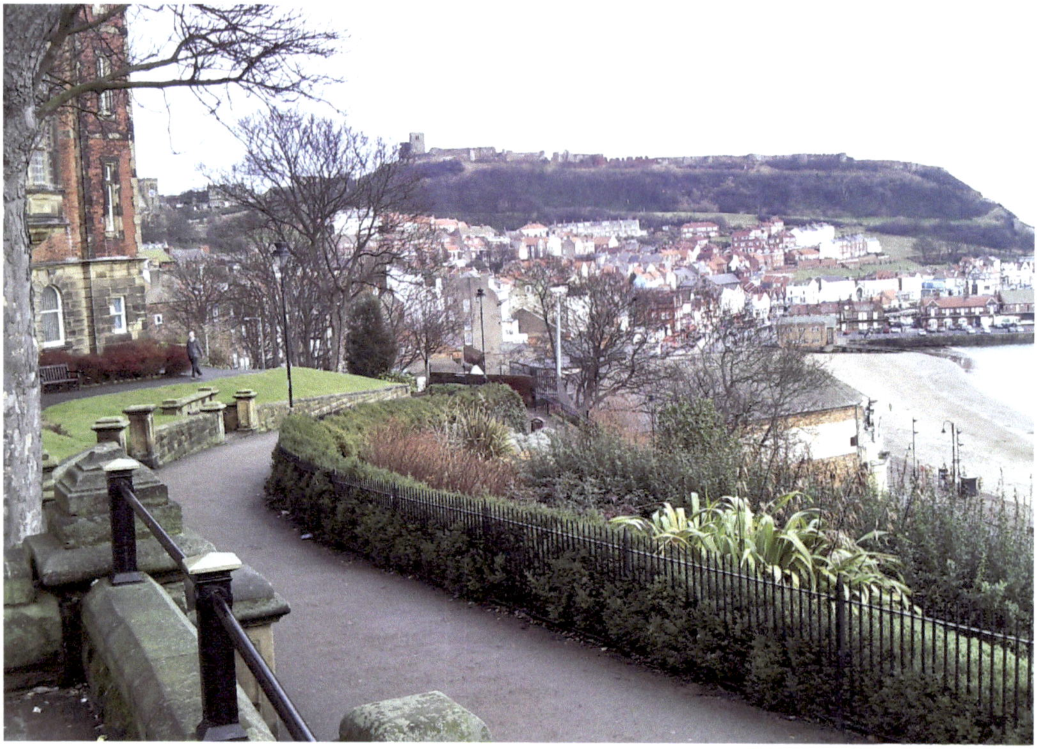

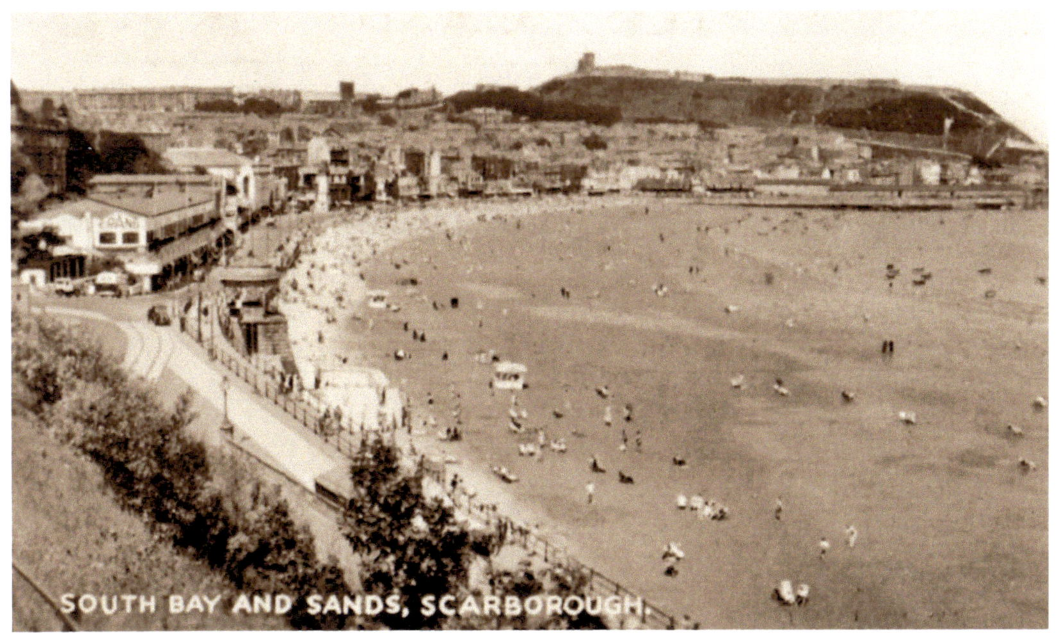

South Bay

Another 1950s view of the South Bay from the pathway leading to The Esplanade. The Grand Hotel is partially visible on the left with its promenade entrance below. Again, there are very few road vehicles present with only the odd motor car on Foreshore Road and a lorry, along with a coach at the promenade entrance of the Grand Hotel. The view along Foreshore Road has changed considerably in the years since this picture was taken. The sands are reasonably busy with holidaymakers here and at least the sands still remain busy today, even with competition from sunnier climes. The old town can be seen in the background and the harbour is on the extreme right. The whole bay is overlooked by the castle. Another popular feature of the seaside holiday is the donkey ride along the beach.

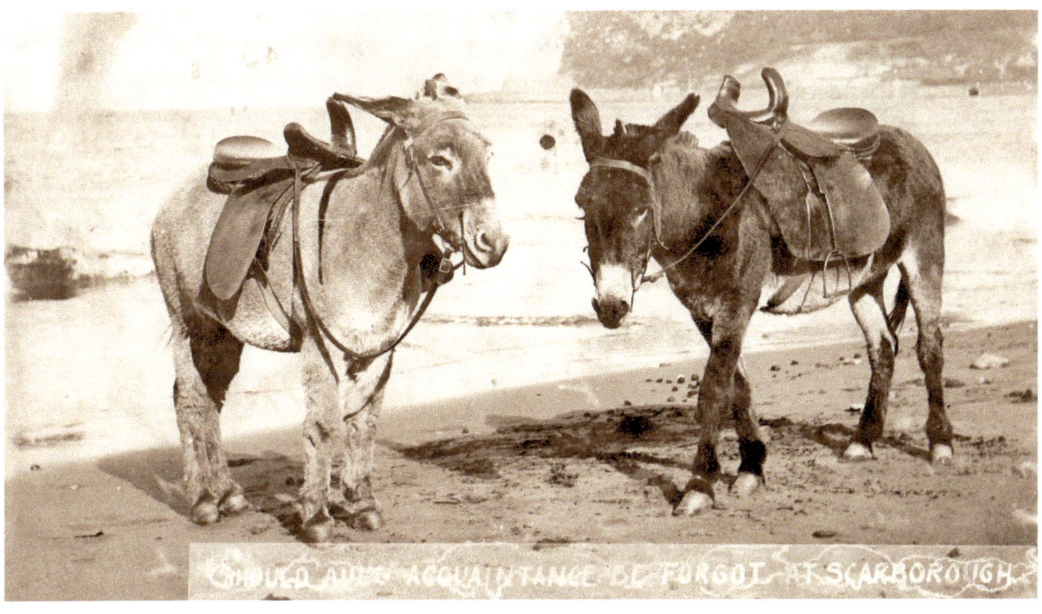

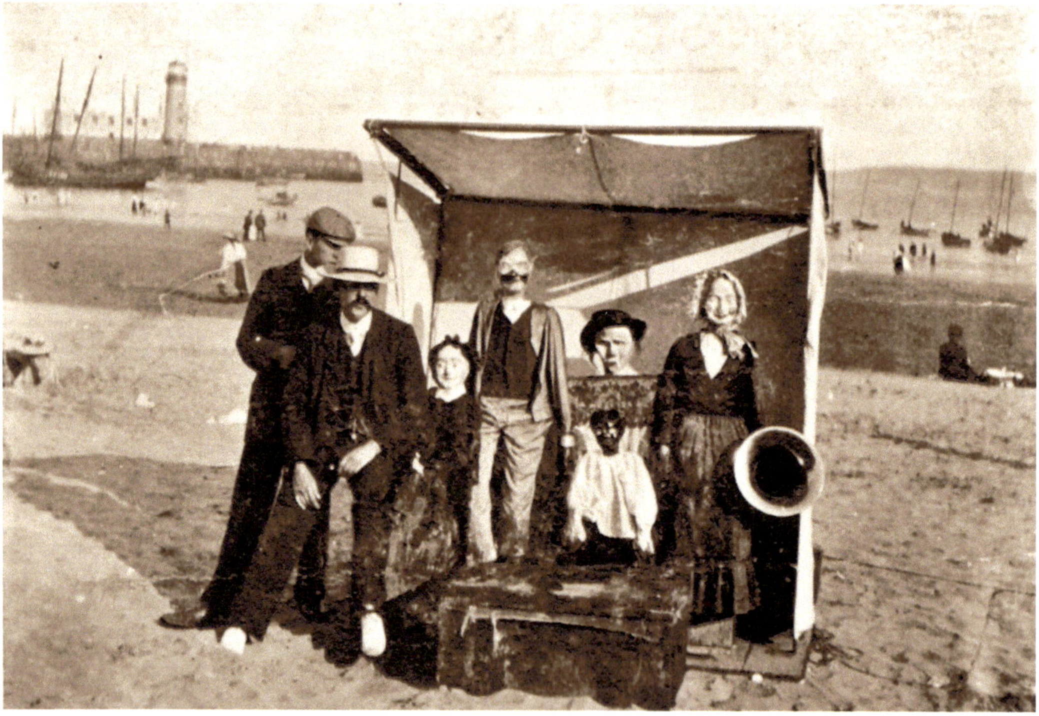

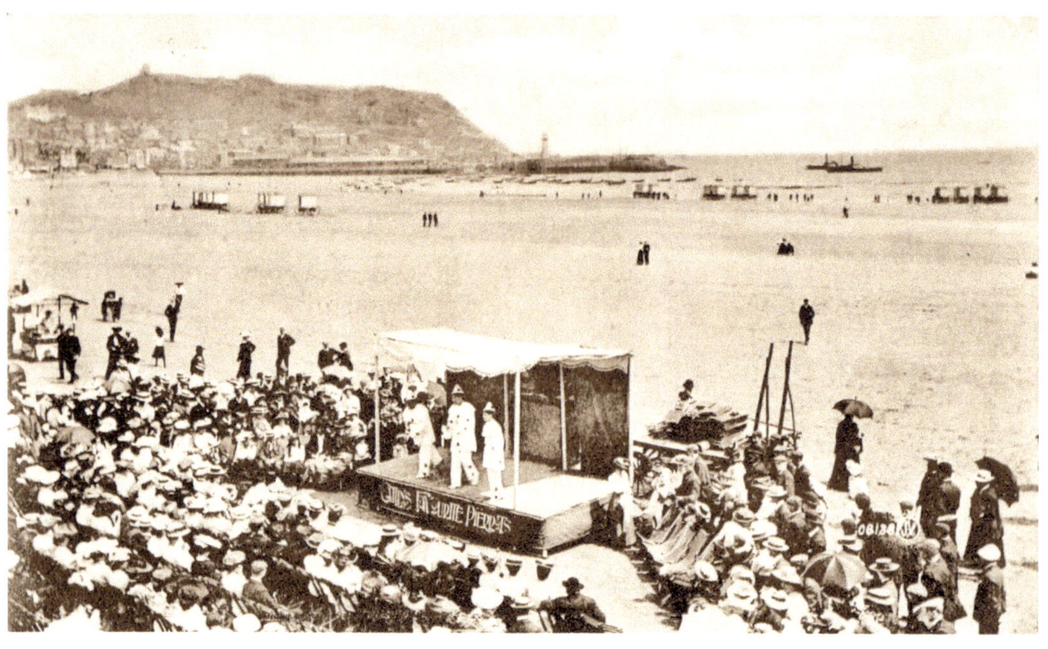

South Bay Beach

Puppet shows have often been a popular form of amusement for holidaymakers and Scarborough was no exception. One such show is seen on the South Bay beach during the early years of the twentieth century. Also popular at this time were Pierrot shows, seen here on South Bay beach prior to the outbreak of the First World War. The harbour and the lighthouse can be seen in the background and there appear to be plenty of boats on the sea.

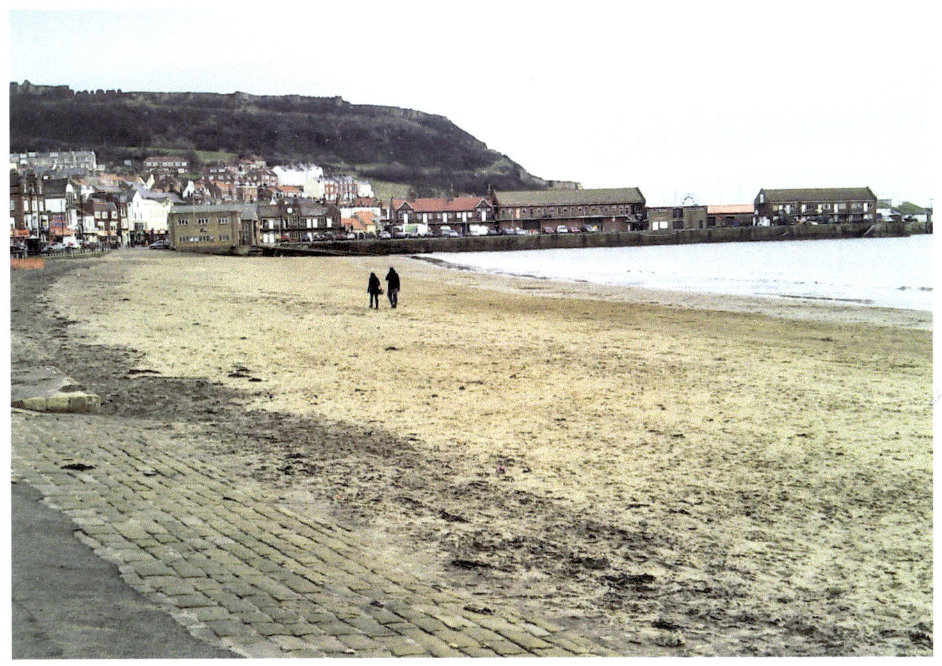

South Bay Beach

The beach on South Bay in January 2011 with a couple of people walking along the sands towards the harbour. The other view shows South Bay looking towards the Grand Hotel. The bright red building just below the hotel is an amusement arcade, which still does a fair amount of business even in the winter, which gives an indication that there is still an opportunity for tourist trade in this post-Christmas period.

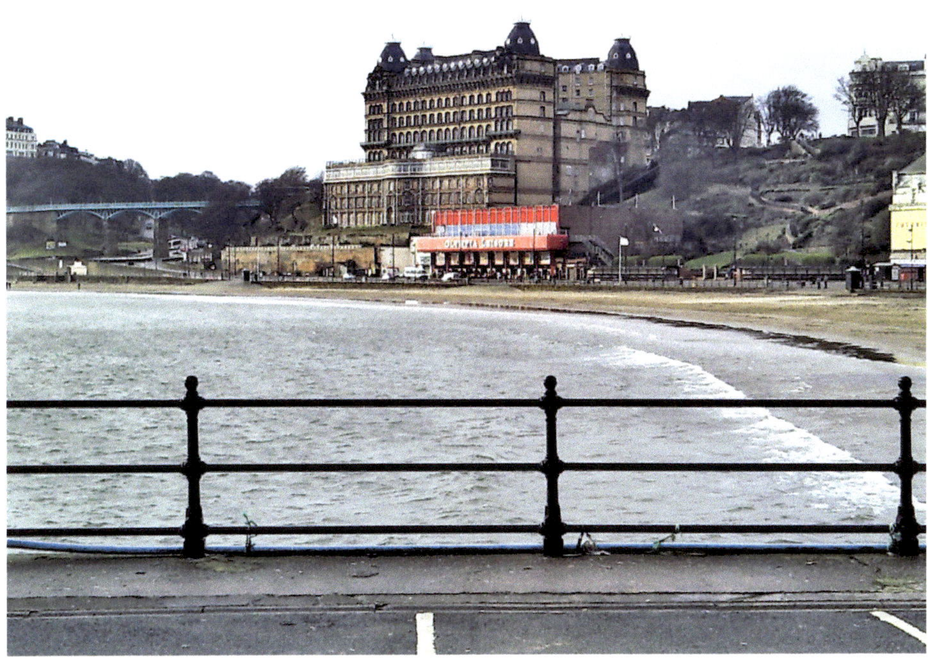

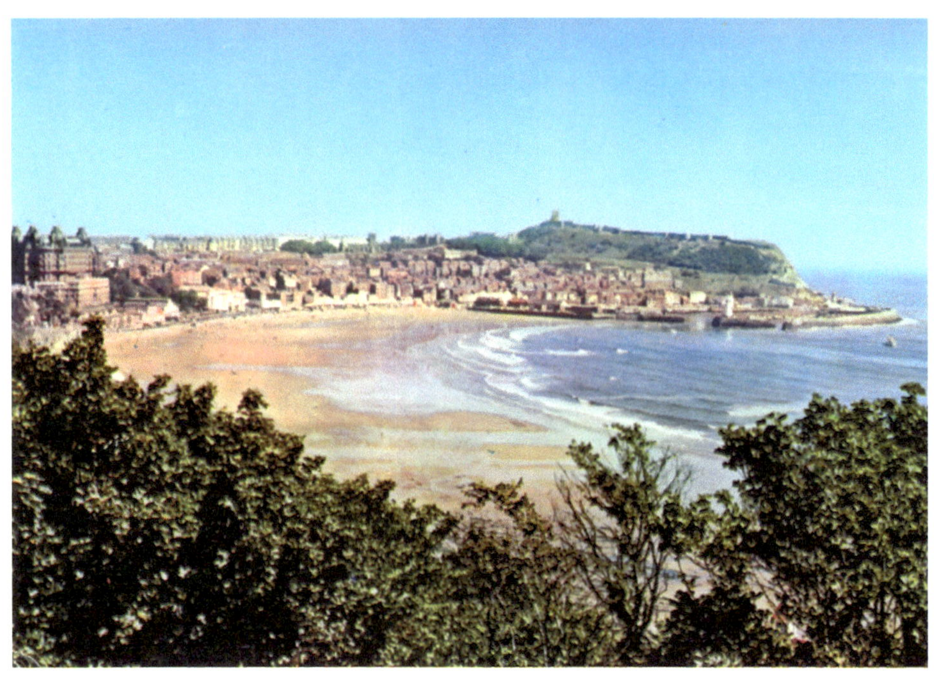

South Bay Beach

South Bay in the 1950s looking from The Esplanade. Close to the harbour is the Golden Ball public house in 2011 with the usual Poundshop next door and in the distance is the harbourside fairground.

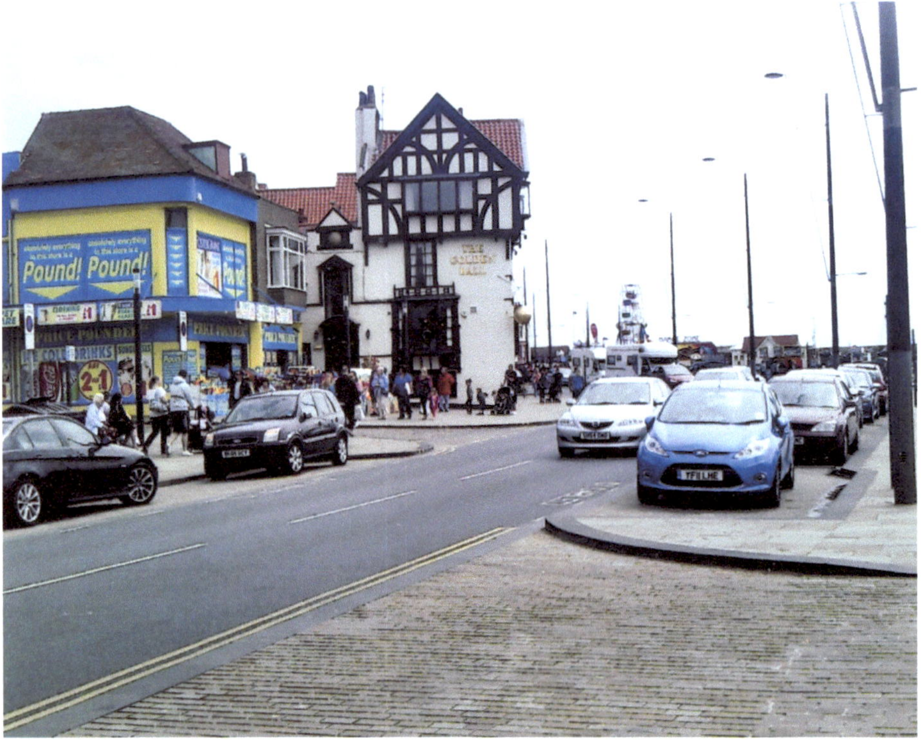

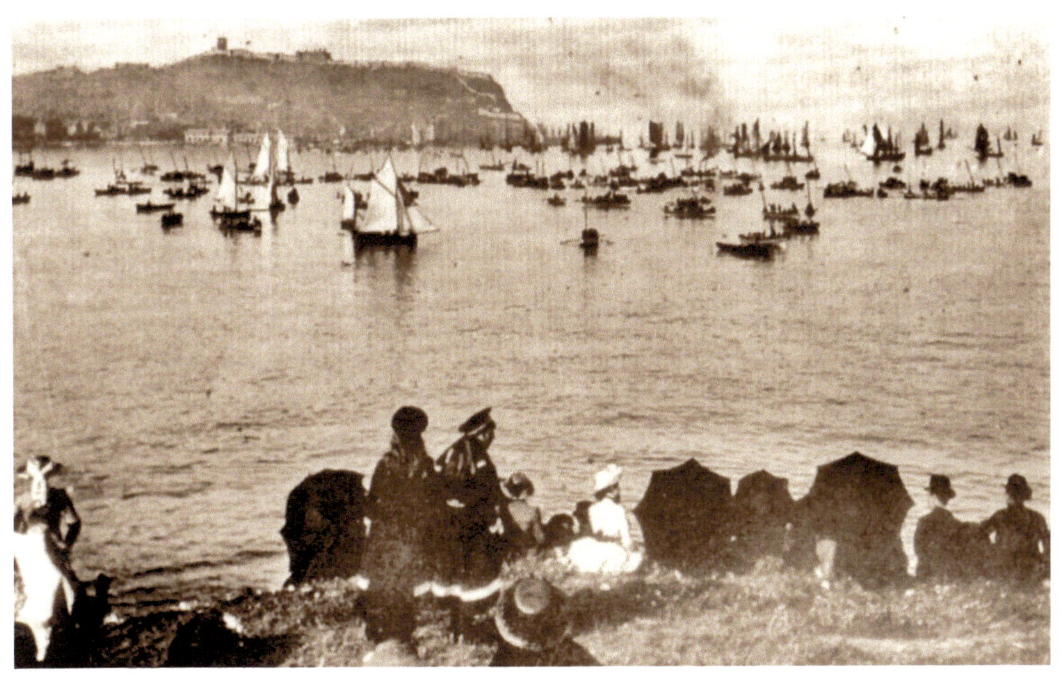

The Seaside

Seaside Scarborough in the late Victorian period as holiday-makers look out at a regatta on South Bay. Umbrellas are in use as protection from the wind, which can be quite strong at times, even during the summer months. The promontory and castle look down on this 1890s view. Below is a view from the harbour to The Esplanade in January 2011 on a cold day. The winter sea looks rather grey and the area appears deserted, although, in truth, there were several people about.

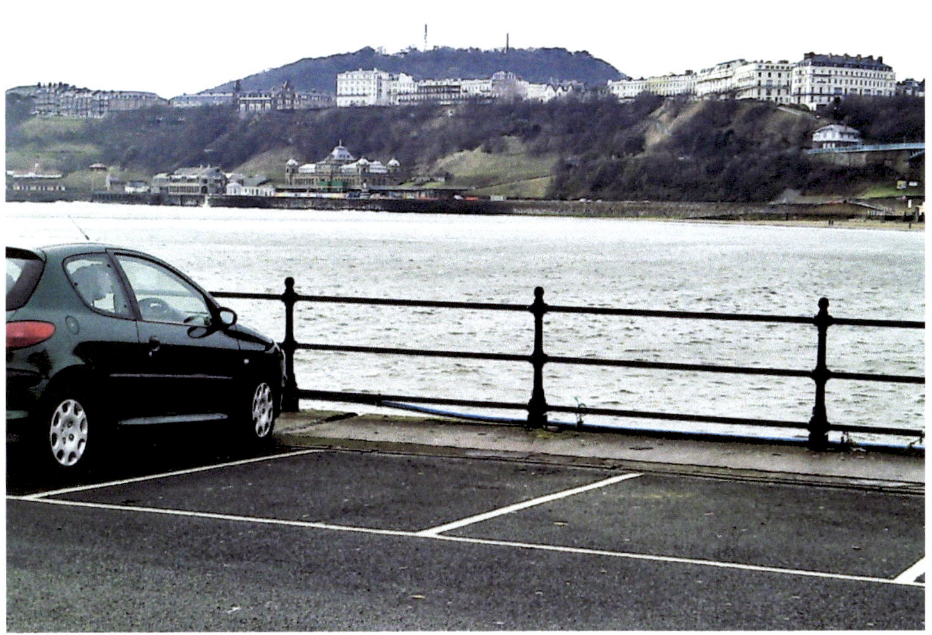

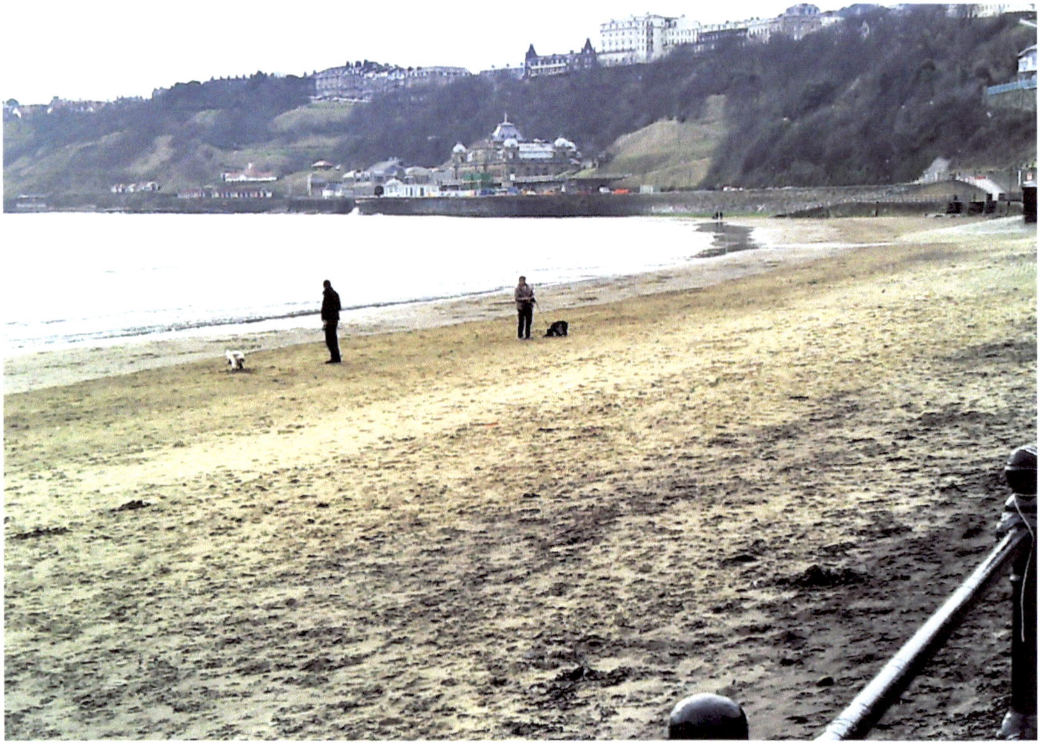

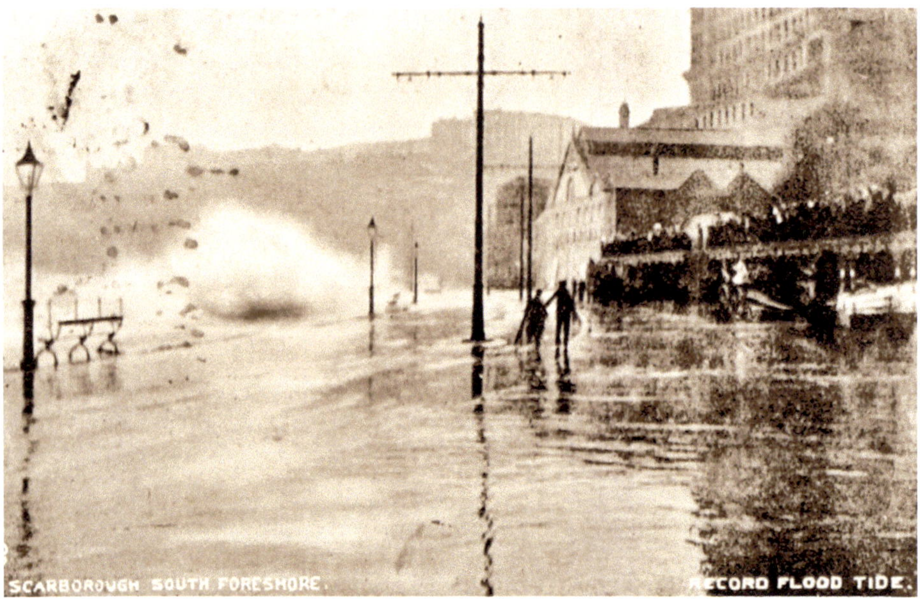

South Bay Beach

A record flood tide on South Bay in around 1905. Such is the height of the tide, Foreshore Road is flooded and waves continue to lash the promenade. It was around this time that the pier on North Bay was washed away and looking at this scene it is probably no real surprise that it did not survive such a lashing. Quieter South Bay sands can be seen above in January 2011, with walkers enjoying a stroll along the beach.

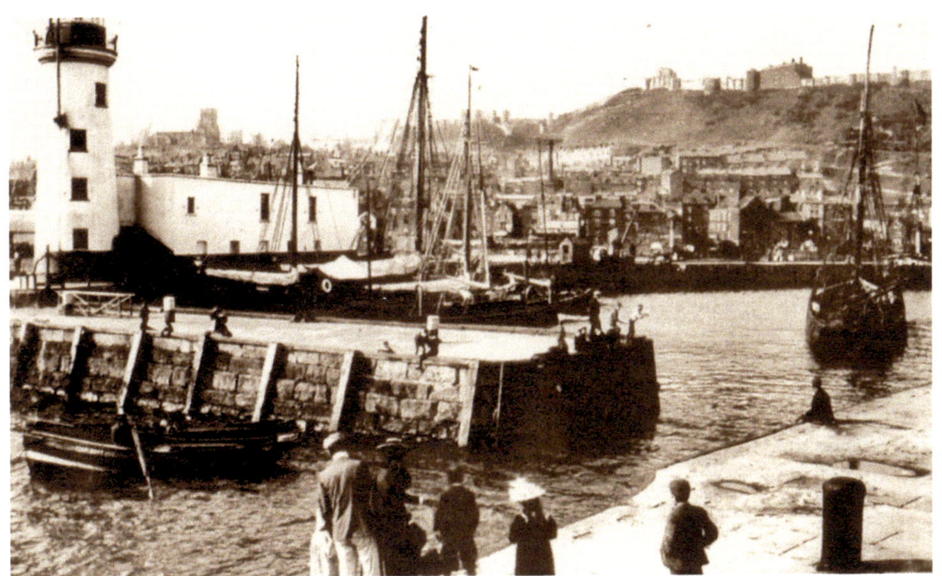

The Lighthouse

The lighthouse at the outer harbour in 1895, as fishing boats have either landed or are about to sail out. A similar view in 2011 shows the harbour entrance and private yachts in view, rather than fishing vessels. The lighthouse was damaged when the town was shelled by German cruisers early in the First World War, when a shell went right through the structure. The town also suffered some severe damage at the same time. The event was used as an aid to recruitment to the army after this with the slogan 'Remember Scarborough', which was designed to increase anger against Germany and encourage men to volunteer to fight against them on the Western Front.

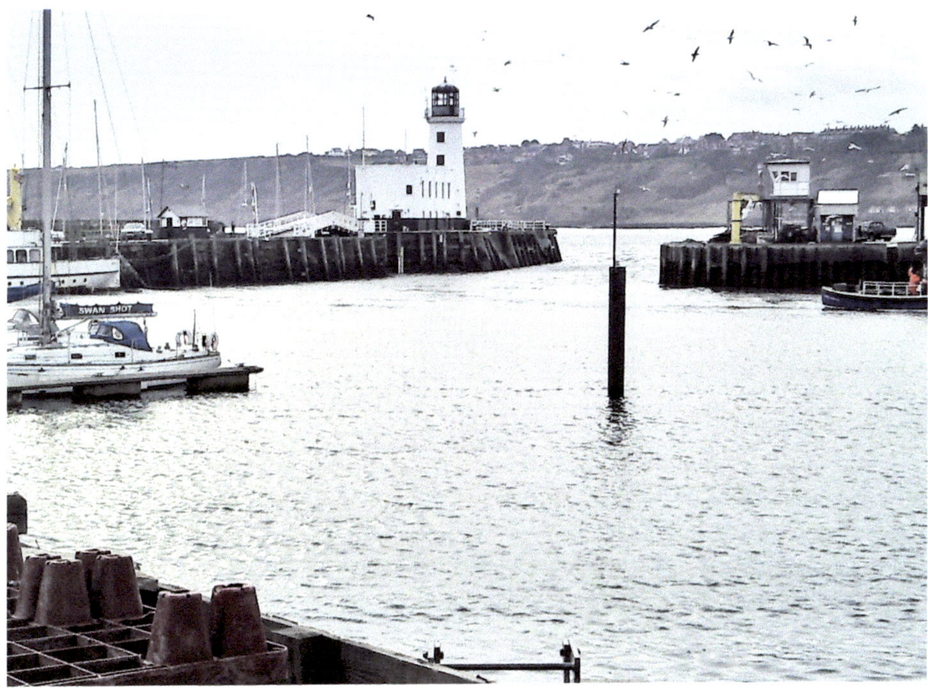

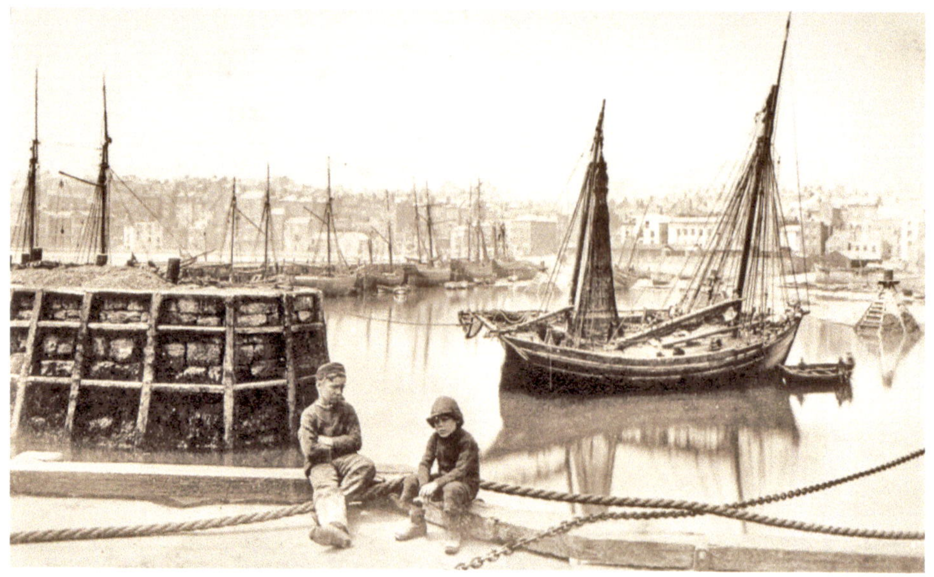

The Harbour

The harbour in the 1890s with several fishing boats in view and a couple of fishermen in the foreground, although the one on the right appears to be rather young to be called a 'man'. The harbour was once the commercial and industrial centre of the town and ships were built here at one time. The cobles (the east coast fishing boats are called this) are still sea-going, but put out with lobster and crab pots. The fish auction sheds are still in existence and there is a collection of fish stalls close to the pier. The modern view shows cobles which have just returned with their catches and give only a sense of how the harbour used to be.

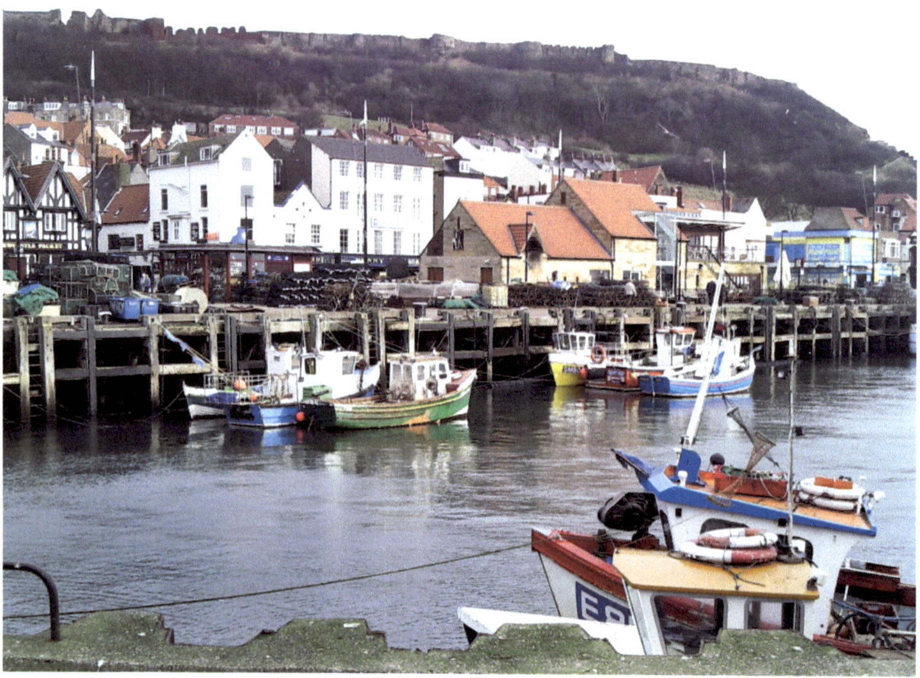

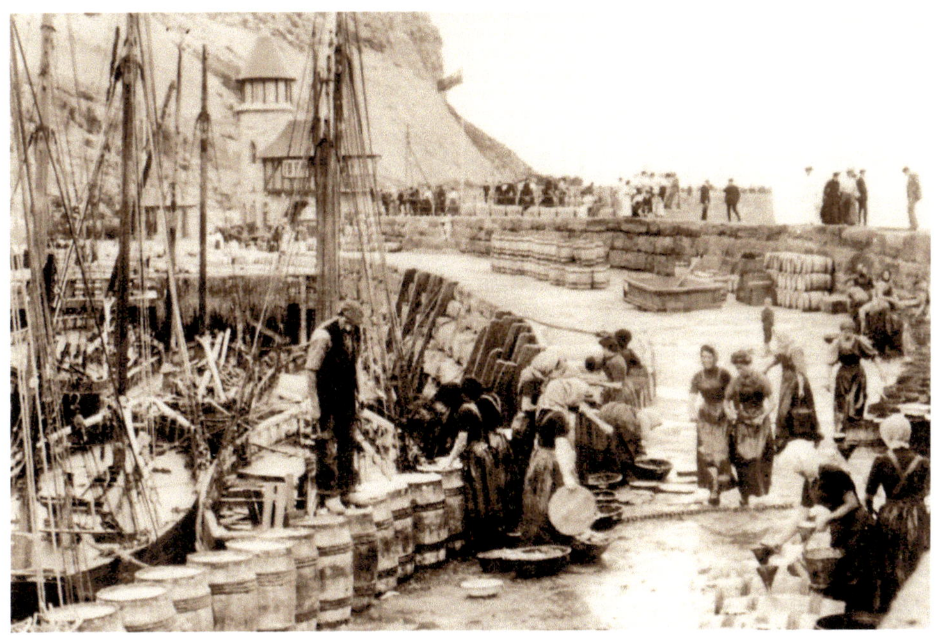

The Harbour

Landing fish at the harbour in the early twentieth century, while women were employed in the gutting and cleaning of the catch before going in for auction or sale. Women found employment in this kind of work and some can be seen packing cleaned fish into salt barrels with more containers in the background ready to be filled. These operations are being watched by visitors to the town. In the background is the rather ornate toll booth at the entrance to the North Bay's Marine Drive. In contrast, the modern period shows crab and lobster pots stacked up against the old auction sheds. There is also a lack of people here; giving an indication of just how few of the local populace are now employed in such occupations.

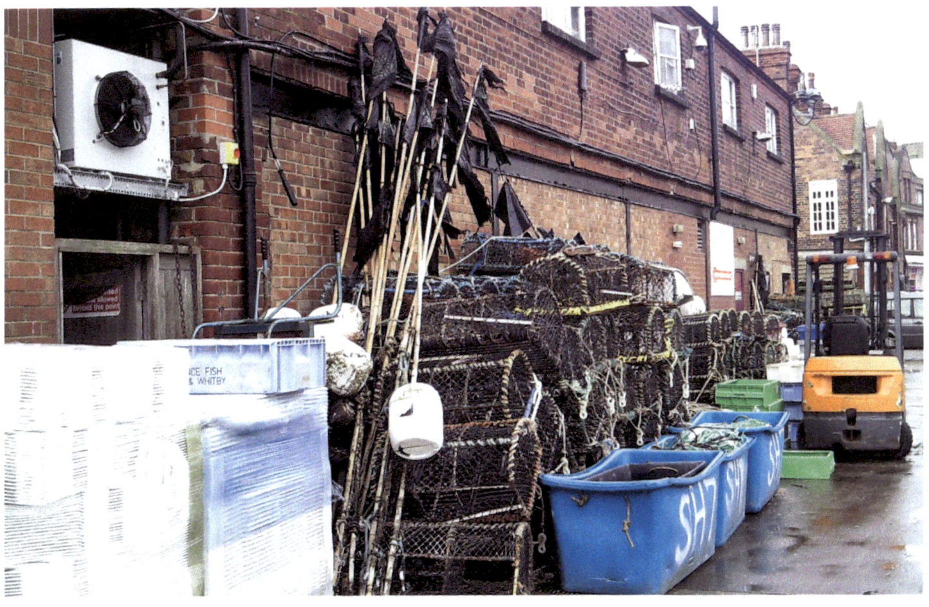

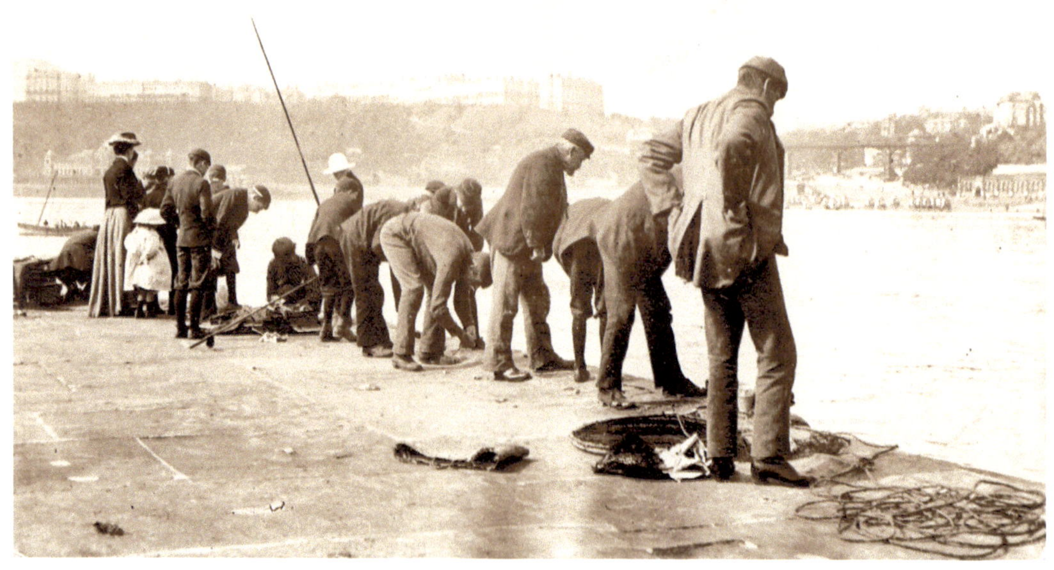

The Harbour

Fishermen on the quayside at Scarborough in the Edwardian period. In the background is The Esplanade with the footbridge linking it with South Bay. Below, fishing boats line the harbour wall at Scarborough with buildings of South Bay promenade in view.

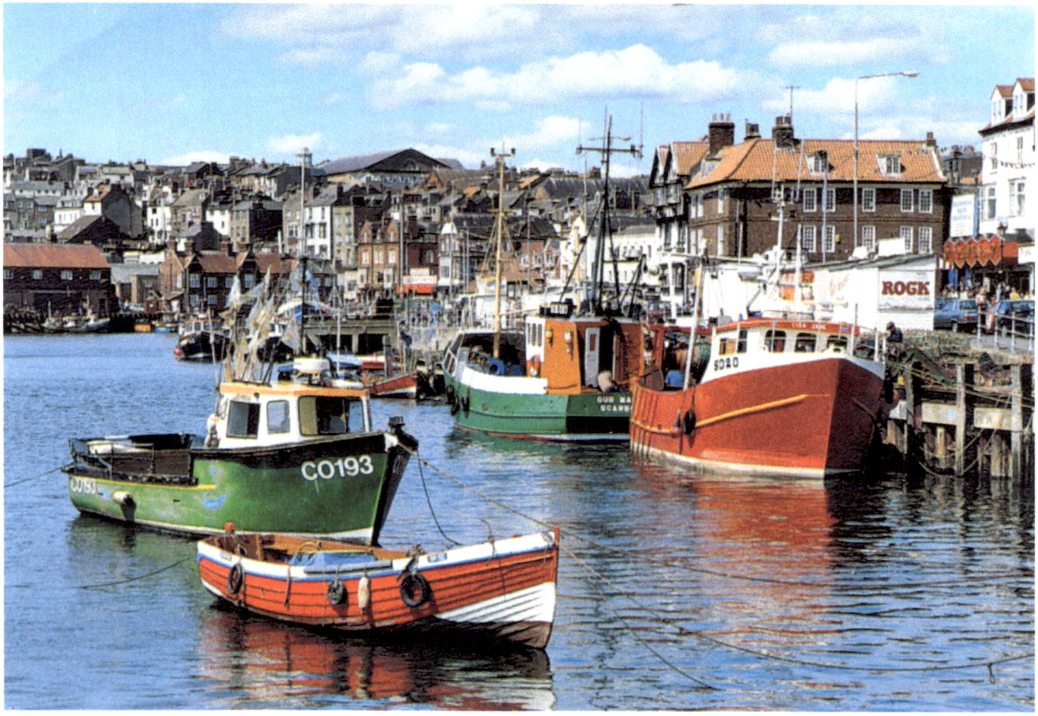

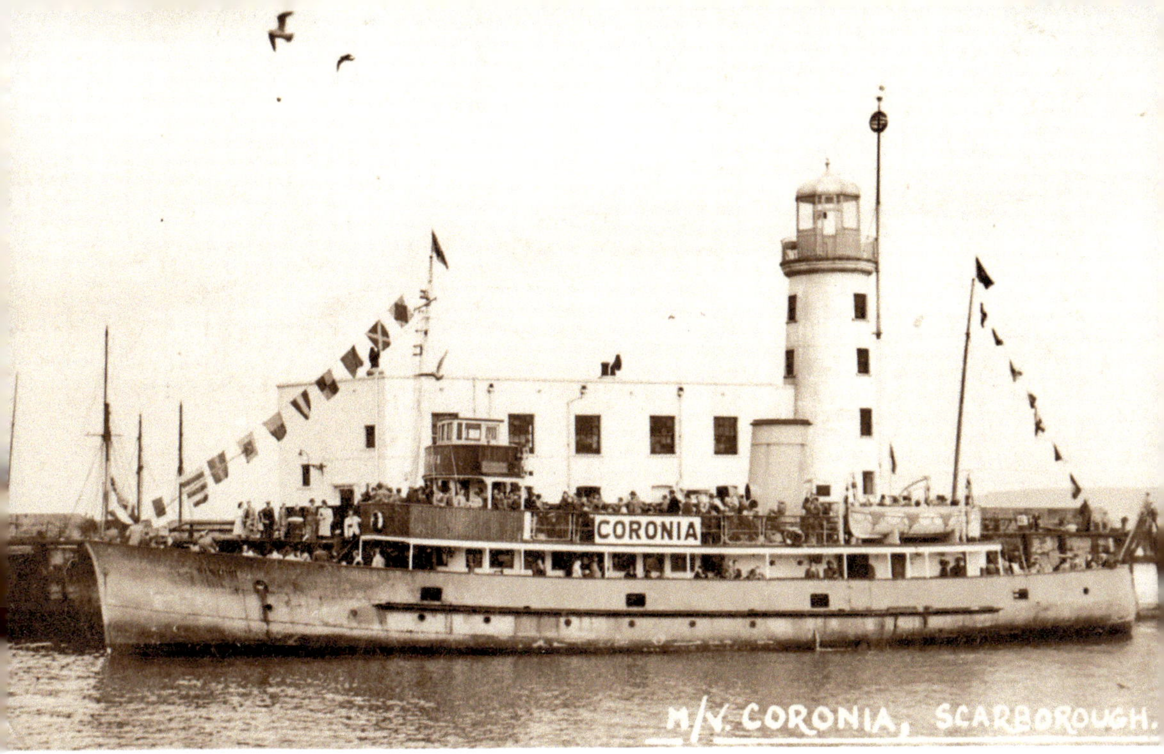

Shipping at Scarborough

The MV *Coronia* at the harbour with the lighthouse in the background. Another view of the *Coronia* leaving the harbour at Scarborough with passengers on a pleasure cruise.

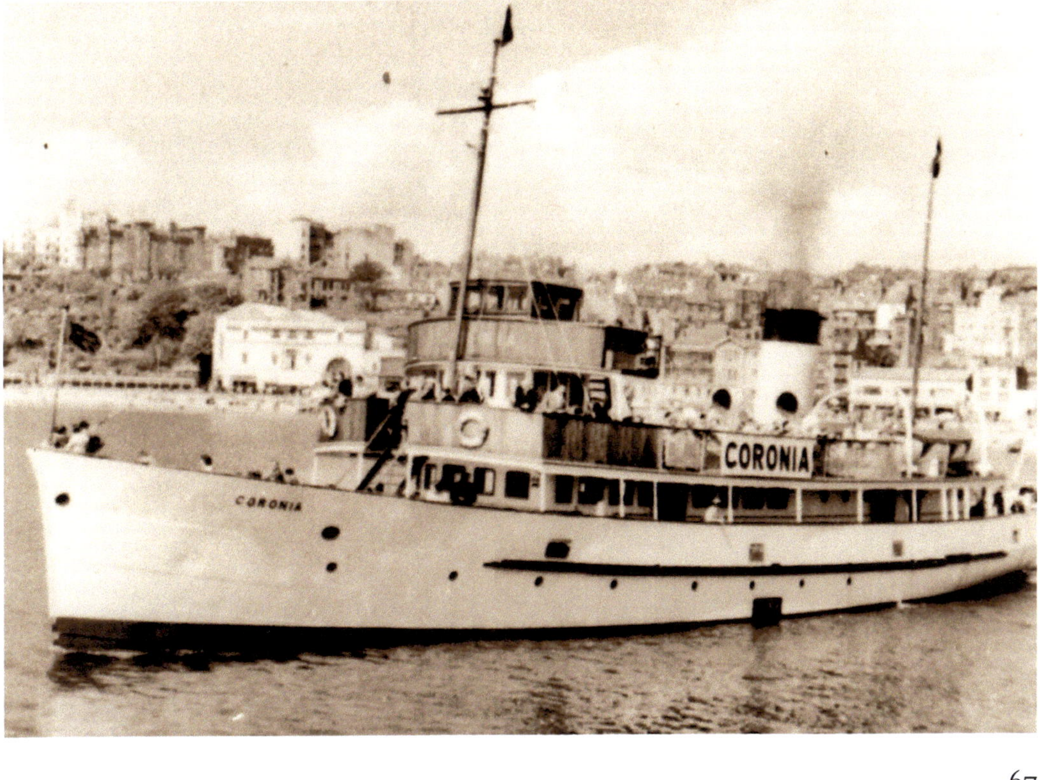

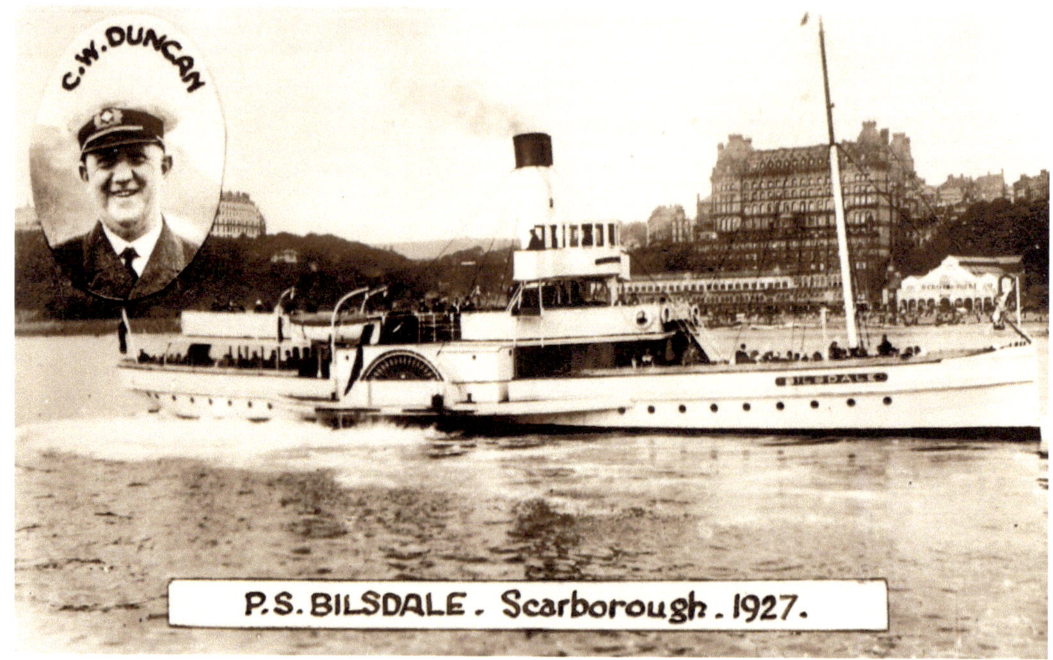

P.S. BILSDALE . Scarborough . 1927.

Shipping at Scarborough

With the Grand Hotel in the background, the paddle steamer *Bilsdale* is approaching Scarborough Harbour during the summer of 1927. The *Bilsdale*'s captain, C. W. Duncan, is inset top right. Below, passing through Scarborough on her final voyage, is Cunarder *Mauretania* on 2 July 1935. Before the First World War, the liner used to call at Fishguard before going on to Liverpool, as passengers could reach London quicker by rail from there instead of sailing through to Liverpool and thence to the capital. Her sister ship, the *Lusitania*, was sunk by a German U-boat off the Old Head of Kinsale, to the west of Ireland, in 1915, which did much to bring the USA into the war.

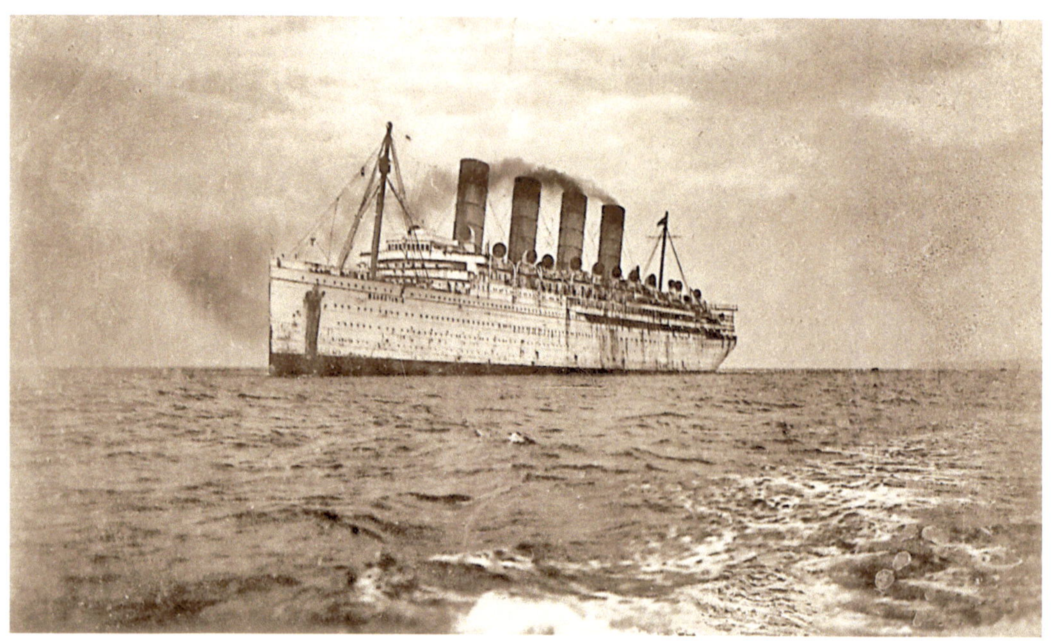

McCain Foods Limited

Along with fish, there are chips and McCain Foods established a factory producing potato based foods at Eastfield, which includes its famous oven chips. Here, in the late 1960s, when McCain decided to establish its works here, contractors are preparing its site for construction of the works. New housing can be seen in the background; some who live there will find this place, as will some of the old fishermen, ironic. The site for the McCain Factory has been cleared ready for construction to commence.

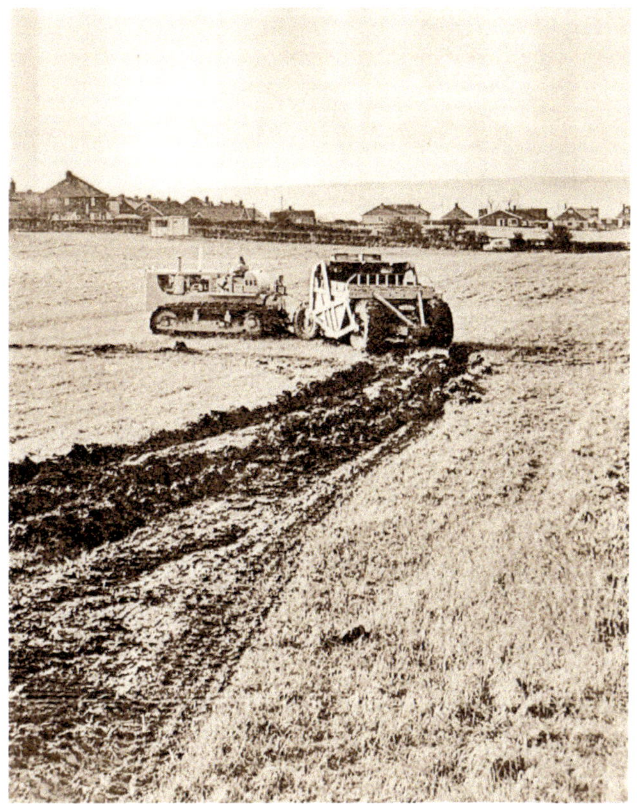

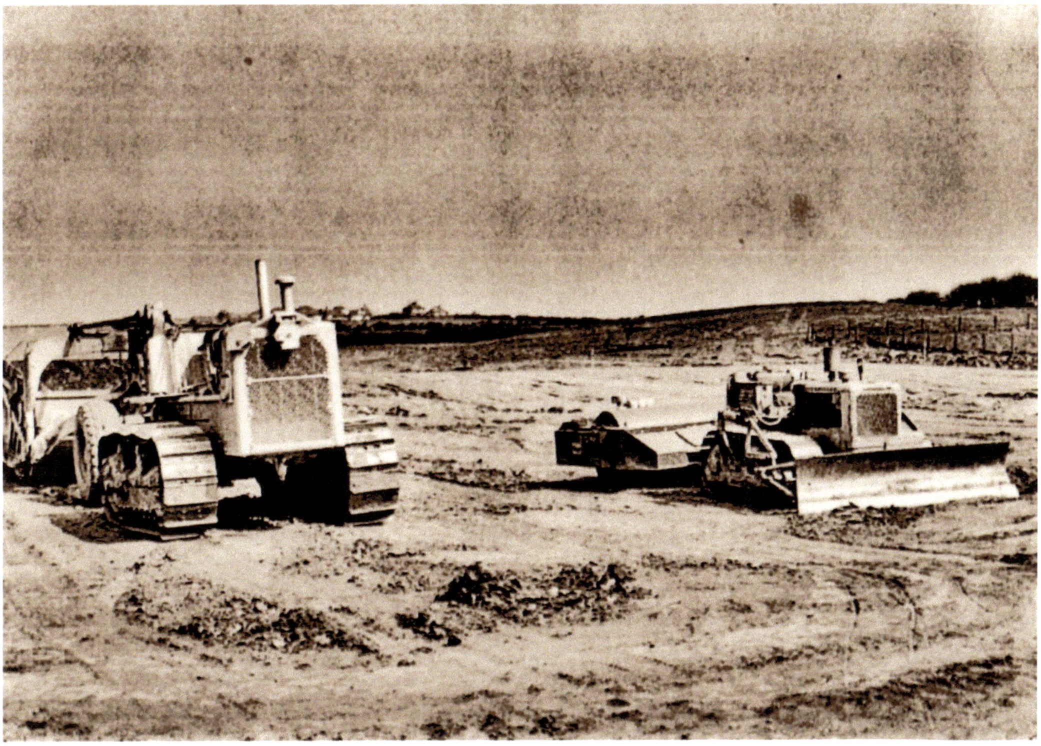

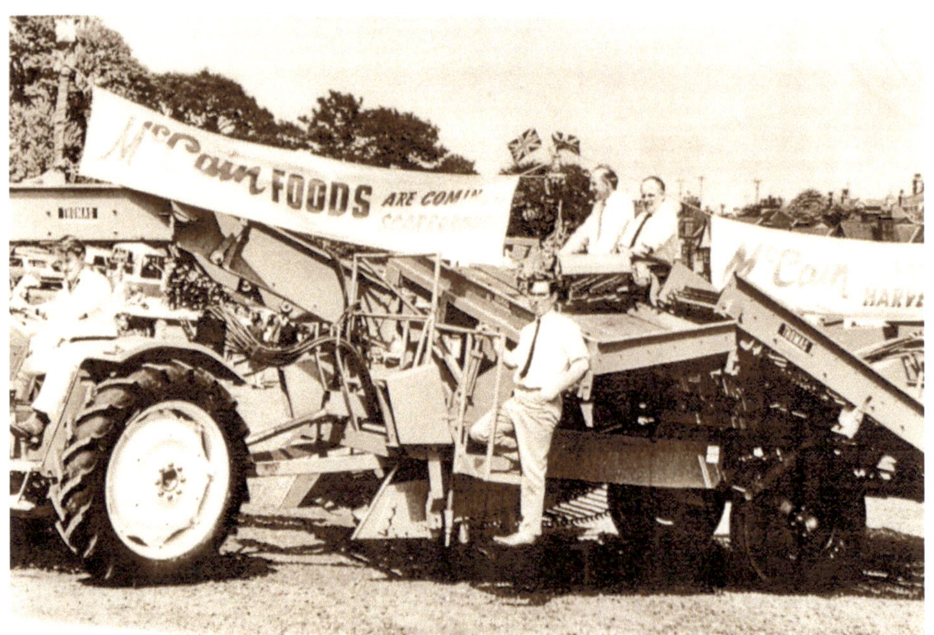

McCain Foods Limited

The McCain Foods company were not slow in advertising the fact that it was establishing a new factory here, as this view of company managers and the excavator, which will be used to prepare the site, displays banners proclaiming that the food company will be present in the town. The framework to the McCain factory is being put in place and it will not be long before production will begin on the site. It will expand quite considerably over the years as McCain develops new products and develops its markets.

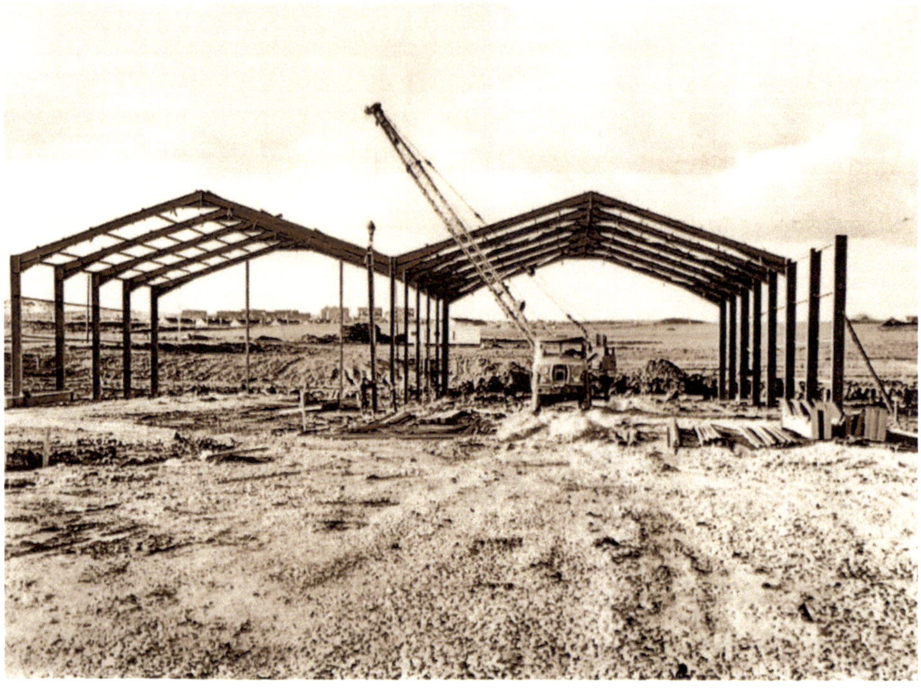

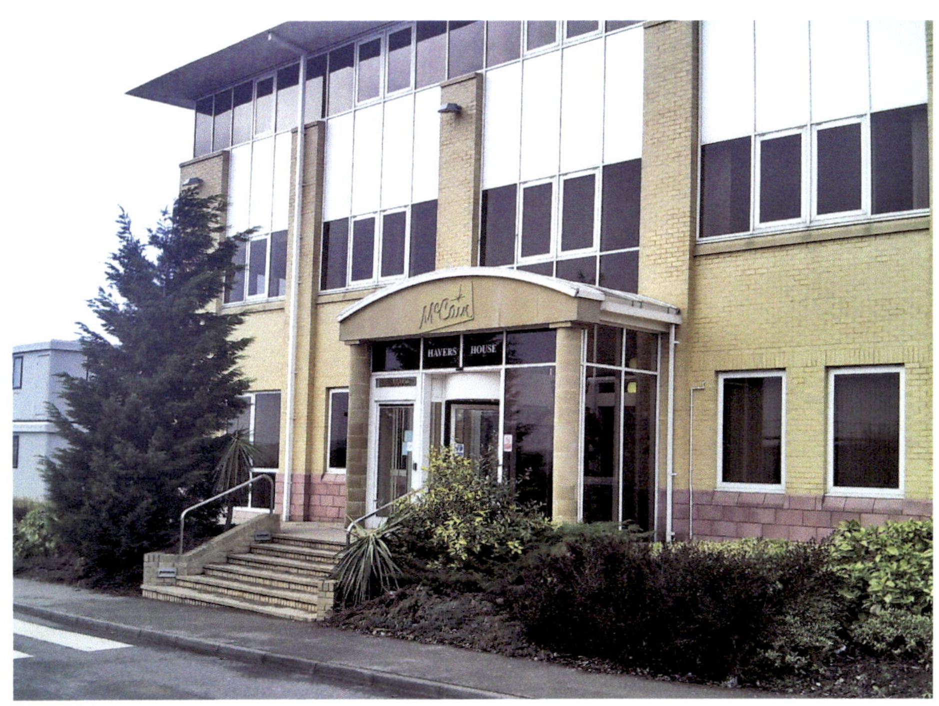

McCain Foods Limited

Head office of McCain Foods at Scarborough in 2011, at the top of Havers Hill. The factory at Havers Hill is where production of McCain potato foods at Scarborough is based. The company employs many local people who once worked in the fishing and tourism industries.

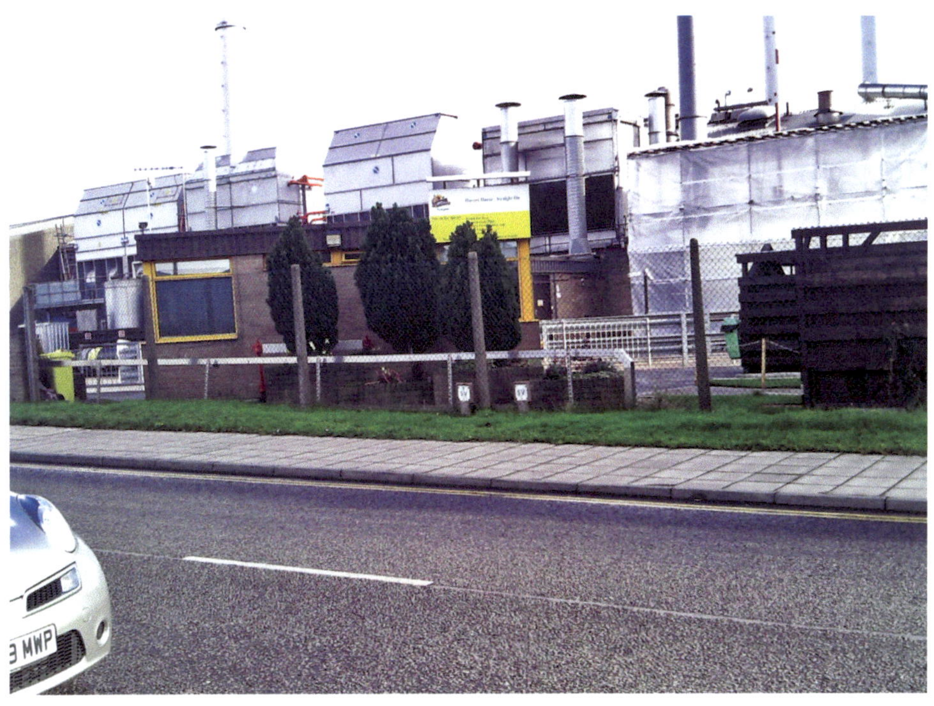

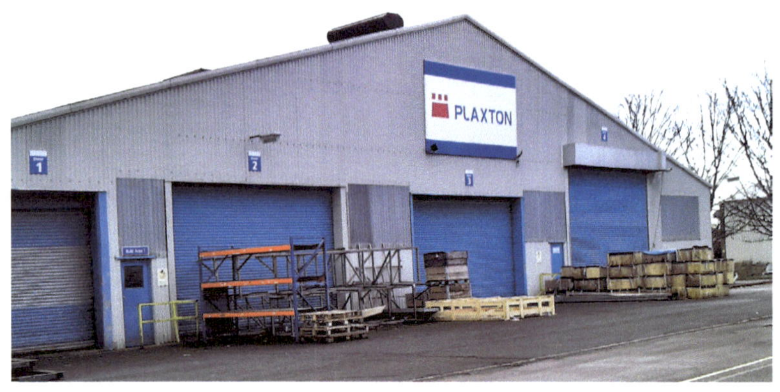

The Plaxton Factory at Eastfield in 2011

The coachbuilding works here was established in 1961, but the company goes back to the early years of the twentieth century. In 1907, Frederick William Plaxton started a joinery shop in Bar Street, off Westborough. By 1914, he was employing plumbers, masons, plasterers and bricklayers, along with joiners. Indeed, it was Plaxton who built the Palladium cinema on Foreshore Road. He also built the Futurist cinema in the 1920s, along with the new Valley Bridge. Plaxton was quite entrepreneurial and opened a works on Castle Road, which specialised in bodywork for motor vehicles. By 1936, he had opened a larger factory on Seamer Road and began building motor coach bodies. During the Second World War, Plaxton's made ammunition boxes and, from 1946, they were making bodies for Bedford, Commer and Austin chassis. They were also building 'Green Goddess' fire engines and mobile canteens for the US Air Force. Frederick died in 1957 and was succeeded by his son Eric who was responsible for construction of the Eastfield site. By 1972, the works employed some 1,300 local men. The work was, however, mostly seasonal, which would have suited some employees, as they could work in the holiday trade in the summer and at Plaxton's in winter when the orders were completed. Plaxton's also built bodies for the new Scarborough 'Park and Ride' buses, one of which is seen at the bus stop in York Place.

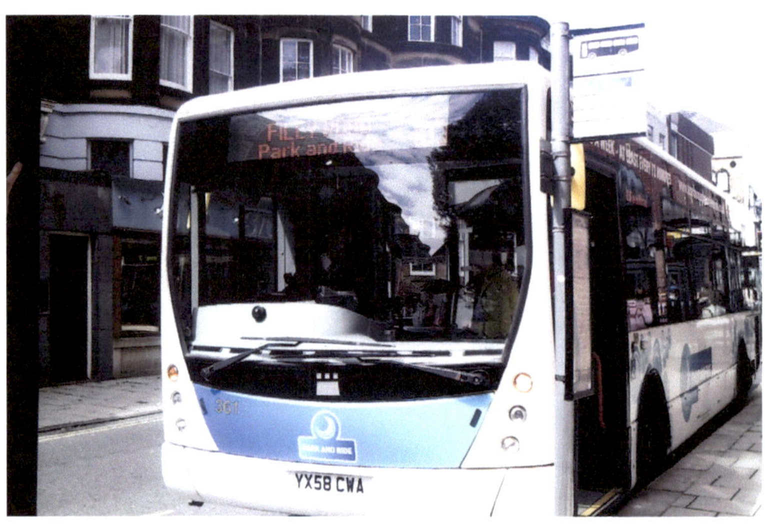

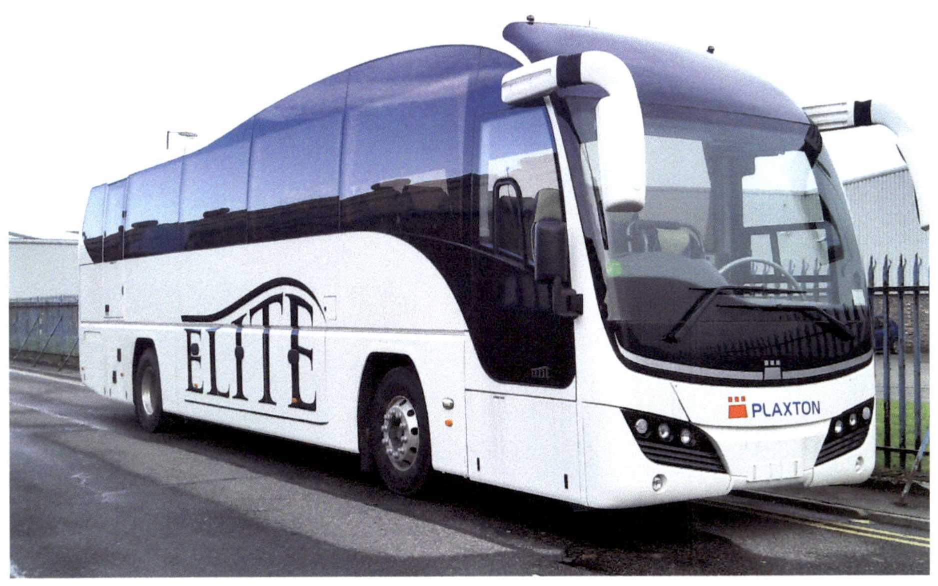

Plaxton's Coaches

The Elite coach, a new design of coach body for 2011, at Plaxton's. The company is now part of the Dennis/Alexander Group; the Scarborough plant concentrates on building luxury coach bodies, while another plant at Sheffield undertakes body repairs. The Alexander works in Scotland builds bus bodies, although Scarborough does undertake such work and actually built the bodies for local 'Park and Ride' buses operating in Scarborough. Along with McCain and Plaxton, there have been other employers in the area, including the 'Pindar Group', which closed only in the last couple of years, and a double glazing company.

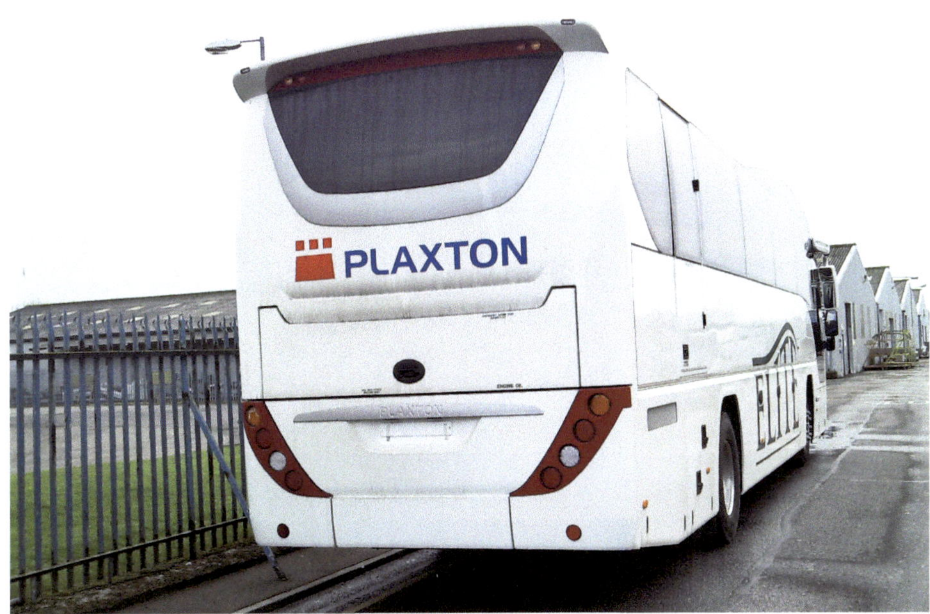

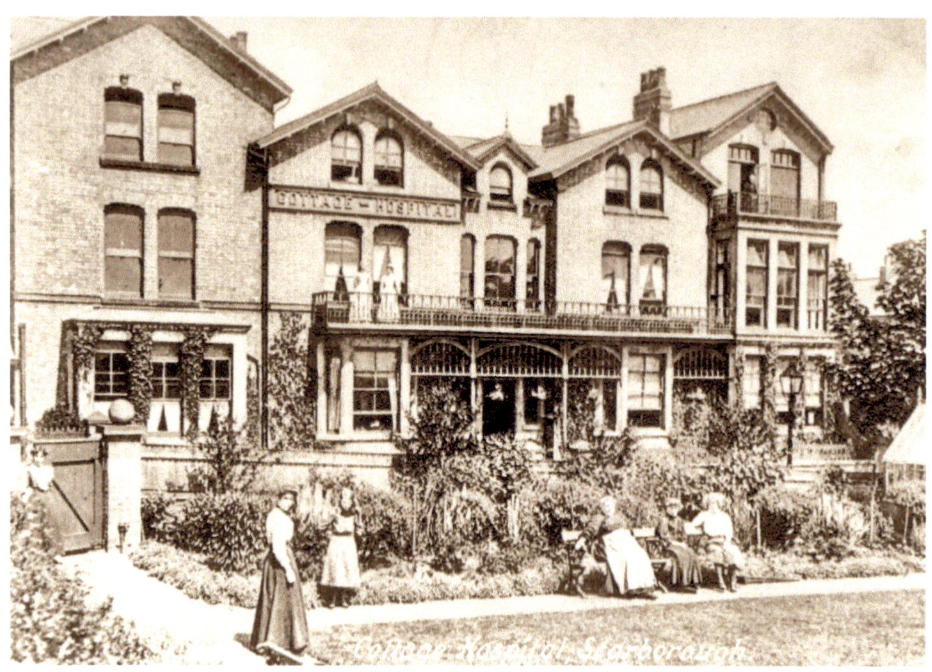

The Cottage Hospital on Springhill Road

The hospital was founded by Mrs Anne Wright, a widow of a Birmingham surgeon, in 1871, and was the first medical hospital in the town, apart from that which existed at the workhouse on Dean Road. The Cottage Hospital served the community until it closed in 1931 due to the economic conditions of the day. Anne Wright was commemorated by the naming of the 'Anne Wright' ward at Scarborough Hospital, which, until recently, was the rehabilitation ward and was situated on the north block.

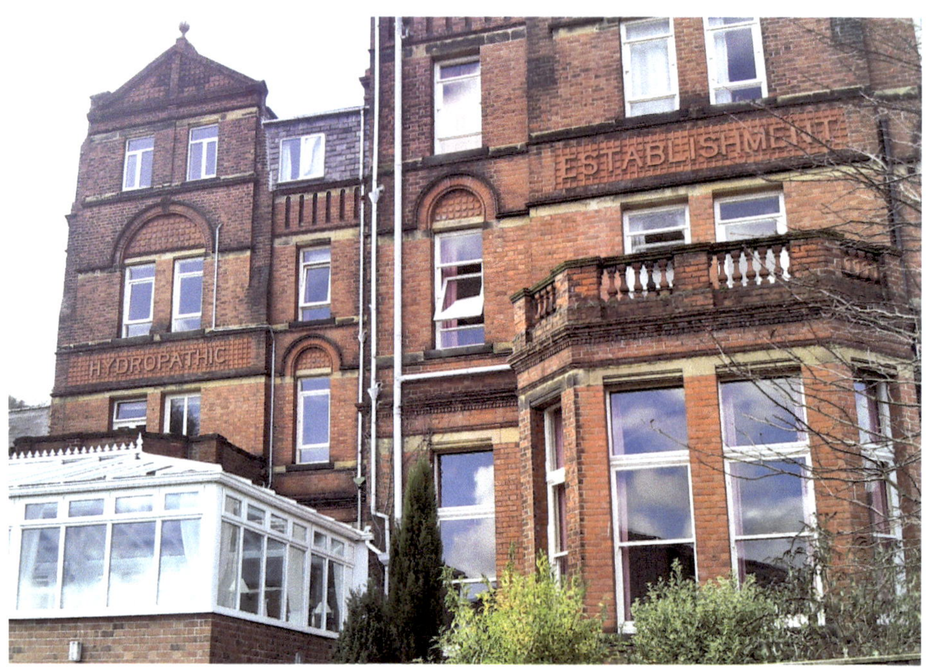

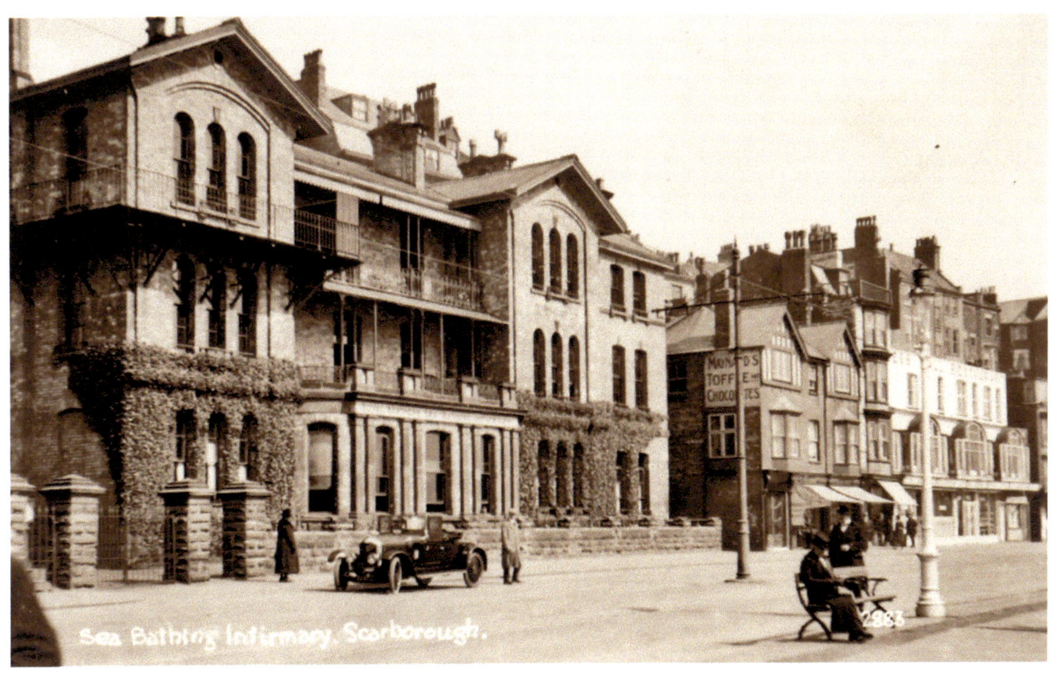

The Sea Bathing Infirmary

The Sea Bathing Infirmary on Foreshore Road, close to the Futurist cinema. The upper view dates back to the 1920s, while the lower view shows the same structure in 2010, during the summer season, the ground floor having been brought into use as a fancy goods shop. At the time the picture was taken, the upper floors were offered for rent. On the left is the amusement arcade, which can be seen in the view from the harbour.

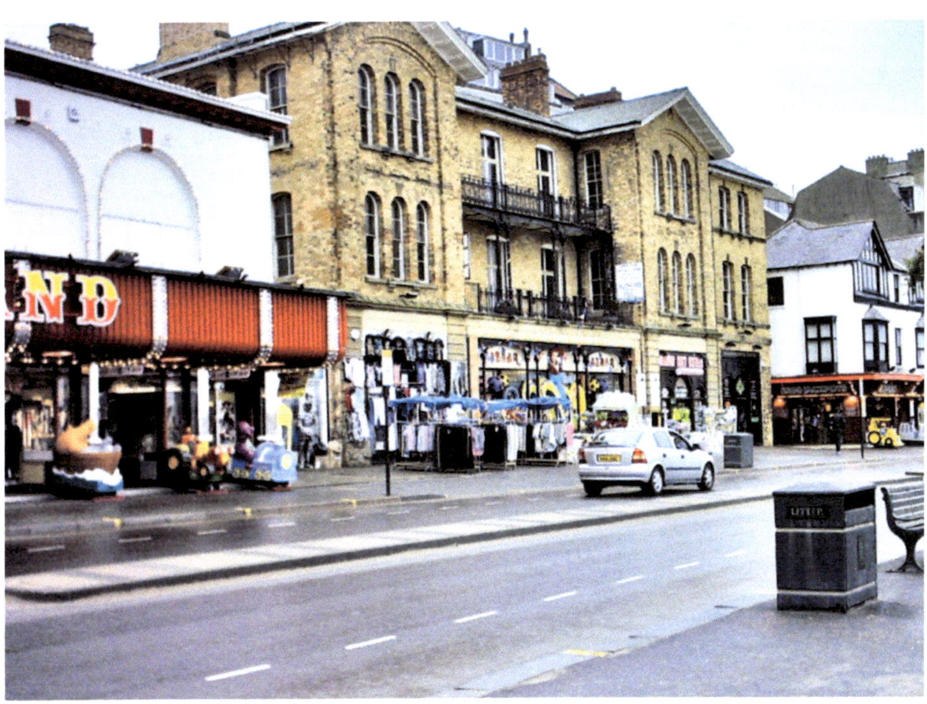

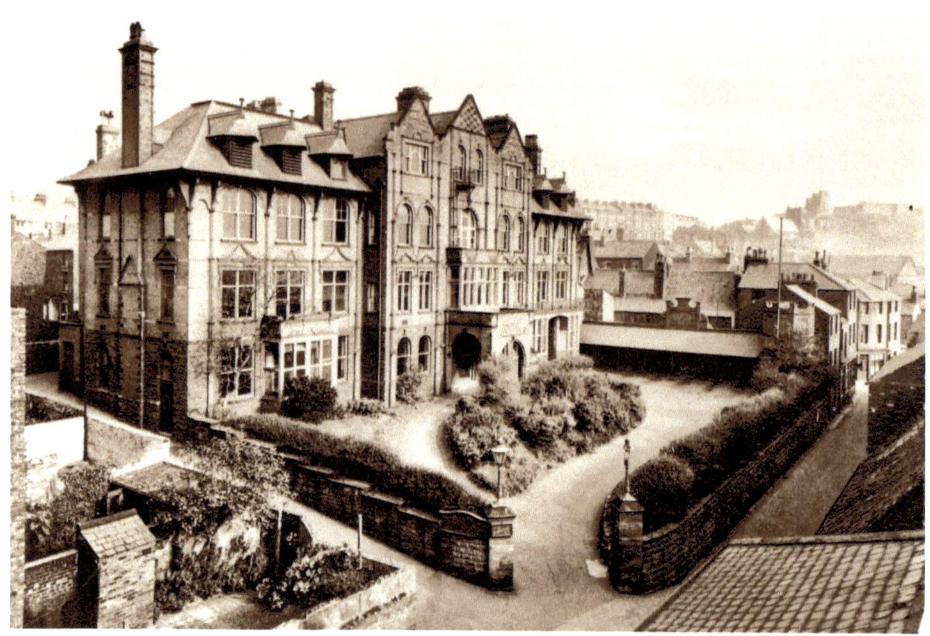

The First Scarborough Hospital

The first 'Scarborough Hospital' opened in 1893 and was replaced in 1936. One John Dale, who had retired to Scarborough in 1882, and was Mayor between 1892 and 1893, donated £500 to launch a 'Hospital Building Fund'. The hospital was situated at Friars entry and was designed by Topwell & Hall. It was built by local men at a cost of £11,300. The hospital eventually had seventy beds before closure. After closure, the building was sold to Scarborough Corporation in 1941, and was used for children who had been evacuated from London during the Second World War. The structure later found a use as Maenson's clothing factory, and then as a base for the local Health Authority until demolition in 1974. The whole site is now a pay and display car park, as can be seen below.

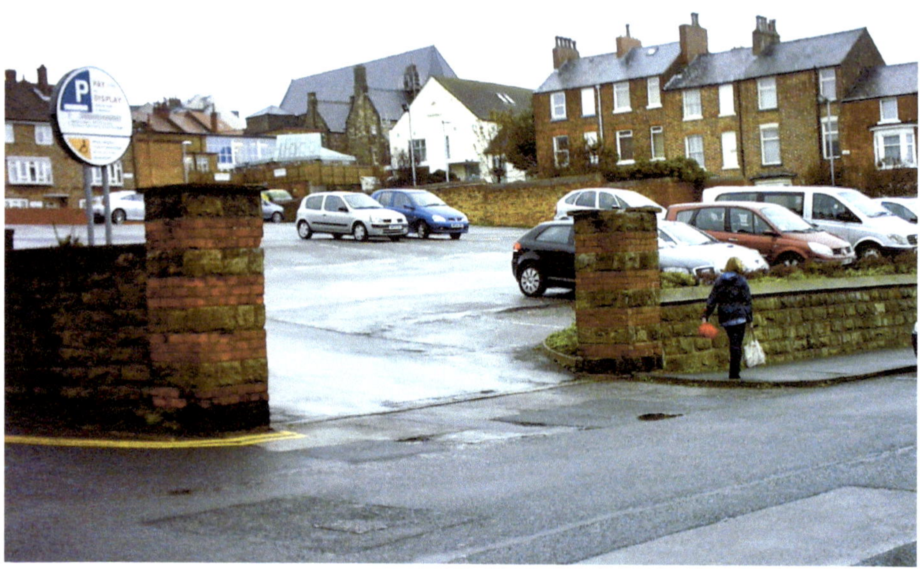

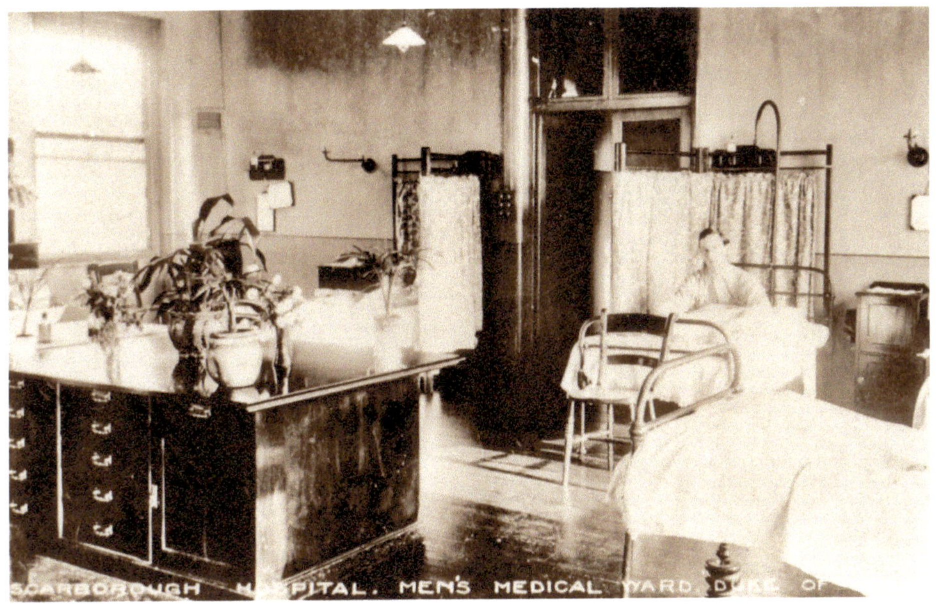

The Men's Medical Ward at the Original Scarborough Hospital

The ward was entitled The Duke of York Ward, the later King George V, as the hospital opened on the wedding day of the Duke and Duchess of York, 6 July 1893. Along with the medical ward shown here, there was a children's ward on the first floor, named after Sophia Adams, and a male surgical ward on the second floor, which was named after John Dale. As can be seen, the ward was rather basic and the steel beds look somewhat uncomfortable, although modern patients still say that hospital beds are uncomfortable even today, despite being fitted with the latest technology. The flooring is polished wood and the furniture, on the left, which probably contained medications, equipment and patient records, is also highly polished. It appears that electric light has been newly installed and wall mounted gas mantles are now out of use. During 1933, the Duke of Kent, along with Sir Kenelm Cayley, are seen inspecting nurses at the old Scarborough Hospital.

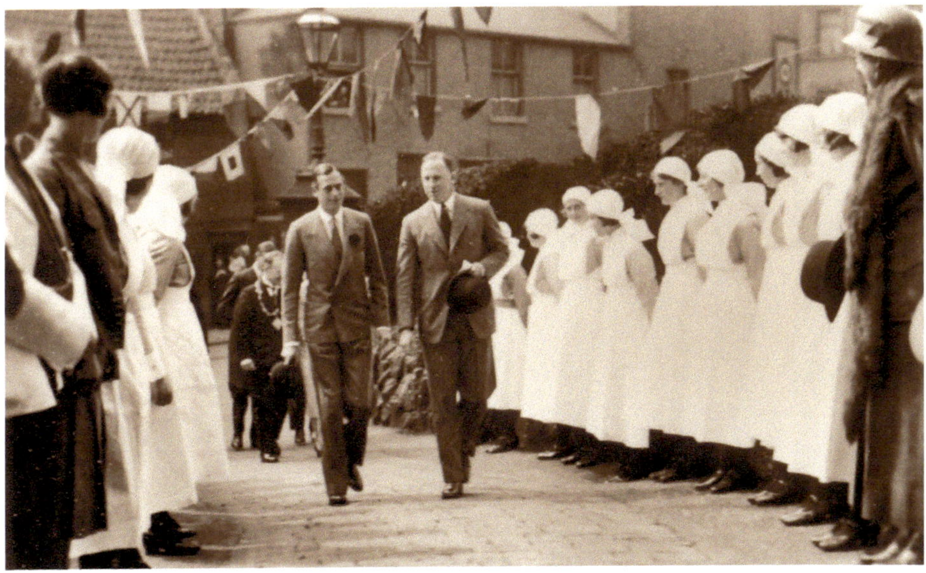

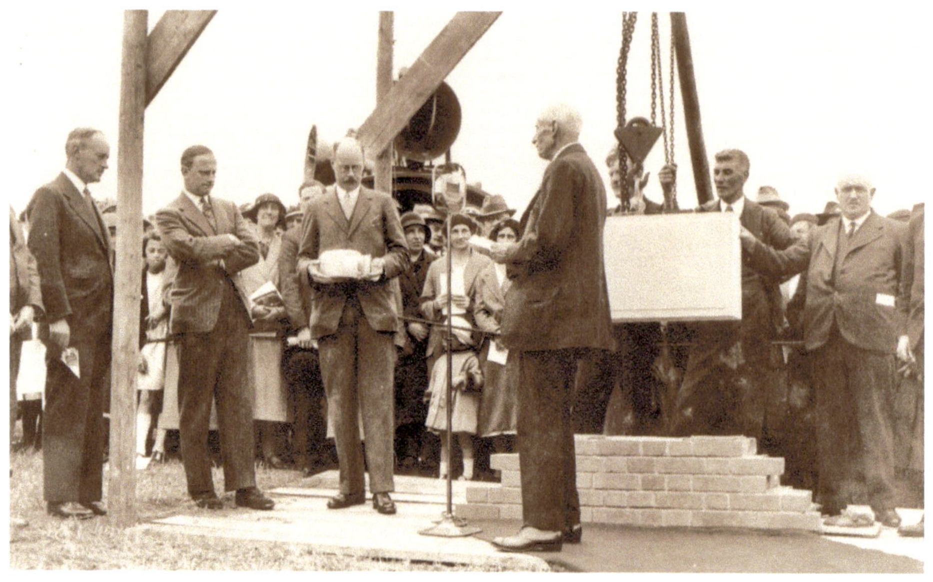

The New Scarborough Hospital

A new hospital was planned on the north side of the town, off Scalby Road, to replace the one opened in 1893 to increase capacity. As a Voluntary Hospital, funds needed to be raised for its construction. Here, the foundation stone is being laid, which is now visible, on the right, at what is now the North Entrance. Members of the public witnessing the ceremony and those who are performing the ritual are, from left to right: Mr W. Marchment, Architect; Sir Kenelm Cayley, President; Mr J. Munby, Honorary Solicitor; Mr C. C. Graham, Patron; and Mr Eagles, Foreman Builder. Below, in 1934, a team of fundraisers are seen with Miss Alice Escolme in charge, who became matron of the new hospital from 1934 until 1962. The children are dressed as doctors and nurses from different periods.

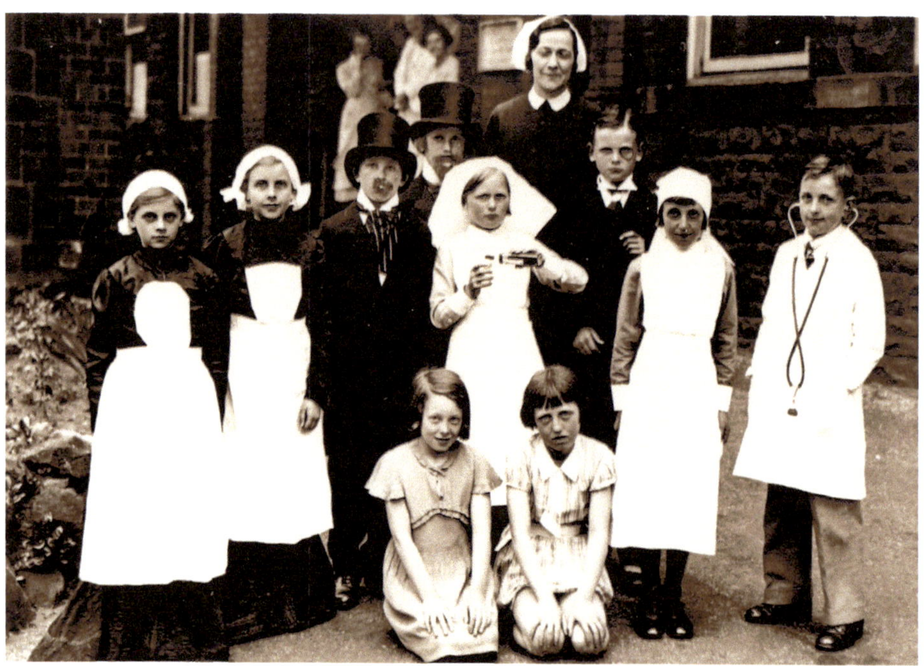

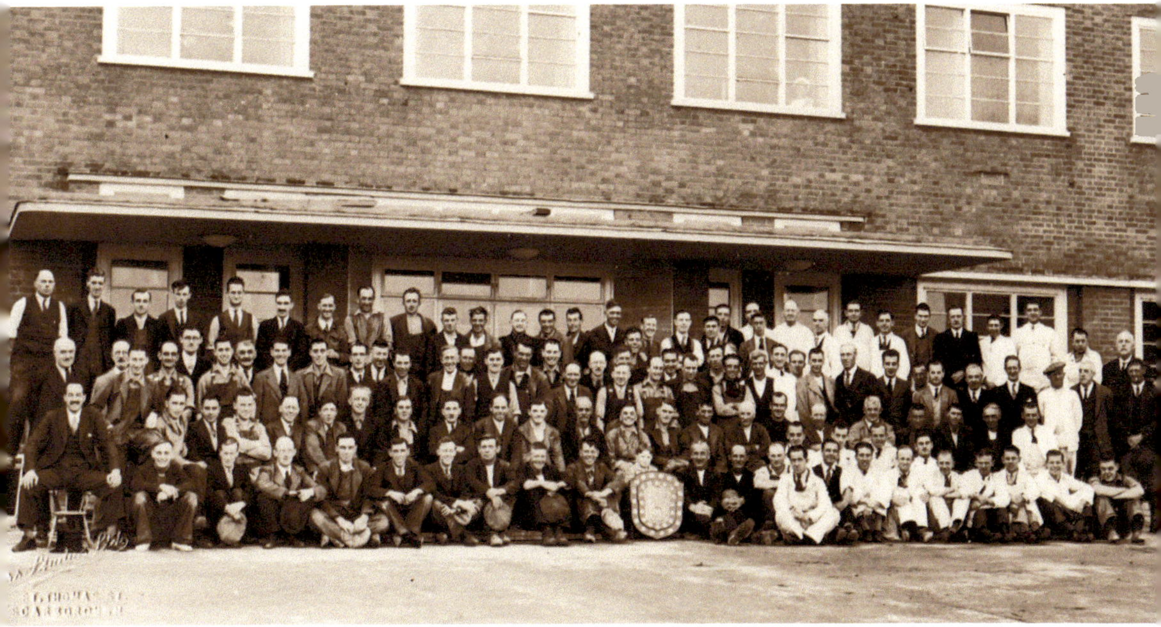

The New Scarborough Hospital

All of those involved in construction of the new hospital are seen here shortly after the building had opened. A nurse can be seen in the upper window taking an interest in proceedings. Below, an aerial view of the construction of the new hospital in 1935.

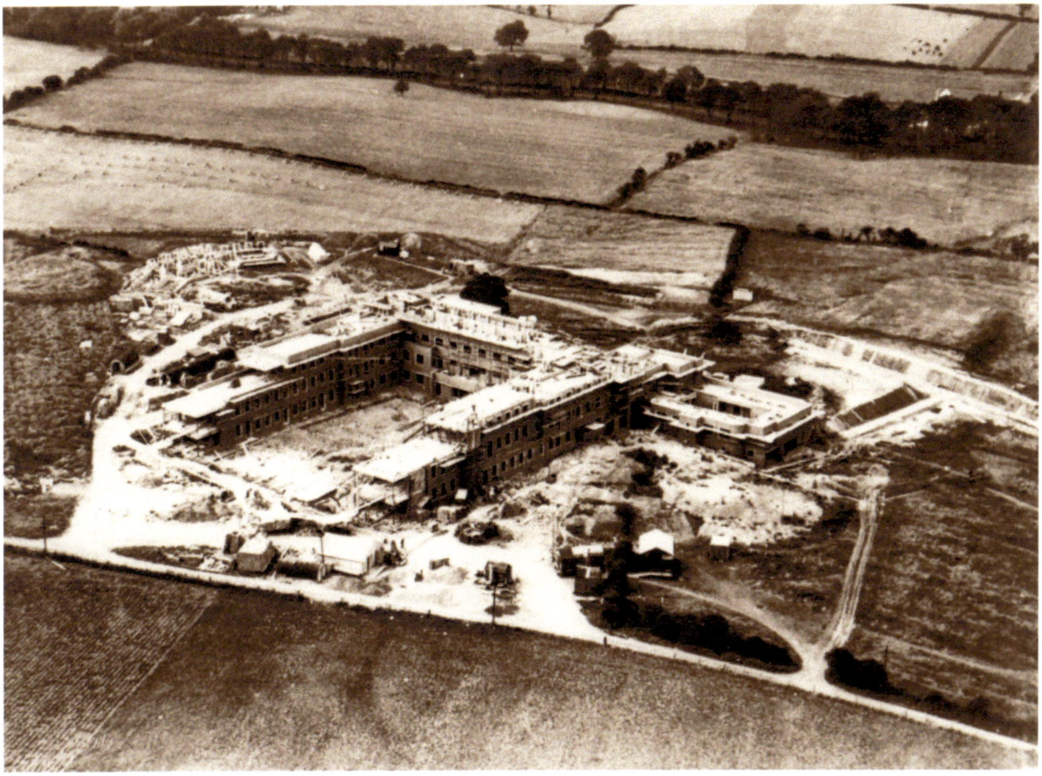

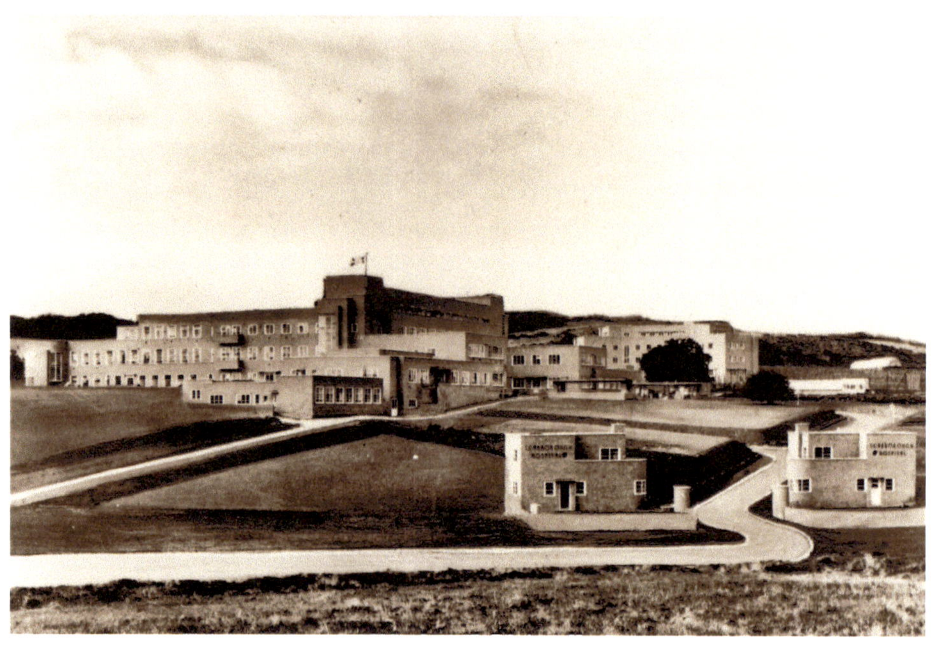

The New Scarborough Hospital

The new Scarborough Hospital when it was completed and ready for opening. When it was opened in October 1936, the building had cost £129,000, and £20,000 was still needed when it opened for public inspection a month earlier. The new hospital had 140 beds, which included twelve for private patients and a further twelve for maternity cases. At the entrance gate are the Porter's and Engineer's Lodges. The grounds were laid out under the supervision of Harry Smith who was a retired Borough Engineer. As can be seen, the hospital was built in the art deco style of the 1930s period. The new hospital was opened for inspection in September 1936 and many of the local population took the opportunity to see it.

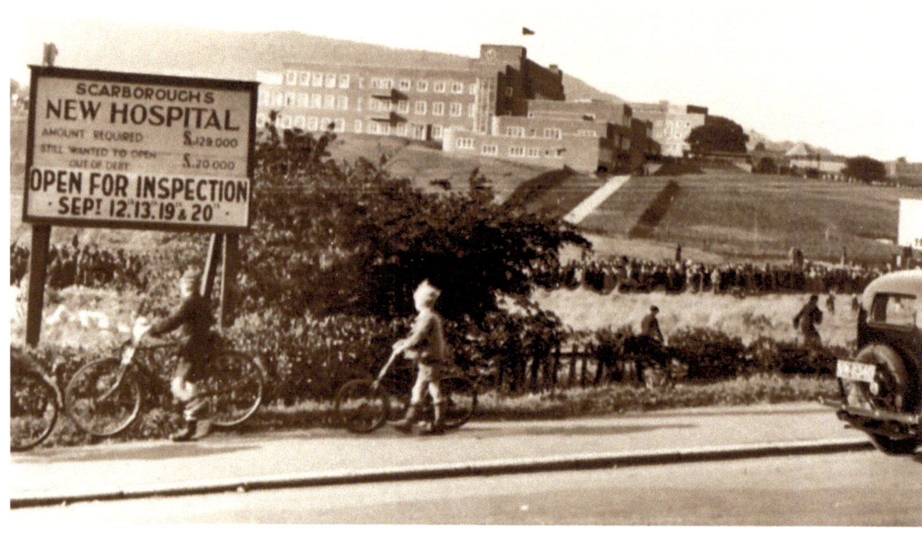

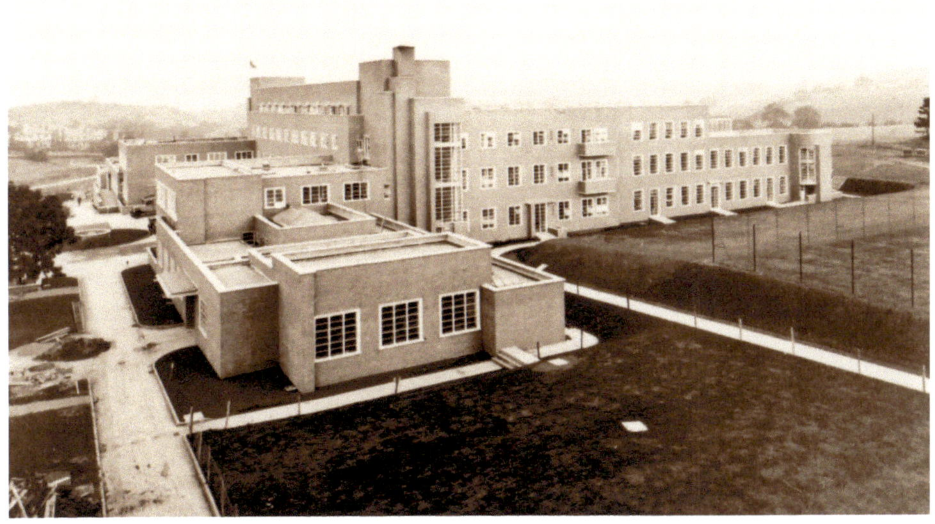

The New Scarborough Hospital

Above, the west wing, kitchen and laundry as it appeared in October 1936. Below, the modern entrance to what is now the North Wing of the original hospital as it appeared in 2010. The two lodges are still visible at the entrance and a notice proclaims that this is the north entrance to Scarborough Hospital in NHS house colours. The hospital became part of the National Health Service after it had come into existence in 1948 as a major reform under the new Labour government. It was this government that also introduced medical care that was free at the point of use, paid for through National Insurance and taxation. Despite many problems and reforms over the years, the principle remains the same, despite some abuse of the system, and a nation is still quite proud of the NHS regardless of its many problems. The main hospital is now screened by bushes and the main Scalby Road passes close by the entrance, unlike when the hospital first opened.

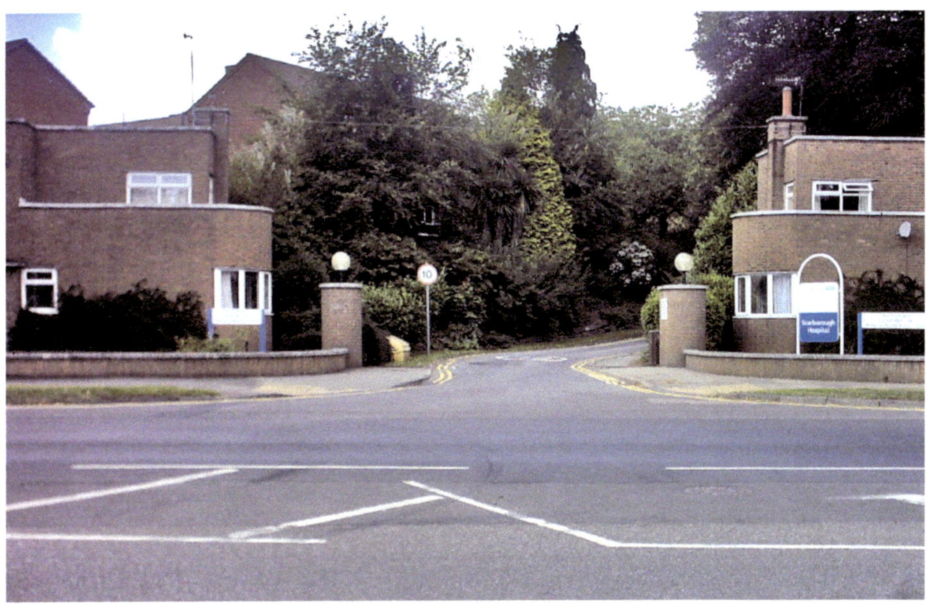

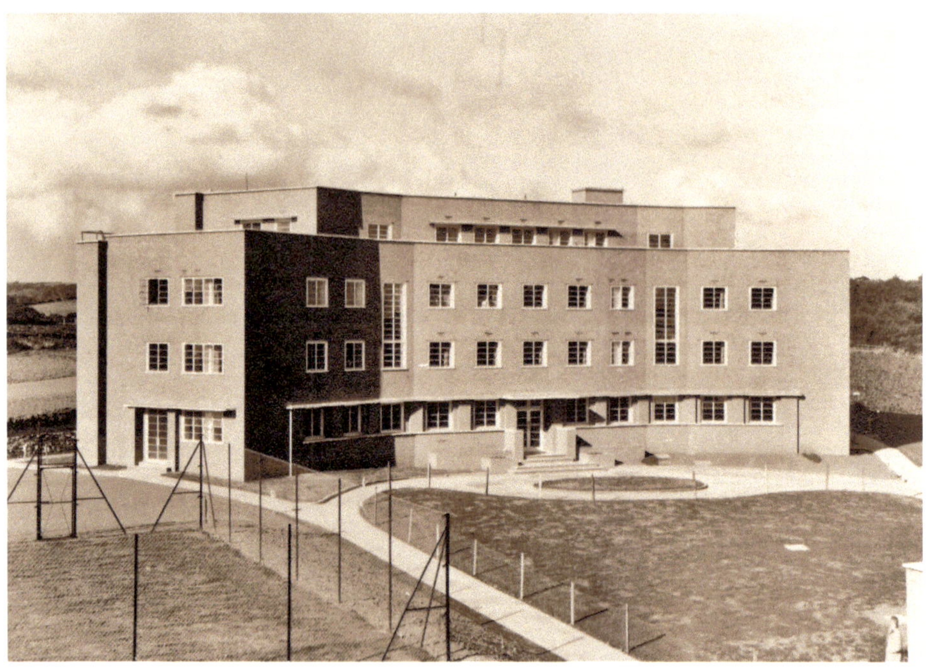

The Hospital Nurses' Home

The hospital Nurses' Home in seen here in 1936. The building had sixty bedrooms, each with hot and cold running water and a wardrobe, along with a bed. The building also housed sitting and waiting rooms, along with a tea kitchen. Night staff occupied the top floor to ensure that they had 'quiet rest'. The building is now the Scarborough and North East Yorkshire Healthcare Trust Headquarters, as seen in the 2010 picture, and it also houses the Occupational Health Department.

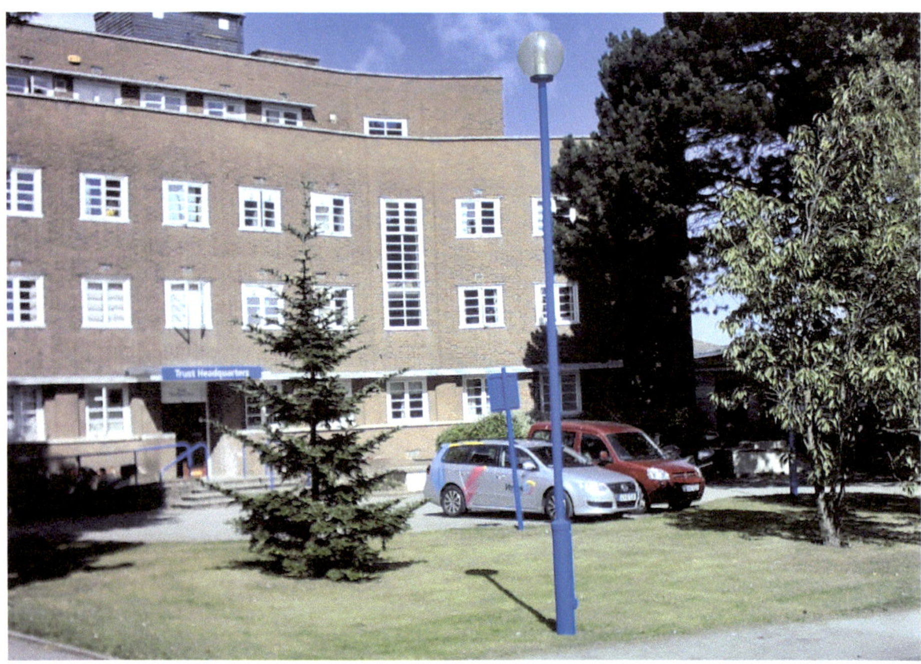

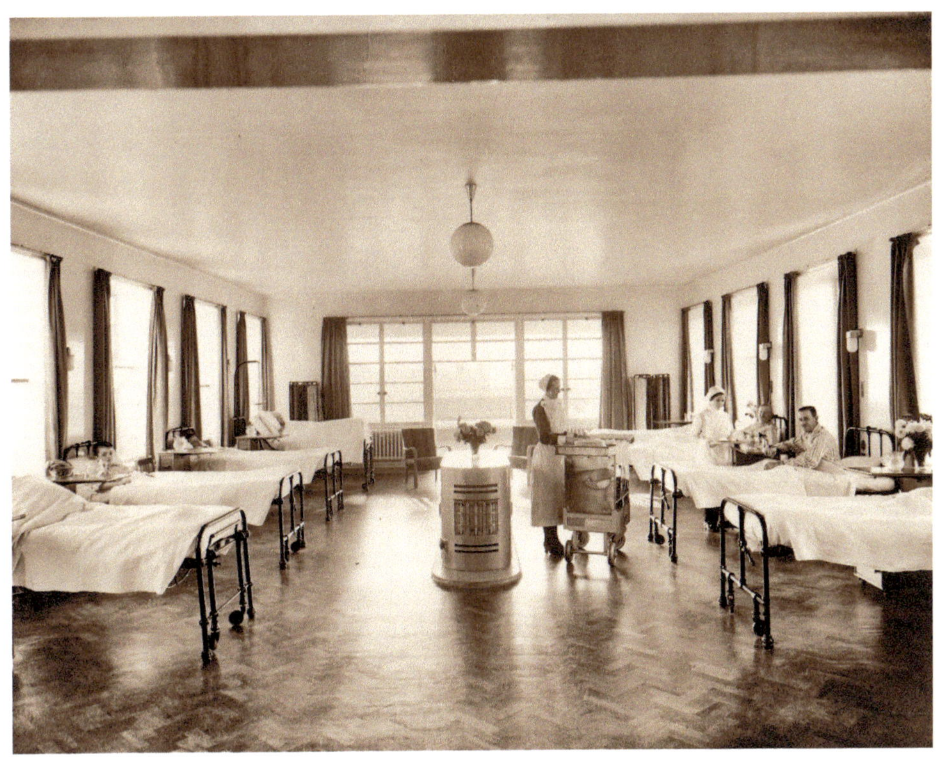

The New Scarborough Hospital

The men's ward at the newly opened hospital with patients, one appearing to be just a boy, in their beds and being cared for by the Sister, who is doing the drugs round, and a member of the nursing staff. In the centre is a metal stand, which will probably contain patient records. The beds that flank the unit are of the latest type, still having steel frames, but with wheels and facilities to be tilted. Little tables are provided at each bed and the beds themselves have their own electric lighting. A parquet floor, which is highly polished, is also provided. This flooring has only recently been replaced and the beds have long since changed. In the background, a balcony is accessed through the open door as it was believed that fresh air was good for recovery; these have now been closed in. Below, nursing staff in the early NHS years. Does anyone remember any of these?

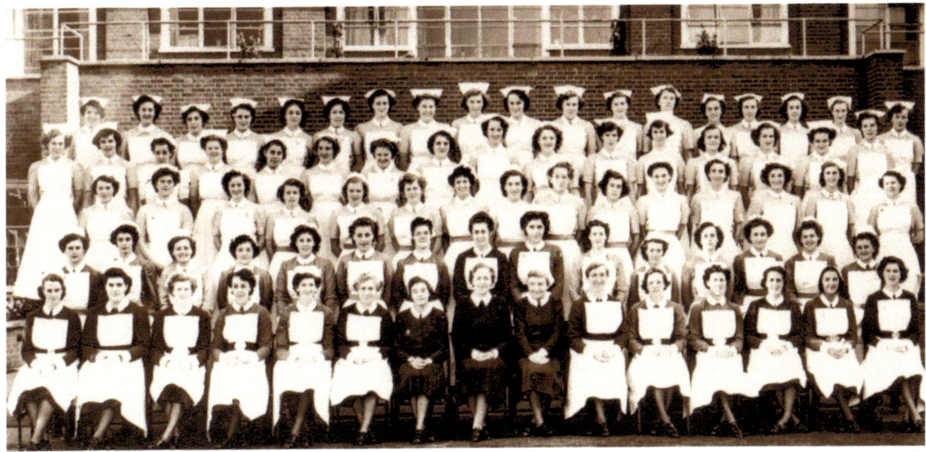

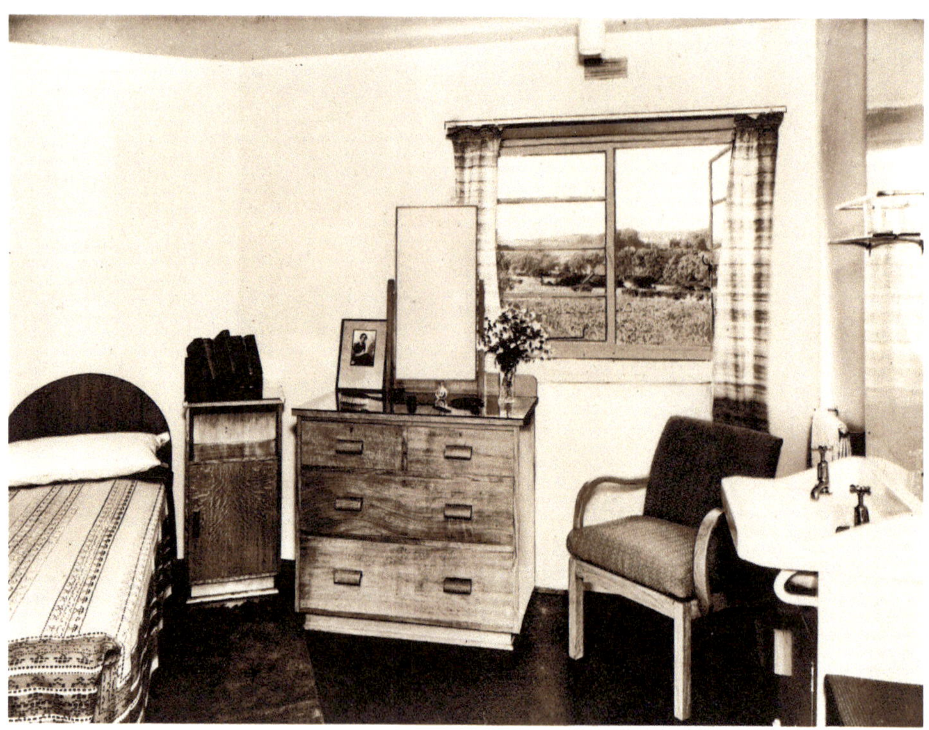

The Nurses' Home

One of the rooms at the Nurses' Home as it was when it opened in 1936. Provided for the staff was a white sink with hot and cold taps, an easy chair, chest of drawers, bedside cabinet and single bed. Unlike today, all nurses were educated at the hospital and all practical training was undertaken here. Below, the first garden party at Scarborough Hospital on 8 July 1937, as the board continued to raise funds for the hospital – these were the pre-NHS days. There were dancing displays, teas served in the centre of the lawn, and a concert party.

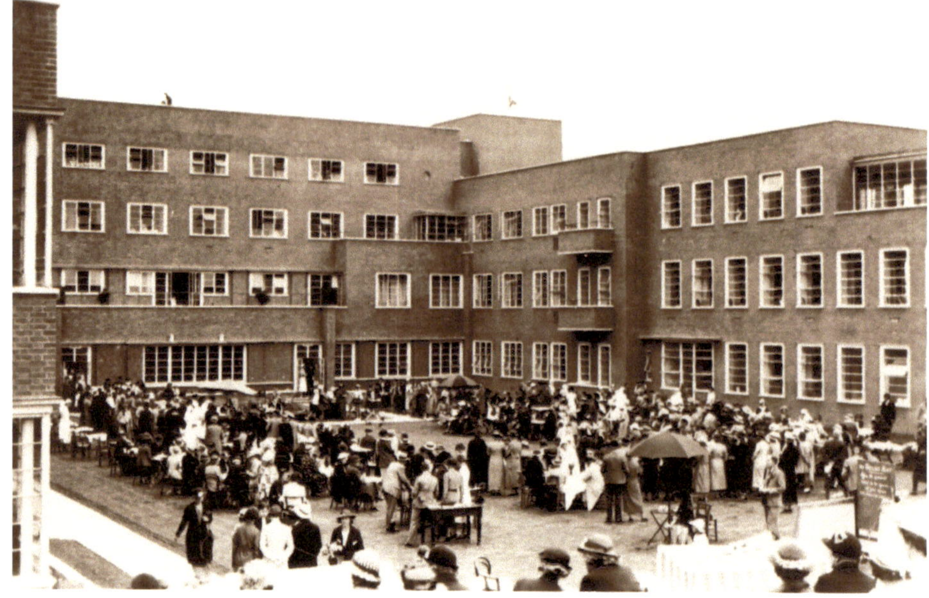

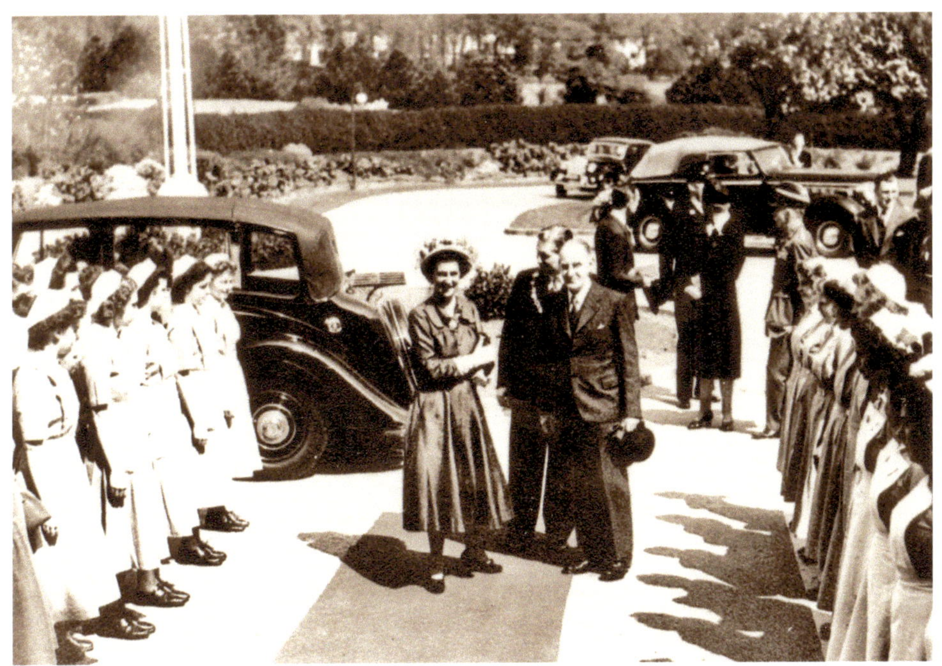

The New Scarborough Hospital

A visit to Scarborough Hospital by the Duchess of Kent in May 1948, twelve years after the opening and shortly before the hospital was to become part of the new National Health Service from 5 July of that year. Below, the Duke of Kent Children's Ward in 1951, complete with a mixture of cots and beds on a highly polished parquet floor. Children are seated at the table and toys are scattered around, including a doll's house, rocking horse and a pair of 'Mobo' ponies.

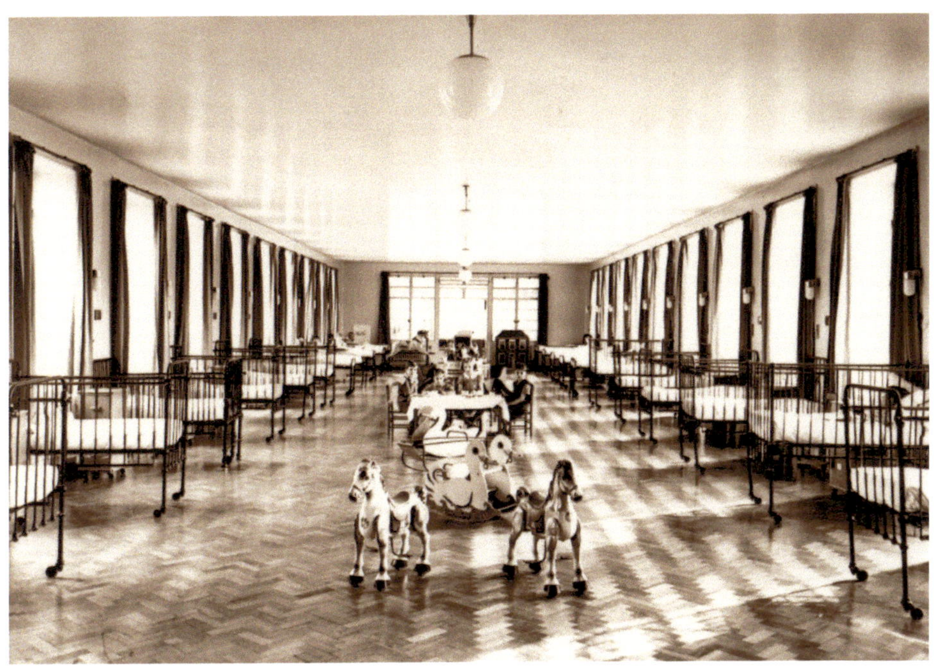

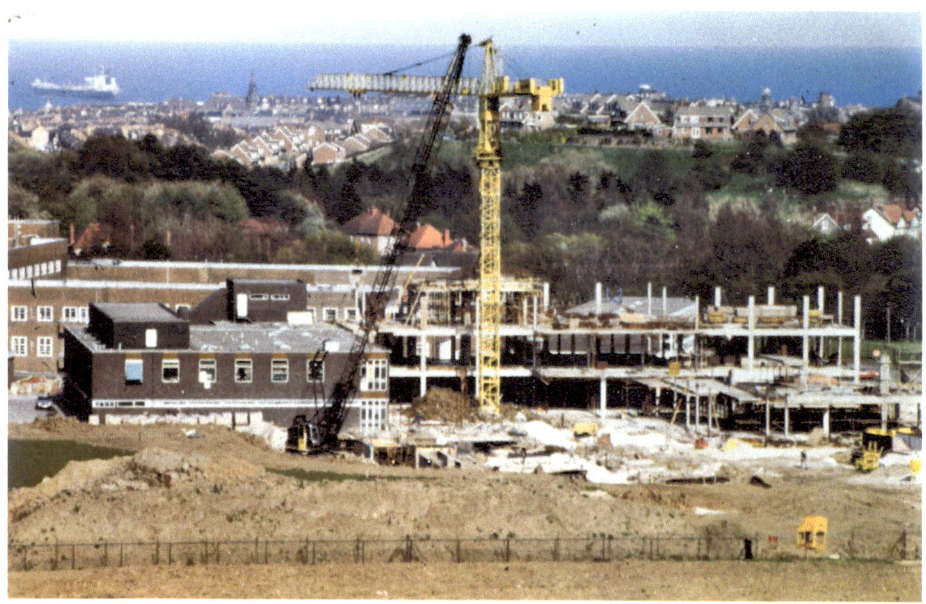

By the 1980s, the original Scarborough Hospital was serving an area as far as Whitby in the north to Pickering, and to Scagglethorpe and Malton in the west. So, a new hospital wing was added and opened by the Duchess of Kent in 1986. Above, construction is underway on the South Wing in 1984. The new wards have been named after trees and the main hospital entrance is now situated here, on Woodlands Drive. The South Wing, as the extension is known, can be seen here on a wet day in 2010. Further extensions have been undertaken here, including new operating theatres and a new medical ward. The hospital also contains a Coronary Care Unit and an Accident and Emergency Department.

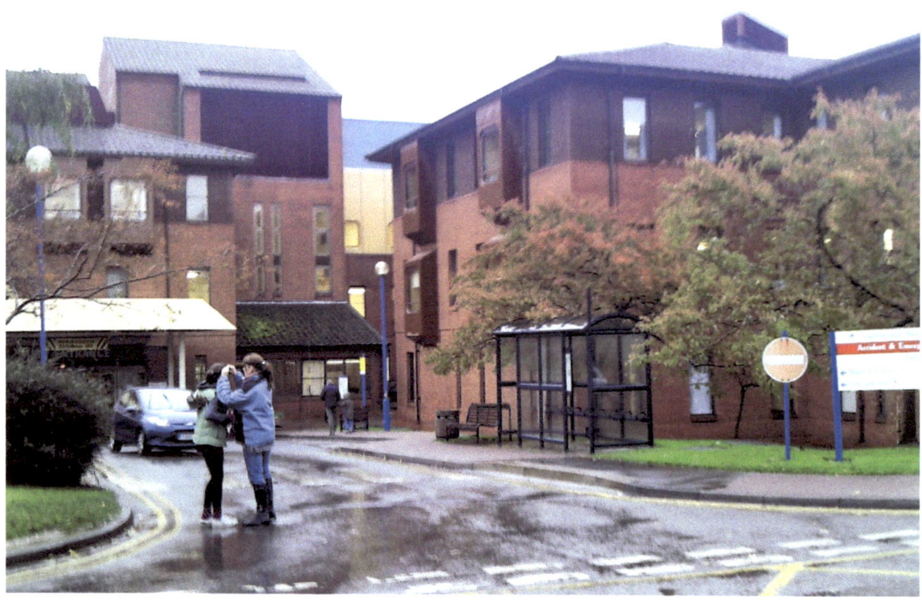

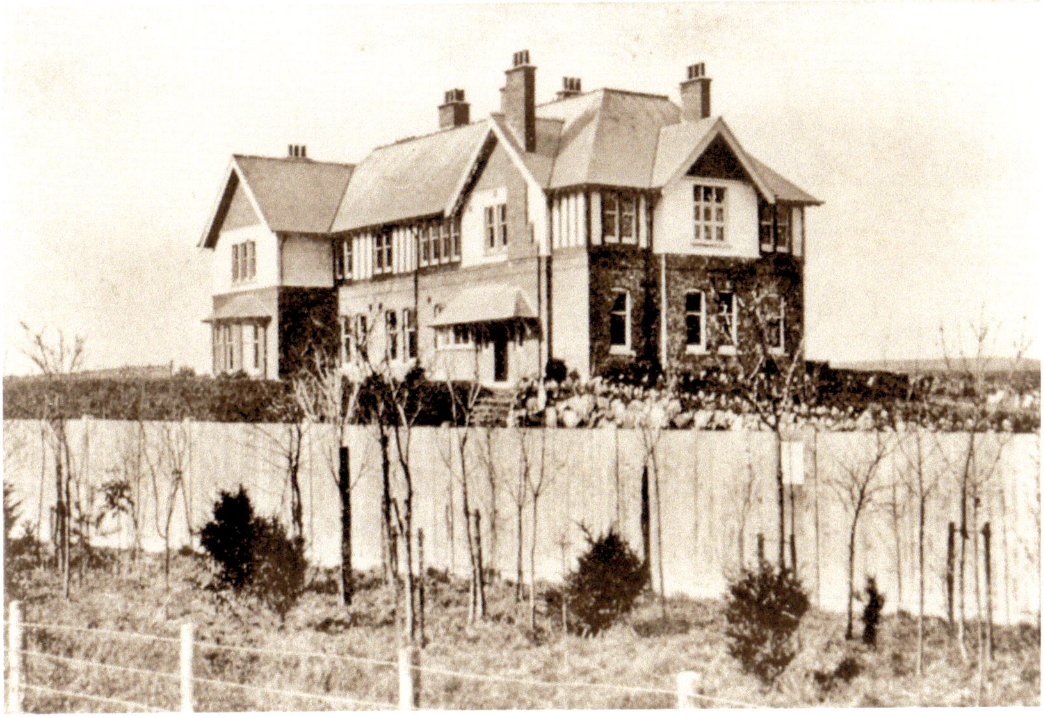

The Sanatorium

The Sanatorium at Scarborough cost £15,000 to build in 1904. It was opened by the then Mayoress Mrs Morgan and was used as a fever hospital and for patients with infectious diseases. It is now Cross Lane Hospital for psychiatric patients, one of its cottages is seen here in 2010.

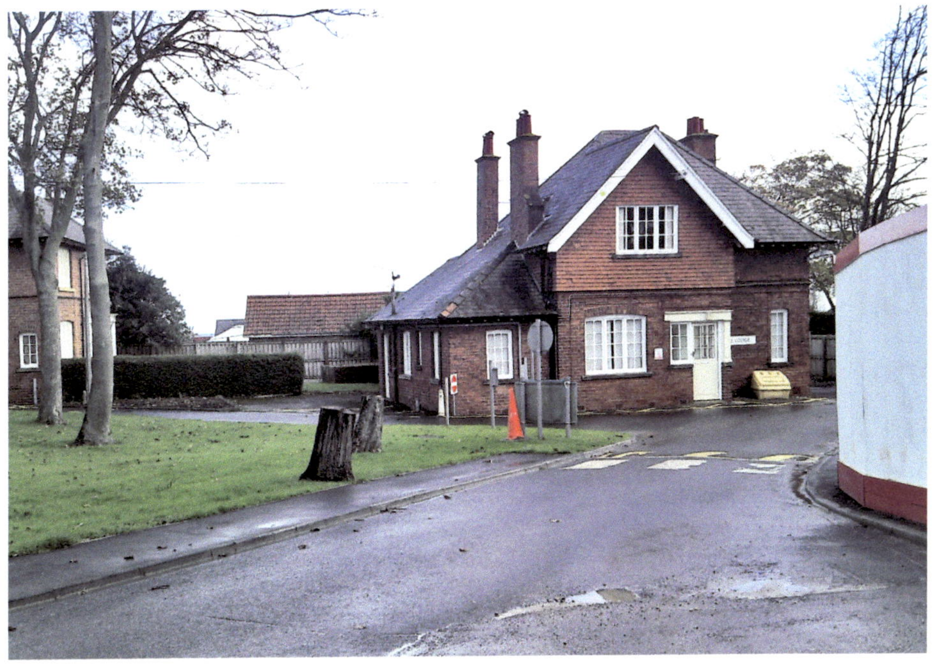

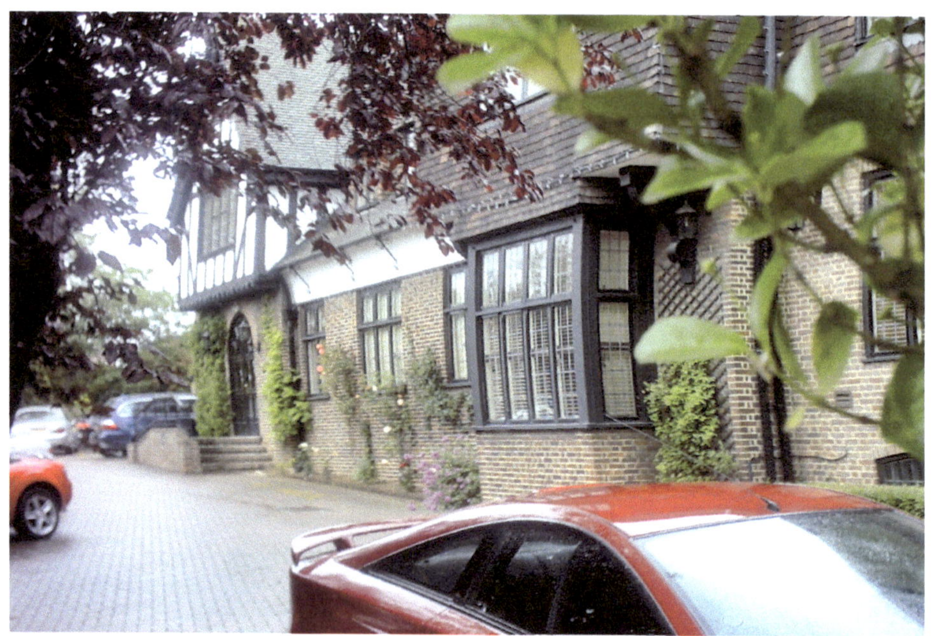

St Catherine's Hospice

An addition to healthcare in Scarborough has been provided over the last twenty-six years by St Catherine's Hospice, which provides services in palliative and terminal care for cancer and other terminal diseases. The Hospice movement had taken hold in the 1980s and such places were being established across Great Britain. Fundraising for such an establishment was begun in Scarborough at around that time, as Hospices are not funded by the NHS. St Catherine's Hospice was opened at the location seen here in 1985. Since moving to its purpose built site, this handsome building on Scalby Road, close to Scarborough Hospital, is now being used as offices. This new, purpose-built St Catherine's Hospice, seen below, provides inpatient and outpatient care.

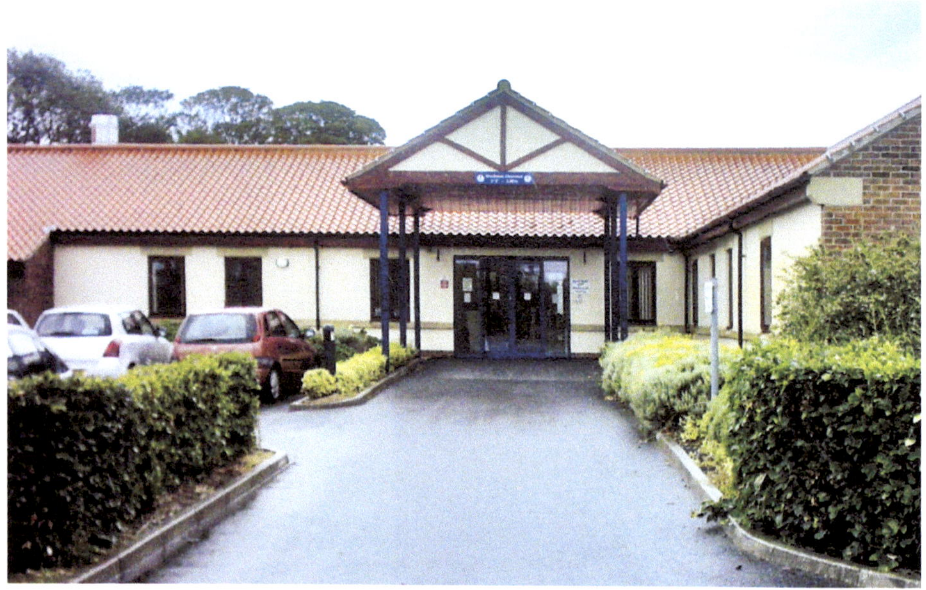

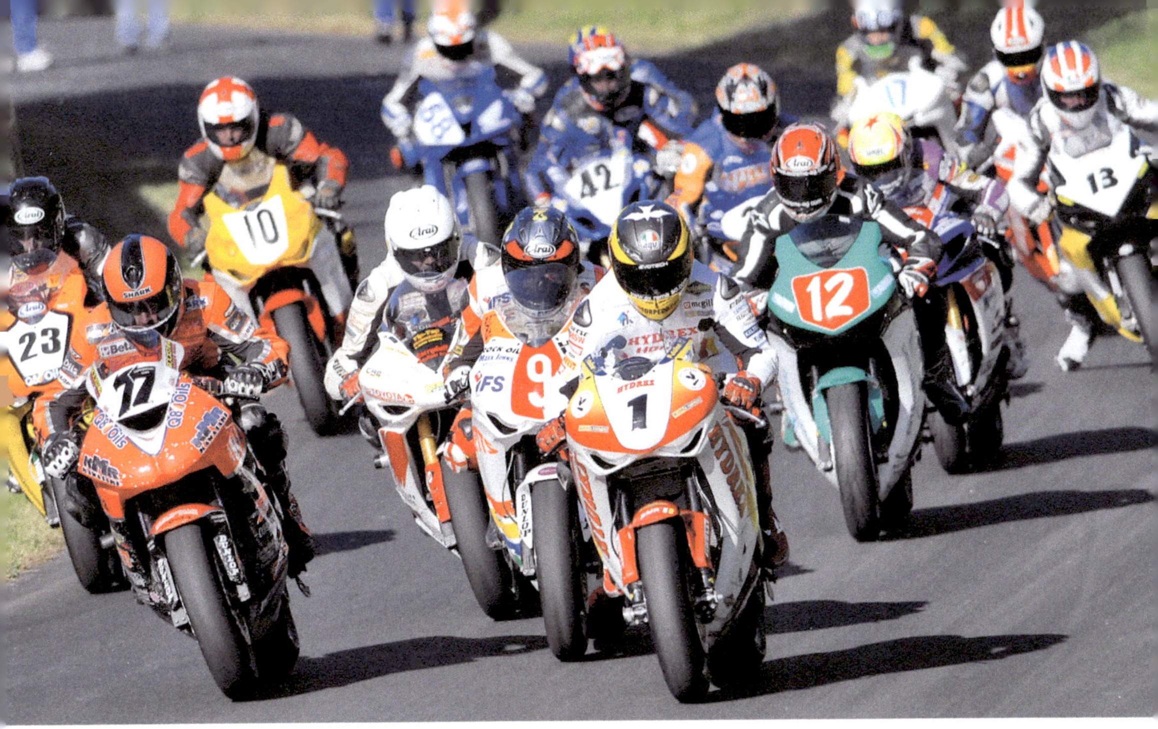

Oliver's Mount

Sport has played a fairly large part in the life of the population at Scarborough, with cricket, football, and motorcycling playing a major sporting role in the town, an example of the latter can be seen here as Formula Three motorcycle racing continues on Oliver's Mount.

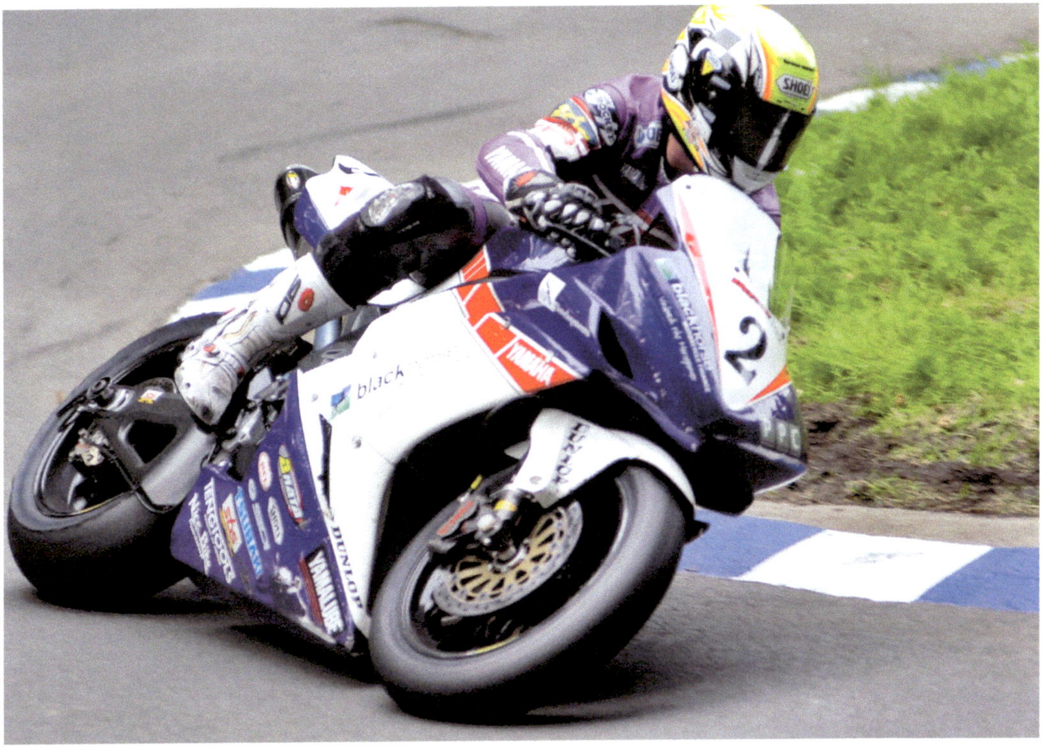

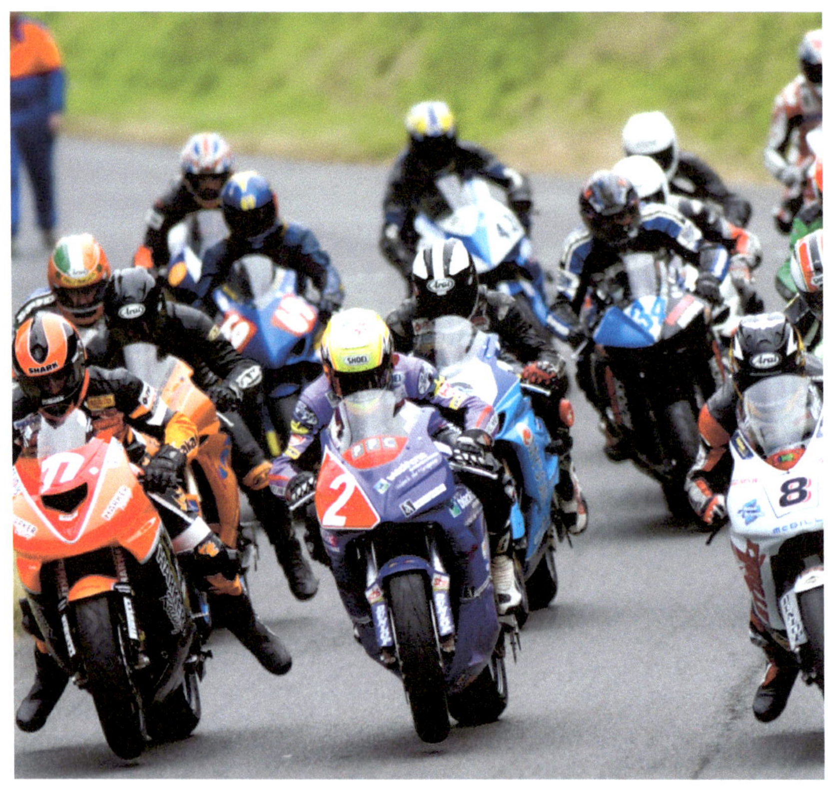

Oliver's Mount and North Marine Road

Another race is underway at Oliver's Mount during the summer. These races attract some famous road racers and include such names as Guy Martin, Ryan Farquhar, Ian Louger, John Mcguiness, Chris Palmer, William Dunlop, and sidecar rider Nick Crowe. Below, the exterior of the Scarborough Cricket Club ground on North Marine Road in 2011.

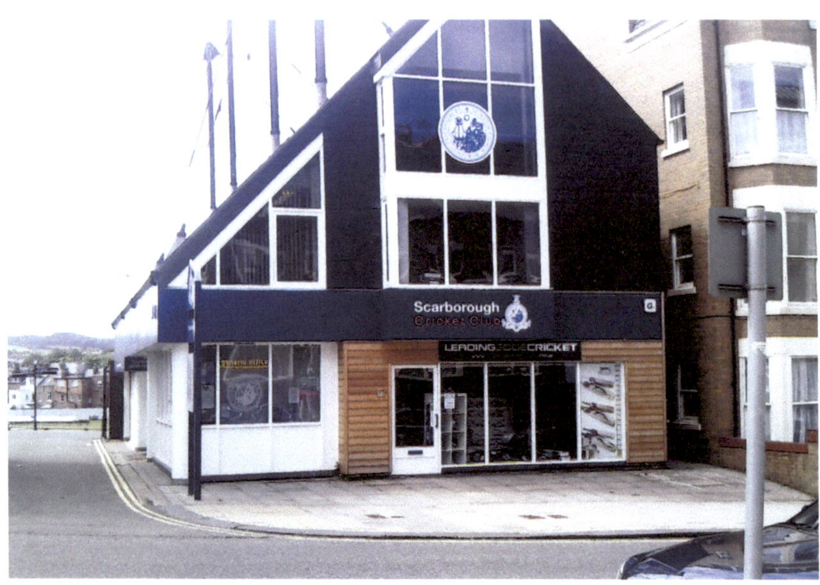

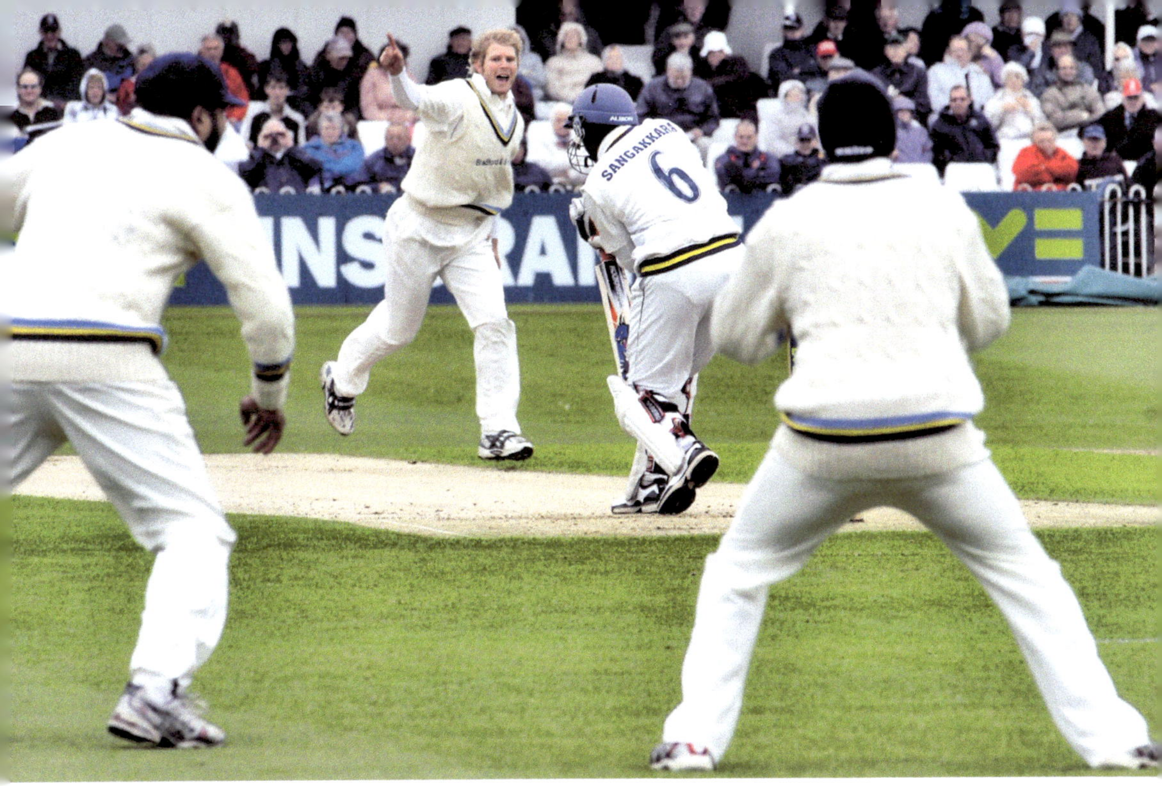

North Marine Road

Another sport played in Scarborough is Yorkshire's favourite, cricket. The Scarborough Cricket Club's ground is at North Marine Road, and Yorkshire County Cricket Club has played matches here since 1878; the annual Scarborough Festival, when the county take on a first class county side, is eagerly awaited by the locals. Here, Yorkshire are taking on Warwickshire in a four day match, the Midland side are batting in this view.

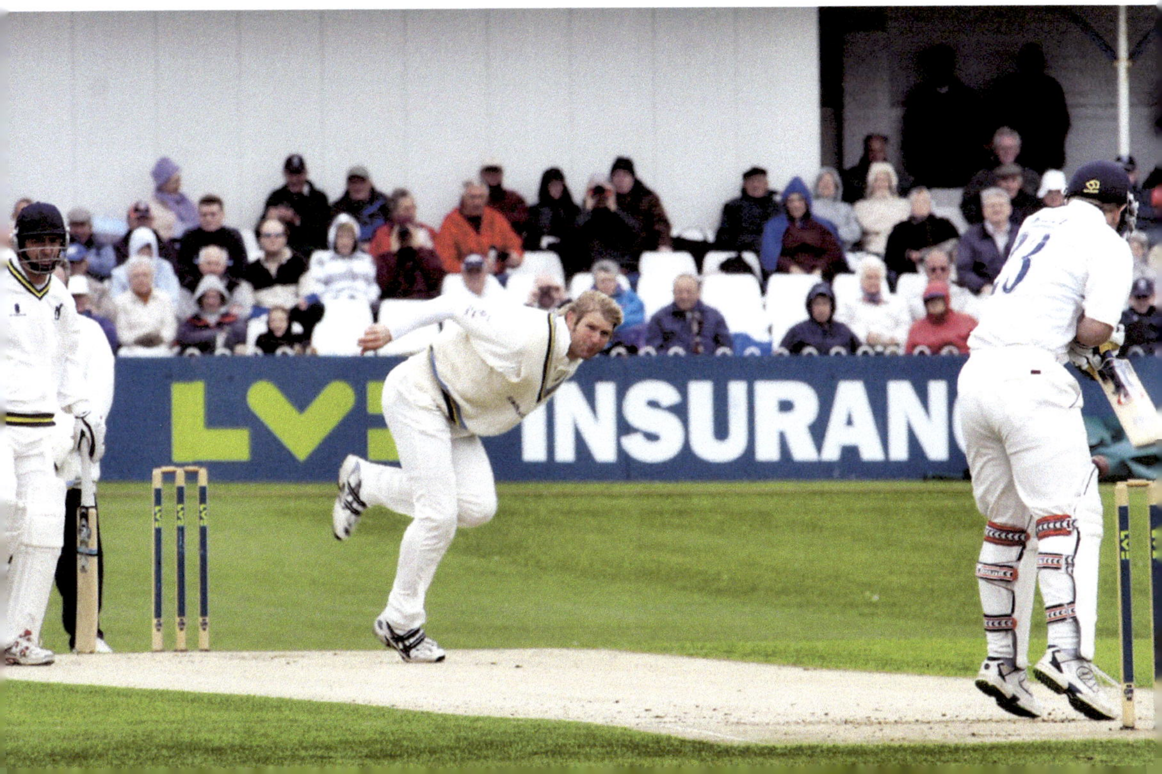

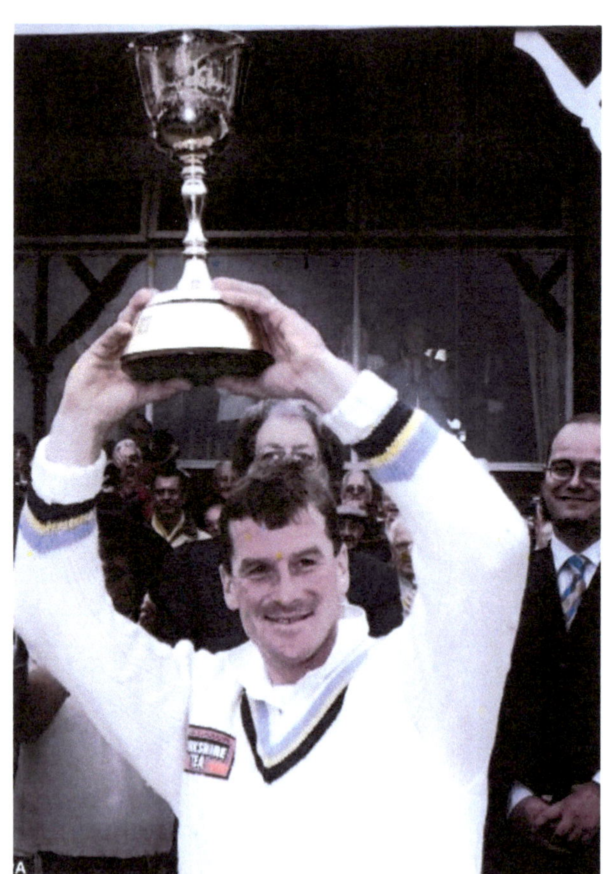

North Marine Road

The Yorkshire captain is seen here lifting the county championship at Scarborough in 2001 after beating Glamorgan at Scarborough. In 2010, Yorkshire reached the semi-final of the 'Pro 40' – a forty-overs-a-side, one-day tournament – where they met Warwickshire at Scarborough. On this day, the Midlands county got its revenge by beating Yorkshire and going on to win the tournament in a year when they had struggled in the county championship and only retained their first division status near the end of the season when all of their international players had returned from England duty. Warwickshire beat Somerset in the final making the West Country county side runners-up in every tournament. Is this a record? In this view, Warwickshire are the fielding side as Yorkshire try to build up sufficient runs to make life difficult for the Midland side. Sadly, they failed to do so.

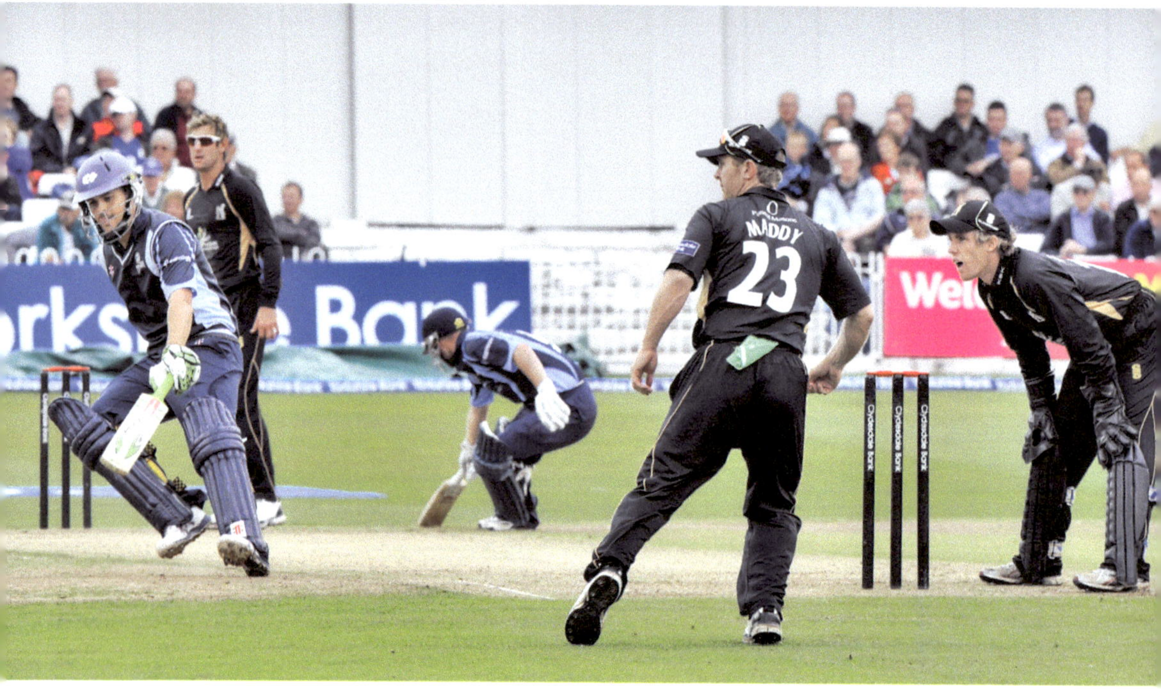

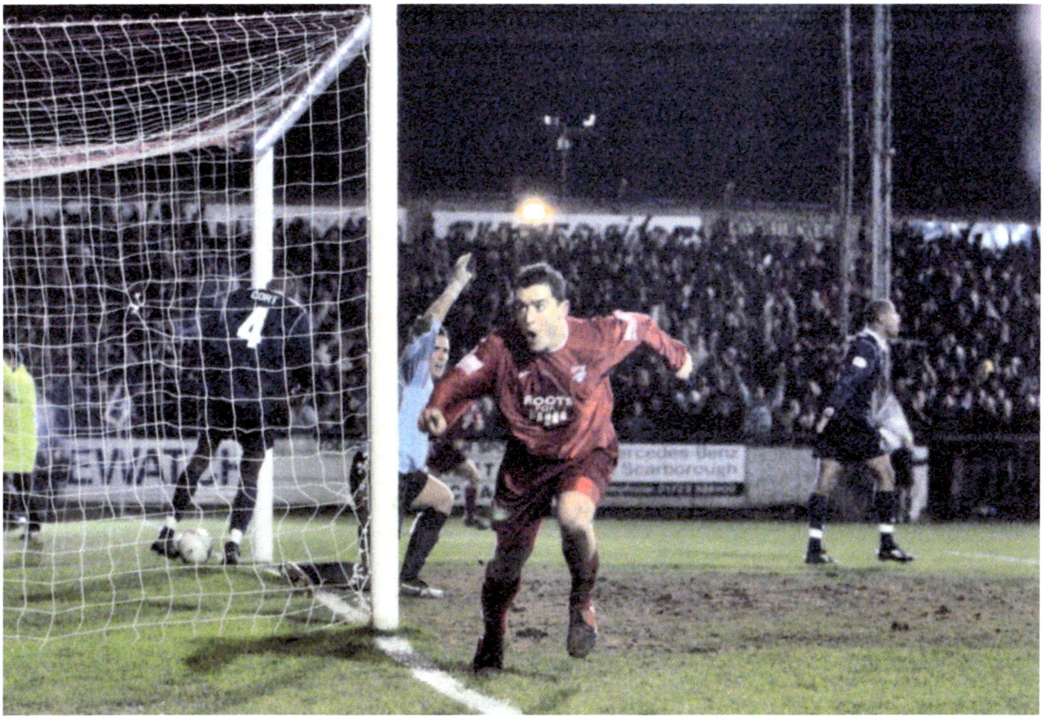

Scarborough Football Club

A floodlit match at the home ground of Scarborough Football Club. The home team have just scored a goal in the third round of the FA Cup, which would bring them up against the mighty Chelsea in 2004; a year when Scarborough had returned to non-league football. Scarborough Football Club had been founded in 1879 and played their first games at the Recreation Ground until moving to the Athletic Ground, becoming the McCain Stadium in 1988, on Seamer Road, where they were to remain until 2007. in 2004, the highlight of a poor season was the Fourth Round FA Cup tie with Chelsea, featured in the view below. Although Chelsea luckily won 1–0, this was not the first time that Scarborough had played the Londoners.

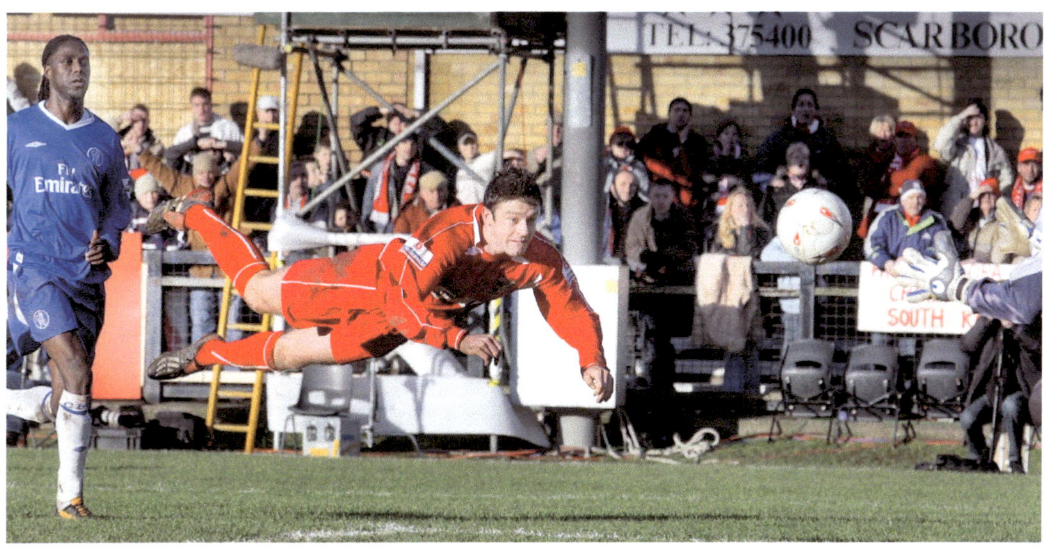

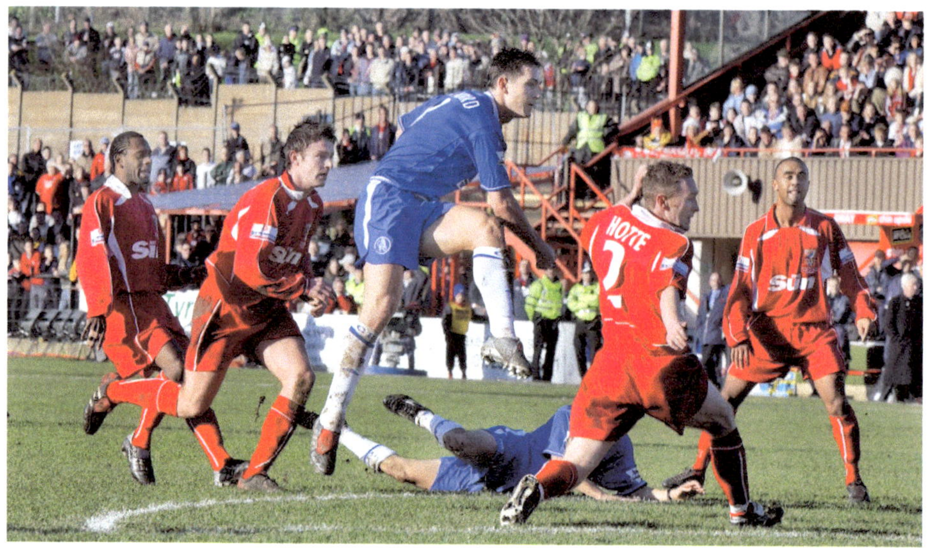

Scarborough Football Club

Frank Lampard of Chelsea heads goalwards in the FA Cup fourth round at Scarborough in 2004. It was John Terry's goal which secured the win for Chelsea on that night. Scarborough were relegated from the Conference in 2006 because the League were not convinced that they were financially sound and the club received a 10-point deduction after going into administration. On 8 June 2007, the Football Association felt that by 12 June, the club would go out of business but a stay of execution was given by the High Court as Scarborough Council had another look at the covenants, but it was to no avail and the club was financially wound up on 20 June with debts of £2.5 million. Following the winding up of the club, a supporter's trust formed a new club, Scarborough Athletic, which gained a place in the Northern Counties League. However, all of their games are played at Bridlington Town's Queensgate ground. Despite this, the ground still stands, as this 2010 view shows, although it is slowly being demolished.

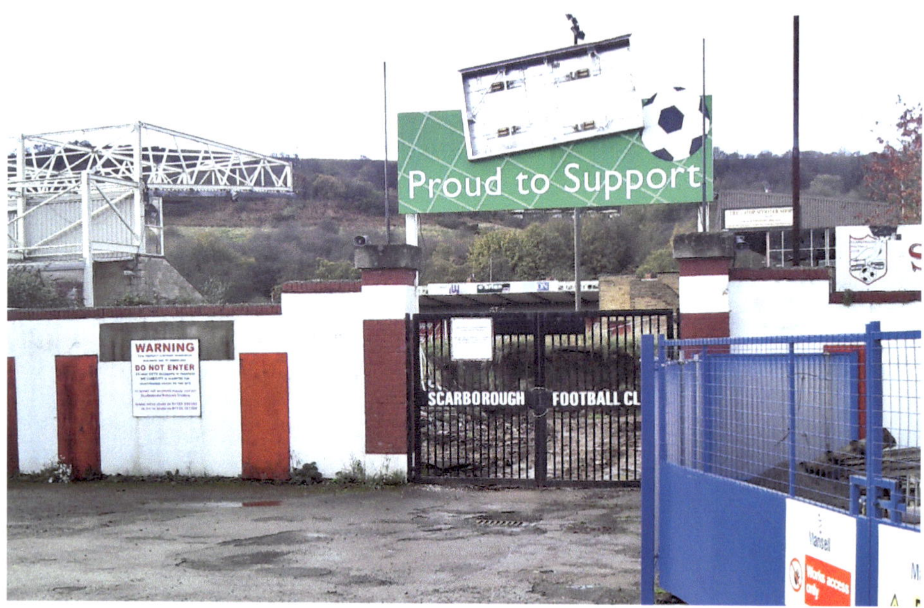

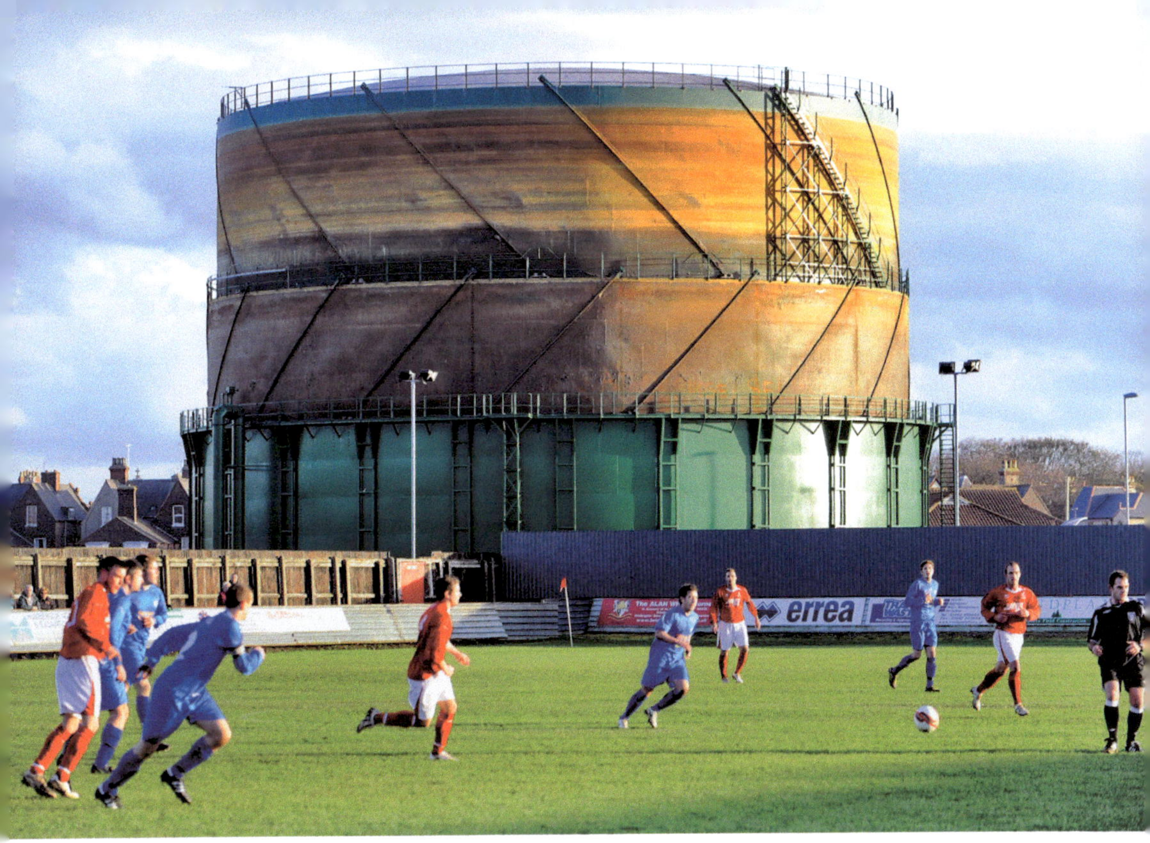

Scarborough Athletic

Scarborough Athletic playing a match at Bridlington. The new crest designed for Scarborough Athletic, with the motto 'No Battle No Victory', which summed up their thoughts at this time. History shows that a Scarborough team could well emerge strongly, the likes of Accrington Stanley in Lancashire went to the wall but have now found their way back to the football league after many years in the wilderness and Wimbledon are on their way back. It is to be hoped that, in the near future, a ground can be found in Scarborough for its own team.

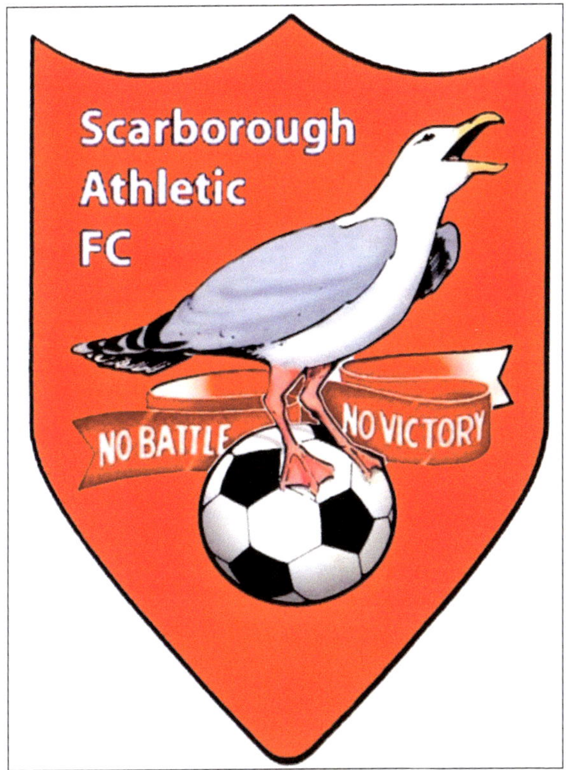

Acknowledgements

Several people have given assistance in the production of this project whose help has made the work so much easier to complete. Therefore, I offer my thanks to Angela Kale at Scarborough library for her assistance in obtaining photographs and information on North Bay. Rebecca Aspin of the Communications Department at Scarborough Hospital provided invaluable assistance on the history of Scarborough Hospital and its predecessors, and provided photographs of this and earlier establishments. The staff at St Catherine's Hospice gave information about the hospice and its work. As far as Scarborough industry is concerned, my thanks go to Andy Warrender of Plaxton Ltd. and Andrew Riley of McCain Foods for their assistance.

Special thanks go to the guys on the Sports Desk at the *Scarborough Evening News* who provided photographs and stories related to the football, cricket and motor-cycling clubs in the town. I enjoyed spending time with them and discussing our sporting interests.

Other assistance has come from Gordon Sharpe, Roger Carpenter and Brian Bowgen, along with Filey library, and Roger Pettican. To all, and anybody I have missed, my grateful thanks.

Finally, may I thank my wife Hilary for her patience and support while working on the project and I hope the finished book will be enjoyed. If so, then the effort was well worthwhile.